CHAM
CHERRIES

For my dear mother and father,
who have brought a lifetime of love
and happiness to my world.

Proud Champions! **Back row left to right:** Tony Pulis, Trevor Aylott, John Williams, Carl Richards, Mark O'Connor. **Middle row left to right:** John Kirk (Trainer), Morgan Lewis, Mark Whitlock, Gerry Peyton, Tom Heffernan, Paul Morrell, Jimmy Gabriel (Assistant Manager). **Front row left to right:** David Puckett, Gary Howlett, Mark Newson, Harry Redknapp (Manager), Richard Cooke, Tony Sealy, Sean O'Driscoll.

THE STORY OF AFC BOURNEMOUTH'S 1986/87
CHAMPIONSHIP-WINNING SEASON

CHAMPAGNE CHERRIES

A Season to Remember!

by Robert Neesam

Foreword by Harry Redknapp

RED POST

Published by Robert Neesam in 2005

© Robert Neesam 2005

Designed by Crispin Goodall Design
Edited by Geraldine Christy

A CIP catalogue record for this book is available at the British Library

ISBN 10: 1-901533-08-5
ISBN: 13: 9-781901-533088

5 Venning Avenue
Bear Cross
Bournemouth
BH11 9QG

e-mail: champagne.cherries@btinternet.com
www.champagnecherries.co.uk

Front cover, main picture: Trevor Aylott scores Bournemouth's third goal from the
penalty spot against Middlesbrough in front of a packed Dean Court.

Acknowledgements

I would like to thank the following individuals who have assisted me in some way in the production of this book. Without their advice, guidance and encouragement throughout the journey this book would not have been possible.

Mum, Dad and Amanda, who have supported and encouraged me throughout this endeavour.

Scott Harrison, Chief Librarian at the 'Bournemouth Echo', for his continued support with my research and infectious enthusiasm from the outset.

Kevin Nash, Head of Features from the 'Bournemouth Echo', who willingly shared his experience and provided invaluable advice and help at a critical time.

Neal Butterworth, Editor at the 'Bournemouth Echo', who kindly agreed to allow the use of a small selection of photographs from the 'Bournemouth Echo' library.

Leigh Edwards, a local football historian, who readily provided me with current information regarding the 'Where are they now?' section.

Jeremy Smith for his continued technical support with the manuscript.

John Carter at the Bournemouth Football Association, who provided access to research the local amateur football records.

Paul Handley, a local photographer, who kindly agreed to allow the use of a small selection of action photographs taken by him during season 1986/87.

Neil Vacher of Collect & Co at AFC Bournemouth for his support, advice and encouragement.

Harry Redknapp and Mark Newson, the Cherries' championship-winning manager and captain, who both accepted my invitation to provide the Foreword and 'Captain's corner' for this book and gave me the opportunity to talk to two of my heroes.

Peter Phillips, AFC Bournemouth Chairman, who has supported the book to benefit the club and gave me permission to use the club crest.

It has not been possible to establish who owns the copyright to a small number of the photographs. Apologies are offered in advance if any infringements have occurred.

About the author

Robert Neesam was born in Bournemouth in 1962 on the day when the Cherries were beaten 4-0 by Fulham in a League Cup encounter at Craven Cottage. He made his first appearance standing on the Dean Court South End terrace in 1970, watching Ted MacDougall and Phil Boyer terrorise Third and Fourth Division defenders, where he suffered the first of his many AFC Bournemouth heartbreaks involving a promotion near miss. He left Oakmead Boys School with 5 'O' Levels and after a spell as resident DJ at the local youth club he began a sensible career as a young teenage insurance broker.

A midfield dynamo in the mould of Bryan Robson and playing amateur football in the Bournemouth Sunday League, he was voted player of the season in 1988/89, but never received his England call-up. Overlooked for his silky soccer skills and realising that insurance lacked a little in excitement, he embarked on a new career within Human Resources, specialising in the Training and Development arena while continuing to be a true AFC Bournemouth fanatic.

Still desperate to express his musical knowledge and wanting to put something back into the local community, he joined Hospital Radio Bedside as a volunteer and has presented a variety of radio programmes over the years, including match day commentary from Dean Court. In 2002 he graduated with an MBA and now currently works for a city investment bank. A lifelong Cherries devotee he can always be found during the football season at Dean Court on a Saturday afternoon.

Contents

Foreword by
Harry Redknapp

When I was approached to write the foreword for this book I was only too pleased to contribute and say a few words about what was a truly remarkable championship-winning promotion season for AFC Bournemouth in 1986/87. I have very fond memories of my time at Bournemouth as a player in the early 1970s. Manager John Bond signed me to play alongside the likes of Phil Boyer, Ted MacDougall and Mel Machin. This was a fantastic Bournemouth team that sadly underperformed and just missed out on promotion. Bournemouth also gave me my first step up into professional football management and I had some wonderful times at the club, winning the Freight Rover Trophy at Hull and beating Manchester United in the FA Cup in front of a packed Dean Court.

The championship and promotion-winning season of 1986/87 has to be the icing on the cake. I was so proud to be the first and only manager to date to take Bournemouth out of the old Division Three and I think we achieved it in some style with a record tally of 97 points and with a team that only cost me £50,000.

Before the season started I had sold Colin Clarke to Southampton in a deal that benefited everyone and gave me the flexibility to sign a number of new players in the summer. If I'm honest, despite the new faces, I didn't think we really had a chance of promotion, especially after the dreadful run of results in our pre-season friendly matches. But we got off to a good start and were able to keep the momentum going, despite some setbacks along the way. I remember bumping into a Cherries supporter in Christchurch town centre when we were top of the League and he said, 'You won't go up, the council won't allow you to.' Apparently there was some old wives' tale that over the years had said Bournemouth didn't want promotion. It was absolute rubbish and I told that supporter 'We'll go up!' and I proved that I'm a man of my word!

The players that season were superb and the team spirit throughout the squad was fantastic. They gave me one hundred per cent effort on the pitch and worked hard on the training ground. They had the will to win and never gave up. They were individual leaders in their own right and each had their own character, a wonderful bunch of players. Some of them needed strong management off the pitch as they liked to go out on the town, so they were often grounded on a Thursday night!

My captain Mark Newson was a great leader on the pitch and he also gave me options by playing out of position when we had injuries. He scored some vital goals for us. If Mark were playing today he would be a Premier League player at the top level. I already had Tommy Heffernan; he was a real tough character whose party trick was to head a cricket ball! But I felt we needed a bit more steel in the squad. Tony Pulis was a tough competitor and added some bite for us in midfield. I'd seen him clatter our own hard man Keith Williams the previous season and knew he could do a job for us, so I drove all the way to Newport in the pouring rain to watch him play, only to find that he'd been left out of the team. We chatted over a cup of tea and a biscuit and I decided to take a chance with him. Carl Richards was another unproven player I took a gamble on and it paid off. When I signed him as an amateur from Enfield he had no idea who Bournemouth were and thought we were an obscure non-League side. He was as quick as lightning and supporters nicknamed him Bruno.

I signed goalkeeper Gerry Peyton on a free transfer and he was outstanding that season, a true professional, as were Paul Morrell, Robbie Savage, Sean O'Driscoll and Mark O'Connor. The First Division experience of Mark Whitlock and Davy Puckett made such a difference to the team and I was upset when I lost David to a bad injury. During pre-season I felt we lacked someone up front who could hold the ball up and act as a target man. I heard that Trevor Aylott was available from Crystal Palace and snapped him up. He was a great player. I later added Richard Cooke and John Williams to the squad around Christmas and they made a significant difference. 'Cookie' was a fast and jinking winger and he gave us more balance on the right. 'Willo' was a fantastic signing, a great competitor and a tower of strength at the back. He also gave us the 'Willo forehead' and was superb at getting in the box, flicking the ball on with his head and setting up a goal. After John joined us we only lost two games and he was out injured for one of them!

I remember the supporters, and their singing, especially at the Middlesbrough home and Swindon away matches. By the time we played them both it had become a three-horse race for the title and all three sides had quality players. The season's turning point for me was the result at Port Vale, never an easy place to go. We won 2-1 and I was confident from that moment that we would go on and win promotion. The promotion clincher at Fulham was a special day. There were more Bournemouth fans at Craven Cottage than Fulham supporters and they made a tremendous noise.

I made a tough decision that day to leave out Mark O'Connor and include loan signing Tony Sealy, but Tony repaid my decision with a magnificent goal that he rattled in from 30 yards out. It was the first time in the history of AFC Bournemouth that promotion out of the old Division Three had been achieved. It was a fantastic moment, my Dad was there and I was so proud of what we had achieved. The post-match celebrations flowed into the late evening and several hours later when they wheeled us all onto the coach back to Bournemouth the Fulham Chairman Jimmy Hill announced, 'We've taken more money in booze over the boardroom bar than we have in gate receipts for the match!'

Off the pitch my old friend Brian Tiler was Managing Director at the club and he was fantastic. He never once interfered with what I was doing, yet had the ability to read my mind and willingly gave advice and support when I needed it. He was a great man.

I still don't really know the secret behind the success of the championship-winning season, but I do know that I was enthusiastic and I think I was quite lucky to have a bunch of lads who formed a perfect blend. Bournemouth is a wonderful place and I love the area so much that I still live on the south coast. I love to see the club do well and have a great affection for the Cherries. I spent nine years there as boss, so I will always have fond memories of the club and the town because I had some of the best times at AFC Bournemouth.

Best wishes.
Harry Redknapp

Captain's corner
by Mark Newson

When I was approached to write a few lines for this book my initial reaction was what an honour to be able to say 'what an unforgettable season it was'. Then I thought to myself 'about time too' – such a book has been long overdue. Now don't get me wrong; I don't mean that it was about time someone asked me, but more a case that it was about time somebody wrote something 'nice' about that memorable year.

As captain of the Cherries throughout 1986/87 I have many wonderful memories of the championship-winning season. Two things spring to mind straightaway. The first is how invincible and confident we felt walking out at every match; especially from Christmas onwards, I felt we were unbeatable. The second thing I remember from that marvellous season was what a crap trophy the club was presented with prior to the Norwich promotion celebration friendly at the end of the season. As skipper of the team Chelsea Chairman Ken Bates presented me with a little glass statue to recognise our championship success. OK, I wasn't expecting the European Cup ... but at least a little bit of silverware would have been nice!

I could write something about all the players in the squad that season, but it would take too long, so I will mention just a few. Tom Heffernan was the first player I met on joining AFC Bournemouth and we were room-mates in the hotel the club put us both in. Having played for the Cherries before, he showed me the nightlife in Bournemouth that first season; we had some good times! Davy Puckett's tally was first class that season; he was one of the best finishers I have played with. John Williams ('Willo') will always tell you that one of the main reasons we were champions that year was because of Harry's signing of himself and Richard Cooke ('Cookie') just before Christmas. We three were very close and had some good times on and off the field; it certainly was one of the funniest seasons with 'Willo' and 'Cookie'.

Looking back, although I would never admit it to John, I think he may be right about the signings at Christmas, but the credit has to go to Harry Redknapp. That was and still is Harry's strength; he is very good at finding players at the right time. I have the utmost respect and affection for Harry and his family. I certainly enjoyed and benefited playing under Harry.

The match that will always stay with me from the 1986/87 season was the midweek home game against Middlesbrough. They were just behind us in the table and it was a 'must win' match for both teams. The atmosphere was fantastic at Dean Court. We, of course, won and I scored. Also I remember the Fulham game was such a good day, especially afterwards on that hot sunny afternoon; the celebrations at the end of the match are something that I will always treasure.

'Up the Cherries!'

Mark Newson

1.

My club, my story, my book

Gazing towards heaven I whispered 'Thank you God', kissed the badge on my shirt and exhaled a scream that released a season of stored emotion and tension. Referee Howard Taylor had just blown the final whistle to end the Third Division match between Fulham and Bournemouth on Monday 4 May 1987 – remembered as the greatest day in the history of AFC Bournemouth. It was the date that my Club gained promotion to the Second Division for the first time in a League career dating back to 1923. It had taken an eternity, but after so many heartbreaks and promotion near misses I could finally admit that the roller-coaster love affair had been worth the wait for this moment and I would not have missed one minute of the turbulent journey. But how and where did it all begin?

I blame my father! He is the one who is guilty of commencing my journey on this wonderful infatuation. I even know the date it all started, Saturday 4 October 1970, a bright and sunny, but chilly, autumnal day on the south coast just perfect for romance. But that is where the romance was abruptly terminated. My Dad had taken me to Dean Court, the home of Bournemouth and Boscombe Athletic Football Club, for the League Division Four fixture versus Chester City. I was eight years old and up to that point had only ever seen football in black and white on a TV.

Specific detail remains logged in my memory as though captured and preserved in a time capsule and the memories are still crystal clear today so many years after the event. I remember the colours – the emerald green of the grass, which looked like a new carpet; the fluffy white clouds high in the sky that were racing past as I looked up to the tall silver floodlight pylons; and the red and black hunting jacket, top hat and Union Jack waistcoat of the strange man who paraded around the pitch indicating his match score prediction with white-gloved fingers. Ken Bailey looked up at us and gestured 2-1 to Cherries. The sounds and the smell were new to me as well – the voice of an invisible man on the crackly public address system calling out the teams, and the growing anticipation of the crowd as 3.00pm approached and the air filled with St Bruno tobacco pipe smoke.

The game itself remains a blur, but I do remember being disappointed that there was no commentator to describe the action and no action replay either. Looking back, it just goes to show how influential television can be to a young child.

Bournemouth won 3-1 and as we made our way out of the ground I excitedly turned to my father and asked, 'Can we come again next week?' He explained that the following week the team would be playing away from Bournemouth, but if I was good and Mum was in agreement, I could go to another match. That was it; at the tender age of eight years I had become a Cherries junkie and would be hooked for life. My journey had started, a journey of ups and downs that so many genuine and loyal football supporters have with 'their team'.

Before it was demolished and rebuilt in 2001 the original Dean Court stadium had witnessed many moments of glory and disappointment through the decades and had a pedigree that spanned over 75 years. For those unfortunate enough not to have had the opportunity to visit the ground, a brief explanation might be necessary, if only to describe its wonder and history, the stuff that legends are made from!

The stadium had undergone a series of facelifts and makeovers since its original construction at the end of Edward VII's reign in 1910. A £12,000 investment in 1927 was one of the most significant and the steel framework had been purchased following the closure of the British Empire Exhibition at Wembley and reconstructed to provide the framework for a new grandstand to seat 3,500 spectators. This grandstand, now called the Main Stand, still stood in 1986, arching over and hiding a rabbit warren of rooms and corridors beneath. Despite regular upkeep the wooden benches had remained in place for decades and the blue clad roof supported on thick iron pillars provided unfortunate spectators with an obscured view. I recall early visits to the ground as a boy when I had to bob my head left and right to see the goalmouth action either side of a roof pillar.

In 1936 the Dean Court Supporters Club provided the funds to build a concrete stepped terrace and part-covered roof behind one goal. This was casually referred to as the 'South End' of the ground and in my early days I simply accepted this. Some years later I was to learn that this terrace was actually sited at the west point on the compass. The standing covered enclosure that ran parallel to the Main Stand and along the north side of the Dean Court pitch was referred to as the 'New Stand' simply because it was the most recent one, built in the 1960s. By 1986, though, it no longer looked new at all! The fourth and eastern side of the ground was called the 'Brighton Beach End' and now reserved for travelling fans only. I once asked my father why it was named that way. He pointed out that it was simply a sarcastic name that had stuck from the 1940s and '50s because the original stony surface of the terraces resembled the shingle of Brighton beach.

Since my first visit to the ground, when I perched on my father's shoulders watching John Bond's Cherries from the South End terrace, I had either stood or sat in all four corners of the ground and got soaked to the skin on numerous occasions at the South End. Dean Court was a peculiar kind of place. I sometimes found it a tranquil, peaceful oasis where I could forget my worries and at other times it was the one arena where I could release my frustrations and emotions onto an unsuspecting audience. The playing surface measured 75 yards wide by 111 yards long and the four edges grew only an arm's length from where spectators stood or sat. It was a neat, tidy and compact stadium, but a venue where no player could hide or escape a verbal battering. The close proximity of players to spectators was often the undoing of many a team. Fortress Dean Court was my second home and, although it had begun to look unfashionable and trite by the late 1980s, I loved it dearly.

As I sit in the new stadium today, 35 years on from my first visit, the passion remains. We supporters at Dean Court sing, 'I'm Bournemouth 'till I die'. This passion is in the blood and it will live with me forever. During the football season, no matter where I am at 3.00pm on a Saturday afternoon, AFC Bournemouth will always be in my thoughts. Slice me in half and inside you will find the club crest. I am 'Bournemouth 'till I die'.

That is why I have written this book. It tells my personal story of the memorable 1986/87 football season that ended with Bournemouth being promoted to Division Two for the first time in their history. I consider myself fortunate to have been able to witness such a remarkable season as I followed my Cherries physically and spiritually home and away during their record-breaking season. Much has been documented on the achievements of the promotion season, particularly statistical, but little from the supporter's angle. I have used my diary and scrapbook of the season to create this book, together with my own memories as a supporter and other sources I am grateful to acknowledge. Being a keen photographer, I have also included a small number of my own photographs taken at matches I attended.

What is documented on the following pages is a football season as seen through my eyes, the paying spectator who was so desperate for his team to finally crack the 'promotion hoodoo'. They include a mix of adventures, stories, personal thoughts and emotions experienced as the season unfolded. I believe they encapsulate the pure joy of watching such a wonderful game, the amusement and banter of the crowd and the fun of travelling to new towns and cities to watch my team play.

It was an education in itself as I travelled to the exotic locations of Blackpool, Chester, Newport, Walsall and Wigan (twice) and other places. Proudly I admit that the emphasis of my ramblings is firmly placed on my team, but I have also included other interesting features, moments and statistics for the season in question. At heart I am a genuine football fan and in love with the sport as a whole, not just Bournemouth. In contrast, football can be a cruel game. I recall the bitter disappointment of defeat; the long journey home after an away game – and the feeling of fear when a crowd turned ugly and I put personal safety first and forgot about the football match in progress.

All genuine football supporters throughout the country have a story like mine to tell. Football supporters amaze and inspire me with regularity. Combined, we are all the spectators, the experts and the critics of a wonderful game. I hope those of you reading these pages will remember your own good and bad experiences of watching 'your team' and enjoy my account of this season to remember.

2.
Unlucky
Bournemouth!

The contents of the trophy cabinet at AFC Bournemouth could be described as a little sparse. When it came to counting the silverware older supporters would usually smile and come out with the old joke that 'trophies at Bournemouth resembled a well-worn carpet, as they were a bit thin on the ground!' There was 'more silverware in the kitchen than there was in the boardroom'. I exaggerate to make a point, but success was generally something experienced by other clubs in the Football League. Of course there is some silverware on display, much of it from the early days and at a localised level, but serious football trophies at Bournemouth are almost as rare as hen's teeth. But why is that the case?

Much has already been documented in other fine publications regarding the Cherries' history and I have no intention of regurgitating a detailed list of historical facts and statistics here. However, the 1986/87 season requires some contextual setting around why it was so remarkable, memorable and record breaking for AFC Bournemouth. For those not familiar with the club, or its past please digest this chapter as a brief historical reference point that sets the scene for what was to truly become a 'season to remember'.

Bournemouth is a seaside town on the south coast of England, twinned with the Israeli resort of Netanya and Lucerne in Switzerland. The town has almost 200,000 residents, some of whom are extremely affluent, but AFC Bournemouth football club have always been and, no doubt, assuming survival is maintained, will continue to be, a small, traditional and less-fashionable club – generally well run, but continually short of finance, always promising much, but regularly failing to deliver on supporters' expectations. Unless a wealthy and charitable white knight appears in the future, this is how it will continue to be and we supporters must all accept that fact.

Formed from the disbanded Boscombe St John's Lads Institute FC in 1899, my fledgling club Boscombe FC had a long wait before finally being elected to the Football League in 1923. Coincidentally that was the same year a very young entrepreneur Thomas Frizzell founded the motor insurance firm where I began my financial services career some fifty years later.

Looking back now it was concerning to learn that in the early days the players wore cherry red and white striped 'Southampton style' shirts. This was at a time when the club played its matches at Castlemain Avenue in Pokesdown before moving to King's Park in 1902. To further develop the sport in the town local resident Mr J.E. Cooper-Dean granted the club a long lease on some wasteland next to King's Park in 1910. Volunteers gave their time to tend the land and produce a playing surface. The lovingly prepared new ground was named Dean Court after its benefactor. It is unclear how the club acquired the nickname 'The Cherries', but it was probably due to either the cherry red striped shirts worn by the team at that time or due to the fact that the new ground had been erected next to the Cooper-Dean estate, which included many cherry orchards. Either way the name stuck and has been affectionately used ever since.

The rise of Boscombe FC to official Football League status triggered a change in name to Bournemouth and Boscombe Athletic. The new name gave a much wider recognition and fairer reflection of the two growing boroughs of the town. Playing in that very first season of the Football League Division Three 'Southern Section' against teams such as Merthyr Town, Queens Park Rangers and Aberdare Athletic was a massive step up for the club. At the end of that first season it was no great surprise when the team finished second from bottom on goal difference, but above Queens Park Rangers, and so were forced to seek re-election. A further re-election scare came in 1933/34 as the club once again finished the season second from bottom. Progress remained slow, but at least it was being made! In the '30s and '40s the club steadily built upon its foundations, but that is where the excitement ends, as a series of mid-table performances continued up to the outset of the Second World War. With the backdrop of war, season 1939/40 recorded Bournemouth's highest League home win against an allegedly slightly inebriated and unmotivated Northampton Town. It was a one-sided game that ended 10-0. The following day war broke out and the season was abandoned with the result expunged from League records. Unlucky Bournemouth!

As the country struggled to get back on its feet after the war the first piece of silverware was proudly collected when Bournemouth won the League Division Three (South) Cup. The final against Walsall was played at Stamford Bridge on 4 May 1946, with the Cherries winning 1-0 in front of 19,715 spectators.

Two seasons later and the club made its first and serious assault to date on the Third Division promotion race. In an incredible season that saw the average home gate reach 16,853, including a staggering 25,495 against Queens Park Rangers, Bournemouth won 24 games and amassed a total of 57 points. Unfortunately, the team finished as runners-up to Queens Park Rangers in the days when only the Champions were promoted from the Third Division. Unlucky Bournemouth!

The 1950s' teams promised much, but, just like their predecessors, failed to deliver in the League. Cup football was the one notable exception. The FA Cup giant-killing side of 1956/57 brought cup fever to the town, and were eventually presented with the Sunday Pictorial 'Giant Killing' cup in recognition of their scalps. Having disposed of Burton Albion, Swindon and Accrington Stanley in the first three rounds, Cherries were drawn away to First Division glamour side Wolverhampton Wanderers and, against all odds, won 1-0. Round five produced a home draw and a 3-1 victory over more Division One opposition, Tottenham Hotspur. Having cast the Londoners aside, Bournemouth drew First Divison leaders Manchester United. The 'Busby Babes' won 2-1 with a decisive and hotly disputed penalty and the Wembley-bound dream was cruelly shattered. Unlucky Bournemouth!

The swinging '60s provided Bournemouth supporters with several more roller-coaster seasons containing relegation dogfights, mid-table mediocrity and the occasional frustrating promotion near miss. The most notable promotion failure was during season 1961/62 when the club, under the direction of manager Bill McGarry, finished third in Division Three. Only a 2-3 defeat at home to Grimsby Town in March ultimately prevented Bournemouth going up instead of Grimsby. Portsmouth finished the season as Champions with 65 points and Grimsby as runners-up with 62 points. Bournemouth ended the season in third place with 59 points. This time only the top two sides were promoted. Unlucky Bournemouth!

The general opinion throughout the town was that Bournemouth did not want Second Division football and had no ambition to ever secure football at a higher level. Having failed to secure a coveted place in the Second Division, and now famous for a mid-table finish, it was only a matter of time before

19

the unthinkable happened. Despite new signing Ted McDougall finishing the season as top scorer with 20 goals, disaster struck.

At the end of season 1969/70 Bournemouth were relegated to the basement division for the first time in their history, ending a record 47 years as a Third Division club. The Cherries, equal on points with Gillingham, were relegated on the goal difference of just one goal only. Unlucky Bournemouth!

The 1970s heralded a turbulent decade that began with a fresh impetus. At a time when Glamrock ruled, leather-clad Suzi Quatro invited us all to head down to Devil Gate Drive and Noddy Holder encouraged all young males to grow ridiculously long sideburns, Bournemouth's ambitious and wealthy Chairman Harold Walker recruited flamboyant manager John Bond from West Ham. The output of their partnership meant Walker invested heavily and Bond spent wisely. Success was instant. Cherries, in their new Inter Milan style red and black striped kit, were promoted back to Division Three at the first attempt as runners-up to Notts County. Even the club crest got a makeover in the form of a David Ginola lookalike with a 'blow dry' to match. This was to promote a modern image of the club, with former player and commercial manager Dickie Dowsett influencing the design.

The following season of 1971/72 witnessed the pinnacle of the Bond era and I consider myself so lucky to have witnessed Cherries playing some scintillating football in front of huge crowds. The visits of Aston Villa, Notts County and Brighton all attracted attendances of over 20,000 and Non League Margate were annihilated 11-0 in the FA Cup. That day remains crystal clear in my memory – I watched in wonder as my hero Ted MacDougall scored 9 goals and had two more disallowed. I recall amusing moments from that match, including MacDougall punching the ball into the net, then rubbing his face as though he had headed it in the goal. The referee was not fooled and ruled out the goal while Ted looked perplexed at the decision. Even funnier was the scoreboard at the Brighton Beach End, which stopped at 9-0 because there was no more space for a double figure goal tally. The *pièce de résistance*, though, was the continual look of horror on Margate keeper Chic Brodie's face each time he picked the ball out of the net. The poor guy didn't put a foot wrong all afternoon, yet still conceded eleven goals! Later that season, on Saturday 12 February 1972, Bournemouth made their debut on BBC TV's 'Match of the Day' as 48,110 at Villa Park watched Aston Villa host AFC Bournemouth. Ted MacDougall scored a wonderful goal to silence the home crowd. BBC commentator Barry Davies described the build-up and execution succinctly – 'MacDougall … Scott on the right … Boyer on the other post … MacDougall … what a classic diving header!' During the second half the Cherries began to fade and eventually lost the match.

Their season then faltered on the final end-of-season run-in and promotion was not meant to be. Bournemouth ended the season in third place and still only the top two sides were promoted in those days. The disappointment was magnified by the fact that Bournemouth had amassed the highest ever total of points for a side not to be promoted. Unlucky Bournemouth!

Rumours from the past began to resurface and for the first time I personally experienced the phrase, 'Bournemouth don't want promotion'. I disregarded it as nonsense, but gradually as I entered my teenage years I regularly encountered similar comments from older more knowledgeable Cherries supporters and even began to believe it myself! The high-energy momentum and push for Division Two slowly drained away and was never regained. I recall two further seasons of promise and disappointment that followed, but included the recording of a club song 'Here come the Cherries' and an official club name change from Bournemouth and Boscombe Athletic Football Club to the more European and succinct AFC Bournemouth. In 1973 Bond left and drained the young Cherries' talent by taking much of the squad with him to Norwich. There, with the nucleus of that early '70s Bournemouth team he achieved promotion and an appearance at Wembley in the 1974/75 League Cup final. The common joke at the time was that Bournemouth had finally achieved success and promotion, but were now called Norwich! The player exodus led to disaster and Bournemouth slipped back to the basement division in 1975. The story was a familiar one with a heavy ring of *déjà vu*. The Cherries, equal on points with Aldershot, were relegated again on the goal difference of a mere four goals. Unlucky Bournemouth!

The arrival of new manager David Webb to the club along with comedian Jim Davidson at the start of the 1980s once again injected new life into the Cherries. In 1981/82 Bournemouth finished the season in fourth place and achieved automatic promotion back to Division Three. Harry Redknapp joined the management team as coach the following season and eventually took over the helm during 1983/4. That proved to be a memorable season for the club as they achieved one of their proudest moments in the FA Cup, beating Ron Atkinson's Manchester United 2-0 at Dean Court. Less impressive, but in

21

the same season, Bournemouth won the inaugural Associate Members Cup, winning 2-1 against Hull at Boothferry Park.

For each of the following seasons the Football League secured sponsorship for the competition in different guises and the finals were all played at Wembley stadium. Bournemouth had won the cup in its inaugural season, the one and only time the final was never played at Wembley. Unlucky Bournemouth!

The record speaks for itself. With 63 years of Football League membership to be proud of prior to season 1986/87 the statistics boiled down to the following – two relegations from Division Three, two promotions from Division Four, three pieces of cup silverware, a handful of giant-killing acts in the FA Cup and a ton of disappointment for their long-suffering and success-starved supporters. Statistics were heavily stacked against promotion above Division Three and, like the many thousands of Cherries fans before me, it was chilling to acknowledge that in all probability I might die of old age before Bournemouth achieved promotion to Division Two. The Third Division was a prison from which there appeared to be no escape. Surely one day there would be something to celebrate – but when, and would it be on my watch?

3.
Introducing 'H'

'For sporting services to the town of Bournemouth and influence in the local football club and community he should receive a knighthood.' These were the exact words that I recorded in my diary at the end of May 1987. I had already begun to refer to him as Sir Harry Redknapp. In a long and illustrious list of names that included Harry Lowe, Freddie Cox, Bill McGarry, John Bond, Alec Stock and David Webb, Harry Redknapp became the twenty-first football manager of AFC Bournemouth and achieved the success that had eluded the club since 1923. He had made no secret of the fact that he wanted to be the first manager to lead AFC Bournemouth into the Second Division. Looking back, I now wonder if deep down this holy grail may have been his intrinsic motivation when he became manager at the club. Redknapp often stated publicly that being a player at the club during one of its more successful periods was a great help. He recognised the potential even at that early stage.

Maybe it is something in the air or because it is such a beautiful part of the world to live, but Redknapp has always had a close association with the south and, in particular, south-coast soccer. His original footballing roots were at West Ham in the mid 1960s when, as a young and developing talent, he played alongside the World Cup trio of Geoff Hurst, Martin Peters and Bobby Moore. At that time it was not possible to obtain a greater footballing pedigree. It was Bournemouth manager John Bond who influenced Redknapp to move south and join Cherries in August 1972 for a fee of £31,000. As a nine-year-old child I still have wonderful, but fading, memories of Harry's dazzling wing play at Dean Court as he played alongside Ted MacDougall and Phil Boyer in a glittering Cherries forward line. Redknapp signed on the same day as ex-Everton and Southampton star Jimmy Gabriel and played 101 League games for Bournemouth, scoring five times before joining Brentford in 1976. Like many great stars, a niggling knee injury eventually forced him to exit the competitive football arena.

With playing restricted, Redknapp began to develop his coaching credentials. The bond of friendship with Gabriel flourished and eventually led them both to an opportunity to apply their respective coaching skills in the USA before Redknapp returned home and teamed up with Bobby Moore at Oxford City. His involvement second time around with Bournemouth was twofold. Under David Webb he toiled as player-coach before Webb was sacked and Redknapp took over as caretaker manager in the interim.

His first taste of management in professional football could easily have been his last. I remember listening in horror to BBC Radio 'Sports Report' as it was announced that Bournemouth had been trounced 9-0 by Division Three leaders Lincoln at Sincil Bank. In his autobiography Redknapp explains in detail the circumstances surrounding that unfortunate afternoon, even admitting that Cherries were lucky to get nil! The baptism was far from the auspicious or confident start that Redknapp would have chosen. The facts stated it clearly; his first game as manager and the club had succumbed to its biggest ever defeat in 59 years of League history. Following a further character-building result in the next match, a 5-0 reverse at Orient, Don Megson arrived as the new manager. At the time I remember feeling relieved at the appointment, yet disappointed for Harry, who was genuine and honest and had been the victim of circumstances. Megson's time was short lived and thankfully Redknapp was re-promoted and offered the post full-time in October 1984.

My mates and I often referred to Harry as 'H', our new visionary charismatic leader who had become experienced in leading the club out of relegation battles and been instrumental in building teams that performed well in Division Three, which included masterminding the defeat of Manchester United in the FA Cup and winning the Associate Members Cup. I admired him especially as he had limited resources to work with. Harry had the exceptional ability to spot a young developing player, nurture and coach the talent, and then cash in on the investment generally for the benefit of AFC Bournemouth. His shrewdness in executing a series of inspirational signings and transfer dealings kept Bournemouth solvent for years.

His flair for finding the component parts to build a successful team were evident from the outset. I think the club had a special place in Harry's heart, and he has Bournemouth blood in him, too, as he still resides in the area today. If you asked any genuine Cherries fan about Harry Redknapp, I am confident that they would utter only positive words about his time with the club and the respect they hold for him. Cherries supporters owe him a great debt for his achievements with Bournemouth. He delivered football success to the town of Bournemouth through courageous leadership, passion and commitment. In my humble opinion Harry Redknapp has been the most influential and successful AFC Bournemouth manager in over 100 years of the club's football history.

He became the first and only manager to date to have successfully exorcised the promotion curse and lifted Bournemouth out of Division Three during season 1986/87 – and he did it in style as Champions.

4.
A summer of reflection

Before studying season 1986/87 in detail I want to look back at the previous season and the key events that contributed and led up to the promotion campaign. Promotion is no fluke and if you don't believe me then look at Bournemouth's appalling record if you need to be convinced of that statement. A football promotion success story is a combination of many factors – unless each is present the result is failure. Unequivocal leadership, a strong financial balance sheet, teamwork, hard graft from everyone connected with a football club and a lot of good fortune. These for me are important ingredients in a success recipe. One of the early lessons I learned from the first management book I ever read was that planning and preparation were key to success. The phrase of a management guru springs to mind, 'failing to plan is planning to fail'. These words still stick in my mind as does a phrase from one of my old school mates, 'piss poor planning makes for piss poor performance'. Both are right.

As summer approached and the 1985/86 football season came to a close, I looked back on what was really a mixed bag of a season and year. Although I thought that football was the most important thing in the world, shocking world headlines put my latest season of disappointment into perspective. In January the space shuttle Challenger exploded shortly after takeoff, killing all six crew. February saw the United States controversially bomb Libya in retaliation for terrorist activities and in April a radioactive cloud crossed Europe after a serious nuclear accident at the Chernobyl power plant in the Ukraine. In the local news a £4 million scheme for a Tesco store on Castle Lane would only go ahead 'over several dead bodies' according to council leader David Trenchard. At least there was a royal wedding to raise spirits in July. Andrew Windsor, Duke of York, was due to marry Sarah Ferguson in a ceremony at Westminster Abbey in front of an expected worldwide television audience of 300 million people.

But now summer had arrived, the days were long and the sun shone. I had played football for two local teams in the Bournemouth amateur league, primarily Lloyd's Bank on a Sunday morning (through my school pal Greg Feltham who already played for the team) and occasionally I played for my employer, Frizzell, on a Saturday afternoon when Cherries were away from home. I also played five-a-side on a Wednesday and trained on a Monday. It had been a long season and I was tired.

I thought of myself as a young Bryan Robson midfield dynamo, with a little more finesse, but sadly less commitment, but for both teams I had scored my fair share of goals. 'The Boys' from the Lloyd's Bank team, as I affectionately called them, were some of my best pals at the time. We would watch and play football together and then go drinking at Sinatra's nightclub in Christchurch. With the football season now over came the luxury to lie in bed on a Sunday morning and sleep off a Sinatra's hangover. Cricket had just started. Hampshire were (and still are) my team, but it was the Test Match arena that I really enjoyed. England were due to host India and New Zealand during the summer and, although it transpired to be a disastrous summer test series, Ian Botham would later inspire England on their winter tour of Australia and unleash his unstoppable grip on the Ashes. Even more exciting was the prospect of the World Cup in Mexico. England had qualified and so had Scotland and Northern Ireland – a wonderful summer was anticipated and expected. I was so excited I thought I might burst.

I sat in the garden listening to the Radio One 'Top 40' broadcast and I found myself analysing the lyrics to the top chart song, 'The Chicken Song', the spin-off from the satirical puppet TV series 'Spitting Image'. The ridiculous lyrics included, 'hold a chicken in the air, stick a deckchair up your nose, buy a jumbo jet and then bury all your clothes'. Although some people found the lyrics offensive, the song spent three weeks at number one. For a brief moment I struggled to understand why, but then I remembered the Spitting Image characters and had a little chuckle to myself. As I sat in the late warm evening sun my mind drifted back to football and 'The Cherries'.

Season 1985/86 was not particularly memorable for any special reason. Sure there were highlights for the club on the pitch, but results could only be described as average. Despite giving Everton a fright in the second round of the Milk Cup at Goodison Park and beating eventual champions Reading four out of five times, Bournemouth had finished in fifteenth position, just below mid table. Twenty-four players had contributed throughout, but only three were ever present – Mark Newson, Sean O'Driscoll, and Colin Clarke. Consistent contributions also came from fullbacks Tom Heffernan and Chris Sulley, midfielder and captain John Beck, and central defenders Paul Morrell and Roger Brown.

Brown had impressed me; he always made his presence known to opposing forwards. He was the solid dependable rock that the defence was founded on. A Goliath amongst centre halves and physically strong, at six feet tall he stood as a commanding figure that towered over most centre forwards. Sadly he was in the twilight of his playing career and had already sensibly begun looking at future coaching roles. I hated it, but I had to admit that Cherries would struggle without a player of his capability going forward.

The pinnacle of the season came in July 1985 when Bournemouth Manager Harry Redknapp signed a new striker from Tranmere Rovers. His name was Colin Clarke. To capture his signature Bournemouth had to beat numerous other clubs, including First Division Chelsea. Tranmere wanted £80,000 for Clarke, but Bournemouth offered only £10,000. Eventually a League tribunal stepped in and fixed the fee at £22,500, which all parties accepted. The deal almost fell apart at the eleventh hour when Chelsea tried to lure Clarke from under Redknapp's nose, but Clarke was a gentleman and despite the temptation he stuck to his word and signed for Bournemouth. In his autobiography Redknapp described him as having a 'terrific attitude'. This was just one of several examples of Redknapp's incredible ability to spot a bargain and execute a great deal – a skill he has demonstrated throughout his football managerial career at all levels. I have to add that football supporters are so often critical when one of their players is sold to another club. More often than not they are vociferous in stating that the player was undervalued and a better price should have been obtained. I tend to take a more relaxed view that 'what goes around, comes around' and that you will win a few and lose a few. Supporters are quick to remember the ones lost, but rarely remember the bargains.

Looking back now, Clarke was without doubt a genuine bargain at the fee of £22,500 and I'm sure Tranmere supporters must have been outraged at his departure at that price. The deal looked even more impressive when I read in my copy of 'Shoot' magazine that before Clarke signed for Bournemouth he had recently been called into the Northern Ireland squad and acted as substitute in a World Cup qualifying match against Spain.

In the programme notes of the first home game against Bristol City for season 85/86, Redknapp boldly stated, 'I am convinced that Colin Clarke will turn out to be the most prolific goal scorer at Bournemouth since the days of Ted MacDougall during the early 1970s.' This was a provocative statement that outraged me at the time.

MacDougall was a goal machine and a legend at Bournemouth and his strike rate would be impossible to replicate. To demonstrate my point the League records show that he only ever played in eight FA Cup matches for Bournemouth, scoring seventeen goals, a ratio of 2 strikes in every cup tie. I have already related his nine-goal demolition of Margate in 1971, an event that will always overshadow his performance in the previous season's First Round FA Cup replay when he scored six in the 8-1 thrashing of Oxford City. MacDougall was, still is and probably always will be my hero. No new striker could ever rival 'Saint Ted'. MacDougall used to have a business, 'Ted MacDougall Sports', a shop located in the Poole Arndale shopping centre. In 1971 I had the opportunity to meet Ted with my parents, but at nine years of age I was too shy to say anything to him and just stood motionless in the presence of the great man with my jaw agape while he served customers. Redknapp was wrong, no one could eclipse 'Super-Mac' and his 49 and 42 League and Cup goals during seasons 70/71 and 71/72 respectively, and so I doubted the rhetoric and Harry's faith in his new signing.

However, Harry Redknapp recognised a quality bargain and knew exactly what he was saying, and as the season progressed I humbly and rapidly retracted my opinion. By the end of season 85/86 Clarke had notched a total of 35 League and Cup goals for Bournemouth. The best of his 35 came on 31 March at Elm Park when Cherries visited League leaders Reading. The home side were leading 1-0 when Clarke picked up a loose ball in his own half, crossed the halfway line and at 35 yards out hit an absolute screamer, which literally smashed into the top corner of the net. The ball travelled so quickly that some wag in front of me quipped that the Bournemouth supporters behind the goal had sucked it into the net. It was the best Bournemouth goal I had seen since Ted MacDougall's diving header against Aston Villa in 1972, in front of the BBC TV 'Match of the Day' cameras. It really was that special.

Standing behind the goal, my fellow Bournemouth fans and I had enjoyed a spectacular view of a stunning goal, with one exception. Three minutes before this memorable moment the guy next to me, with whom I had shared a half-time post-mortem on the first 45 dismal minutes, decided to go and take a pee. At the critical and beautiful moment when the ball smacked into the back of the net, his only view was that of a begrimed and foul-smelling Elm Park urinal. As Reading kicked off again he rushed up and asked me what had happened. I just told him that he'd missed the best goal he'd ever be likely to see a Bournemouth player score. 'Shit,' he said, 'what a f***ing time to go for a piss.' Clarke's goal set up a remarkable 2-1 away victory against a very good Reading team that included beanpole striker Trevor Senior, and the Berkshire club ended the season as promoted champions.

Colin Clarke finished the 85/86 season as the Third Division leading scorer and was only just pipped as the country's leading marksman by England's Gary Lineker. In recognition of his scoring success, Clarke was called up again into the Northern Ireland squad and then into their World Cup squad. As early summer approached, I started to wonder if Bournemouth could retain an International player for another season. My fears soon were justified. On 13 May the Bournemouth 'Evening Echo' ran the back-page headline, 'Substantial offer by Italians for Cherries striker'. Clarkie was the transfer target of Italian club Torino. No figures were quoted, but AFC Bournemouth Chairman Rodney Barton stated, 'It is very sad for clubs at our level when they have to part with players of the calibre of Colin Clarke; finance and falling gates have made the decision for us.'

What was also interesting was the fact that the Italians could not complete the signing before 30 June (remember this date) because of foreign-player restrictions in their league. That meant that Clarke was technically still a free agent and would go to the World Cup in Mexico as a Bournemouth player. I was beginning to feel dizzy!

5.
Mexico '86
– Clarke's World Cup

You might ask what relevance the World Cup has in a book about AFC Bournemouth – well, quite simply, in 1986 another little piece of AFC Bournemouth history was made. The thirteenth World Cup confirmed Diego Maradona as the greatest player on earth. Sadly for the most popular sport on the globe it also confirmed him as the greatest cheat. For Mexico '86 the home-nation mascot was named Pique, a cartoon character that looked like a large green chilli wearing an oversized sombrero and proudly sporting a typical Mexican moustache. England were drawn in Group F with Morocco, Poland and Portugal. Northern Ireland were drawn in Group D with Brazil, Spain and Algeria. Scotland were in the 'group of death', Group E, with Denmark, West Germany and Uruguay.

Mexico '86 was special; it resurrected for me fond memories of Mexico '70, my first World Cup and arguably the last romantic tournament, with its classic sun-bleached images, fuzzy TV colour pictures and Hugh Johns' and David Coleman's crackly commentaries. There was Pele, Bobby Moore, that save by Gordon Banks, that miss by Jeff Astle, the legendary Brazilians, an incredible semi-final between West Germany and Italy, which followed England's unthinkable defeat at the hands of the Germans despite leading 2-0. I hated Gerd Müller in those days and took great satisfaction from using his picture as a dartboard on my bedroom wall. Mexico '70 will always hold a special place in my heart, but sixteen years later the anticipation and excitement was just as strong.

All three home nations got off to a poor start. Scotland lost to Denmark, England lost to Portugal and only Northern Ireland managed a point against Algeria. The second game was worse for England as they managed a 0-0 draw against Morocco, with Bryan Robson dislocating his shoulder and Ray Wilkins sent off. Scotland enjoyed their best game of the tournament, but lost to the Germans. Northern Ireland played Spain and my father and I sat down to watch it live on the television. As the team lists came up on the screen we were delighted; Billy Bingham had included Clarke on the substitute's bench and the TV displayed it as 'No. 14 Colin Clarke – Bournemouth'. The name of my home town and my team had just flashed up all around the world! The game started and within 18 minutes Spain led 2-0. As Dad and I discussed team tactics over a half-time brew we agreed – Bingham had to bring on Clarke at some point in the second half.

As the teams came out I saw Clarkie in the centre circle warming up. 'He's on,' I shouted, as Dad, who had been washing up in the kitchen at that moment, came rushing into the room to watch the second half with me. Within a minute of the restart Clarke had pulled a goal back. While the Spanish defender Ricardo Gallego and goalkeeper Andoni Zubizarreta dithered outside their own goal area, Clarke kept his eye on the ball and looped a brave header over the 'keeper to make it 2-1. Dad and I were jumping about like two school kids and he shouted, 'Good old Colin, that'll put another £100,000 on his value.' Spain held on to win 2-1, but history had been made. Colin Clarke had become the first ever Bournemouth player to play in and score in a World Cup finals tournament.

In the final group games Northern Ireland lost to Brazil and Scotland could only manage a 0-0 draw in a violent match with Uruguay. Both failed to qualify for the next phase. England made it through to the quarter-final stage courtesy of a Gary Lineker hat-trick against Poland, where they met first Paraguay and then Argentina. The 'Hand of God' intervened and the rest is history. I remember I sat on the edge of my seat throughout the entire 90 minutes of the Argentina game biting my nails, willing England on to victory. I leapt two feet in the air when Lineker pulled a goal back and then three feet into the air when I thought Lineker had equalised from another John Barnes cross. Watching the replay even now on my DVD, I just don't know how it did not go in. The shock gradually hit home; England were out. From that point the World Cup ended for me and faded into disappointment. Like most of the nation the minute England are out of a tournament the fire and emotion is extinguished and my interest is lost. Having given heart and soul to my patriotic duty it was now time to refocus on Bournemouth.

Clarke gave his Northern Ireland Mexico World Cup shirt that he wore with pride to Harry Redknapp, who stated, 'That was a superb gesture, although my young son Jamie will probably claim it!' I wondered if this was this to be Clarkie's parting gift?

6.
1986/87
Pre-season review

As the summer progressed so did the speculation about Clarke's departure from Bournemouth. Torino, Manchester United and Tottenham were all in the race to secure his signature. It was no longer a case of 'if' but 'when' and even more importantly 'how much?'! During my lunch break on Monday 30 June (remember the date), I purchased a copy of the 'Bournemouth Evening Echo' for the price of 16 pence. The front-page headline leapt out at me – '£400,000 deal for striker'. The speculation was over and the facts were presented on the front page. Colin Clarke was not Italy bound, but had surprisingly signed a deal that would take him from Dean Court to neighbours Southampton. Redknapp agreed when originally signing Clarke that if a bigger club wanted the striker he would be released. The fee was a new club record. Under the terms of the transfer, one third of the fee would go to Tranmere, but it still left the Cherries with a massive financial boost to help clear some of their debt. At the time £400,000 was big money for one player, but all I could think of was that Clarkie had gone. What made it more painful to accept was that he had travelled along the M27 motorway and joined local rivals Southampton.

At the time it seemed insignificant and of little relevance, but as well as the fee, Bournemouth were also to have two Southampton players as part of the deal – central defender Mark Whitlock, who had made 61 appearances in seven years at Saints, and striker David Puckett, who had 95 games under his belt at the Dell. Both had First Division experience and could prove useful additions to the squad. As colleagues and I discussed the Clarke deal next day at coffee and lunch breaks it was unanimous. The sale of Cherries star man would help the club financially, but it made any realistic chances of AFC Bournemouth being promoted to Division Two seem extremely remote. My colleague Ken Bichard captured the moment as he sighed and mumbled, 'I think we'll struggle this season' and, like the senators of Rome, we all nodded in agreement.

The 99th Football League season, 1986/87, was to be sponsored by 'Today' newspaper and would see more revolutionary change at high level than any one season in the history of the game to date. This was to be the first season when two substitutes would be permitted in both cup competitions and the new play-off system was to be introduced to the Divisions of the 'Today' League. The brainchild of Ron Noades and Martin Lange, the respective Chairmen of Crystal Palace and Brentford football clubs presented the concept to the Football League.

At their Extraordinary Meeting in May it was agreed that the Football League would undergo a restructure, which would include the First Division being reduced to twenty clubs from twenty-two. The First Division clubs' proposals on the restructuring of the League entailed a considerable amount of money being passed over to them in respect of TV, sponsorship etc. that was previously shared equally by all clubs. The Chairmen of the lower divisions had to explore how alternative funds might be made available to supplement those being conceded to prevent a Super League breakaway.

The initial idea was to introduce something for the fans to provide extra excitement at the end of the season. The view was taken that there were not enough successful clubs each season. So if the top six clubs in Divisions Two, Three and Four were able to win promotion automatically and/or to be involved in end-of-season play-offs to win promotion that would mean that many more clubs would have an interest right through to the closing stages of the season with a chance of being successful. Come the final end-of-season results it meant the top two in the division would achieve automatic promotion, giving the next four clubs finishing below the chance to battle it out for the final promotion place. Besides stimulating the interest of the fans, which would help all the clubs in the end-of-season games and increase gate receipts, it was intended that the play-offs should produce a certain amount of money for a fund to be distributed to all clubs outside the First Division.

Up to 1985/86 all clubs were only allowed to field one substitute for League and Cup games, but at the start of season 1986/87 the FA approved the rule to allow two substitutes in the FA Cup and Littlewoods Cup matches. If the experiment were successful then this rule change would be adopted for League fixtures next season.

One final significant change to the League structure that would not impact on Bournemouth, but would add towards the end-of-season excitement, but terrible fear for those involved, was the introduction of the 'Trap Door'. This required the club finishing in 92nd position in the 'Today' League Division Four to drop out and be replaced by the Champions of the GM Vauxhall-sponsored Conference League. For the first time ever, non-League clubs were given an automatic promotion place to play for.

Let me just put something into perspective here. Selling your star player, relegation and even losing the FA Cup Final will give you and your club heartache and disappointment in the short term, but you will get over it. If your team drops out of the Football League it is devastating and soul destroying, possibly resulting in the end of professional football in your town. In footballing terms I cannot think of any worse fate.

At the end of the previous season Reading, Plymouth Argyle and Derby County were promoted to Division Two, while coming in the opposite direction were relegated Carlisle United, Middlesbrough and Fulham. Tumbling out of Division Three were Lincoln City, Cardiff City, Wolverhampton Wanderers and Swansea. Promoted from the basement to replace them were Swindon Town, Chester City, Mansfield Town and Port Vale.

Bournemouth announced a new sponsorship deal with the brewery firm Coopers of Wessex, who had provided a £10,000 boost to sponsor the Cherries' new all-red kit for the forthcoming season. The new season League fixtures were published in June. Cherries would start with an away trip to Brentford. I made a careful entry of each match in my diary and against the Brentford away entry I wrote, 'Bugger! Once again I will miss Brentford away. I am cursed.'

Football hooliganism, once known as the 'British Disease', had continued for many years to be a major concern throughout Europe and had shrouded English football with a dark and dismal record. There was a growing frustration about the inability to curb or redirect the anti-social behaviour of the minority of football supporters who constituted the problem. It terrified me. The 38 dead Juventus fans in the Heysel Stadium continued to haunt any debate about the causes and cure of football violence. In the majority of cases during the early 1980s Bournemouth matches had passed peacefully, with only Millwall fans causing some concern, primarily due to their reputation, but other clubs had been less fortunate. It was a disease that impacted on every club and, as impatience grew, some decided to tackle the problems themselves.

Interesting events were taking place in the First Division. On the face of it, Luton Town's decision to ban away fans from matches at Kenilworth Road for the forthcoming season seemed an excellent idea. During the 1984/85 season not only had there been appalling scenes when Millwall fans invaded their pitch, fought with police and ran amok through the town, there had also been 190 arrests and 96 casualties throughout the season. The toll went down to 102 in 1985/86. However, once the ban was imposed for the 1986/87 season not a single arrest was made inside or outside the ground. But there was an almighty row. The argument against the ban on away fans was threefold. First, it penalised the innocent as well as the guilty. Second, it deprived the game of its atmosphere and, third, it also deprived the away team of valuable vocal support. Luton's counter to this was that it made the game safer, the local residents were not plagued by hooliganism and the club saved a fortune in policing costs.

The damage done by the violence and tragedy at Brussels and the recent pre-season 'friendly' violence abroad did much to tarnish the image of the game. Typically, though, at Dean Court the image was one of friendliness and warmth. There was no record of violence as such, and mum, dad and the family could watch in safety. Having said that, there were still a lot of people who would not visit Dean Court because they felt there was generally trouble at games, and the problem was a significant factor in my own decision to limit travel to away games. Cherries' Chairman Rodney J.C. Barton confirmed that Bournemouth would not be following Luton in banning away fans from Dean Court, but did not rule out the club adopting a similar membership scheme in the future.

Most of the cash from the Colin Clarke deal went to pay off a chunk of Bournemouth's growing debt, although a small amount was made available to Redknapp to strengthen the squad. Exiting the club were Chris Shaw, Chris Sulley (to Dundee United), Mark Nightingale (to Peterborough), Phil Brignull (to Cardiff City), Colin Russell (to Doncaster Rovers for £5,000), captain John Beck (to Cambridge United), goalkeepers Ian Leigh and John Smeldeurs (to Hamrun Spartans in Malta and Torquay United respectively), Colin Clarke (to Southampton) and the talented Ian Thompson (retired due to pelvic injury). Arriving at Dean Court were Mark Whitlock and David Puckett from Southampton. Tony Pulis was signed from Newport County to add strength to the midfield and 6ft 2in Eire International goalkeeper Gerry Peyton signed on a 'free' from Fulham after ten years with the 'Cottagers'.

A fee of £10,000 secured former England Amateur International, but unknown, striker Carl Richards from Gola League side Enfield. Richards was a tall and athletic Jamaican who in professional football terms was green and unproven. His experience was limited and I laughed when I learned that his pre-match meal was a bowl of Weetabix and he described his best ground ever visited as Scarborough. Joking aside, he was no mug and had scored 28 goals for the Gola League champions, including four goals in 25 minutes during one match. He was athletic, strong and had pace, ingredients that Bournemouth needed to inject into their forward line. Redknapp described his new signing as 'having muscles on muscles'.

Then just as pre-season friendlies commenced, Redknapp swooped in August to snap up Trevor Aylott, a much-travelled big target man from Crystal Palace. He was an experienced striker with plenty of First and Second Division experience, having played for Chelsea, Barnsley, Millwall and Luton. He made his first appearance in the midweek friendly match versus Wimbledon and I remember two points from this match. First, like a lunatic, I had rushed from work to get to Dean Court for the start of the game and, second and more relevant, I thought Aylott looked a useful acquisition, while short of match practice. 'Big Trev', as he was to become affectionately known, was no Colin Clarke, but he was big and skilful and in my humble opinion I felt Redknapp had made a good decision. This was the final warm-up game before the season started. Bournemouth performed well, but not well enough. Outclassed by the talented John Fashanu and Nigel Winterburn, the Cherries lost again. Admittedly, pre-season friendly matches are only an opportunity to boost players' fitness, experiment with positions and embed the changes before the real thing begins. For supporters, though, they are an early indication of the team potential for the coming season. Bournemouth's forward line had been completely remodelled from last season, so I had to be patient. But most of the results in the friendly matches were disappointing and a little embarrassing. Redknapp was unequivocal – 'Those matches served their purpose in giving us match play and the results do not count.'

For the record, here are the dismal pre-season friendly match results:

31	July	Parley Sports 0	AFC Bournemouth 4
2	August	AFC Bournemouth 0	Birmingham 1
5	August	Bournemouth Poppies 2	AFC Bournemouth 11
6	August	Weymouth 1	AFC Bournemouth 1

39

7 August	Bath City 1	AFC Bournemouth 0
9 August	Crystal Palace 3	AFC Bournemouth 0
9 August	Woking 2	AFC Bournemouth 1
11 August	Sturminster Newton 1	AFC Bournemouth 3
12 August	Wimborne Town 2	AFC Bournemouth 2
15 August	AFC Bournemouth 0	Wimbledon 3

With six new signings, however, the brief thought crossed my mind that perhaps this could be our year. Maybe we did now have the opportunity to grab that elusive Second Division place which every Bournemouth supporter dreamt about. Yeah right! – I wasn't convinced. We had lost all of our pre-season friendlies against League opposition, not a good omen. The players themselves, though, began with an early belief that they could strike gold this season.

Taking a lead from their confident manager, Redknapp's influence was obvious, instrumental and influential as the orchestrator behind the scenes. His confidence had captivated the squad from the outset and once he had recited the magic formulae the players were quickly under his motivational spell. I liked Redknapp's style of management; he waxed lyrical about his new men, building their confidence, but maintaining a sense of realism. He described new, yet untried, striker Carl Richards as an 'unpredictable player with phenomenal pace', adding, 'but you never really know what he's going to do next. Sometimes even I don't!' Puckett and Whitlock from Southampton brought something else to the party, which Redknapp eloquently called 'a little First Division class from The Dell'. Keeper Peyton was another great signing and would, according to Redknapp, provide 'a more commanding presence in goal'.

Having experimented at the end of the previous season, Harry was now ready to release his sweeper system, which he passionately argued was not a defensive system. Being open and honest, he declared that the pretty patterns of last year's Cherries' play had gone and the club had sacrificed style for steel to deliver results, adding, 'I think we will be a far more physical team this year.' This was encouraging and fighting talk. Bournemouth had traditionally followed the West Ham school of football, preferring to play the game the correct way. Whether it had been an approach adopted since 1899 I don't know, but it had got the club nowhere. To get out of the Third Division a successful team needed that extra bit of steel. It seemed that Redknapp had developed a new strategic recipe by recruiting and collecting youth, experience, talented individualism and battle-hardened seasoned professionals to do a particular job – win promotion.

Redknapp's tough-nut evangelism continued, 'Pulis is one of the hardest men in the Division and we have plenty of ball winners, so we will be very hard to beat.' From my perspective this was all great rhetoric, but would it deliver results? One thing was for sure, though; while I had not yet observed recent-signing Tony Pulis in action, all the talk about his reputation as a hard man meant that I already feared him. His character appeared to be similar to 'Animal' from the Muppet Show, an individual who would let actions speak louder than words. He had been elevated to the status of a rough and tough western gun fighter. Thank goodness he was on our side!

7.
Season 1986/87
(Part 1: August to
December 1986)

In the club handbook issued in time for the pre-season friendly matches, Cherries' Managing Director and Secretary, Brian Tiler, wrote: 'Every new season brings new optimism and enthusiasm. I feel that with the changes in playing personnel and the gradual sounder financial climate we have achieved then our fans can feel more confident of a brighter future. That barrier of achieving Second Division football for the first time has to be broken sometime and it might just be that this season could be the culmination of that dream.'

From a commercial perspective the team had a new all cherry red kit for the season's start following a three-year sponsorship deal with the Icelandic company Henson, which was 50 per cent owned by Aston Villa. Once again there were no pre-match ticket sales at the start of the season and, in keeping with previous years, admission was available on the turnstile on the day of the match. Admission to the South End and New Stand terracing cost £3.00, while a seat in the Main Stand cost £4.50. A seated season ticket would set you back £90.00.

In the draw for the Littlewoods Cup First Round, Bournemouth were paired against the favourites for the Third Division Championship, Bristol City. Bookmakers Coral quoted City at 6-1 for the championship, with other odds including 10-1 Swindon and Walsall; 12-1 Gillingham, Notts County, York and Wigan; 14-1 Doncaster, Fulham and Middlesbrough. The Cherries' chances for the season ahead were not rated highly – Coral quoted AFC Bournemouth at odds of 33-1 for the Third Division title and a place in the top four was a 6-1 shot. You could also get odds on the Cherries to finish anywhere in the League table with relegation positions (21st to 24th) at odds of 9-2! The bookmakers saw Cherries as a team more likely to get relegated than promoted.

AUGUST

Brentford v. Bournemouth – Saturday 23 August

Cherries' campaign began with a visit to Griffin Park. Redknapp had completed his first piece of pre-season homework when he watched Brentford during their friendly match 1-0 reverse at home to QPR on 12 August. I missed this easy trip to the capital because I was on holiday in Greece. It's strange really, but Brentford are my jinx team. Whenever Bournemouth were due to play them away, I was unable to get to the match because of holiday, work or illness! Incredibly the jinx continued for another 18 years before I finally made it to Griffin Park.

This opening game of the season with a new-look side was technically Bournemouth's 2,500th match in the League. Mysteriously, though, this same milestone would be achieved again in the home game with Bolton on 16 September. This confusion needed some explanation and after some brief research I found the answer. The total of 2,499 games played so far included those played at the start of season 1939/40, before the League was suspended because of the war. The fixtures and results from that season are generally not included in statistics, but these figures appeared in the Association of Football Statisticians report. The club had agreed to mark and celebrate the achievement at the home game against Bolton.

Unable to receive UK television or BBC Radio in my hotel in Corfu, and before mobile phones existed, I had to just sit it out in the blazing sun and wait for the game to end; no real hardship. Maybe it was something to do with being Saturday, but there was a queue for the hotel payphone. The wait was painfully slow, but finally after 20 minutes that seemed to last an eternity, I called home and spoke to Dad, who told me that the Cherries had drawn 1-1. Captain Mark Newson was both hero and villain on the day. Newson had given away a 44th-minute penalty for handball, but claimed he was nudged in the back by a Brentford forward and the ball hit his hand.

Playing the role of the unbiased tourist, it sounded as though referee Hemsley had either consumed one ouzo too many, like me, or absorbed too much sun and then crumpled under the pressure of the home crowd. Robbie Cooke converted from the spot. Despite this setback, Newson turned hero in the 85th-minute as he rose to head home the equaliser. As the season progressed Newson developed the knack of regularly popping up and scoring a vital goal. Newson's leadership, inspiration and determination on and off the pitch rubbed off on his colleagues and contributed massively to a 'never say die' team spirit that the players developed. Yet amazingly, like other players, he occasionally got some stick from segments of supporters. Newson would become known as 'Captain Marvel', because as the season progressed we marvelled at his flexibility to play in any position and still score critical goals. As I prepared for a heavy drinking session with the boys in Corfu, I reflected on the result as a point well earned.

Three days later, lying on the beach, I worked my way through a second-hand, shabby, sunlotion-stained 'Sunday Express' that had finally arrived in the hotel shop and for which I had paid three times the cover price. Scrutinising the opening results of the season, I was sickened to learn that in Division One Southampton had beaten Queens Park Rangers 5-1 at The Dell, but to rub salt in my wounds Colin Clarke had scored a hat-trick on his Saints debut. Against this entry in my diary I wrote one comment, 'Bollocks!'

Bournemouth v. Bristol City – Tuesday 26 August
The first home match of the new season was a Tuesday evening Littlewoods Cup first-round, first-leg match against Bristol City. I was still sobering up in Corfu, so missed this match too. In his programme notes, 'Harry's Line', on the 26th, Redknapp wrote: 'We have had the biggest turnaround in players that I can remember during my time with the club. This gives us a strong looking squad of players and I am more optimistic than ever for the future of the club.' He also went on to add, 'I think tonight's visitors under Terry Cooper will be one of our main rivals for a promotion place.' City were promotion favourites, but only 2,631 turned up to watch Alan Walsh score a gem of a goal for the visitors as they held the advantage for the second leg. Although I missed the match, I thought it was summed up nicely by 'Evening Echo' reporter Colin Smith in his write-up: 'With six new signings and Bobby Savage back after an injury enforced absence throughout last season, Bournemouth have to find a new blend.'

There was trouble in the First Division match between Luton Town and Southampton, but not of the hooligan variety. Luton, having banned all away supporters from their home matches and introduced a membership scheme using identity cards, experienced problems with their computerised turnstiles and many home fans missed Luton's fourth-minute opening goal. Critics of the scheme gloated, Southampton lost, but that man Clarke scored again.

45

Bournemouth v. Newport County – Saturday 30 August

Not only was I back in the country – I was back at Dean Court, and took up my usual standing position in the South End of the ground. Walking towards my regular viewing point, I passed three men leaning on a crush barrier, one of whom held a two-foot high green plastic Tyrannosaurus Rex with gleaming white teeth. As I smiled at the man and his inflatable he gestured, 'This is Rex, say hello Rex!' Rex sat with them on the crush barrier and watched this game and also every home match for the rest of the season. I recall that Rex was regularly hurled skywards to celebrate a Cherries goal! Two years later the football inflatable craze took hold on Britain's football terraces. Sadly, Rex was before his time and had peaked too early.

It was good to be back and once again sense the magic and mystery of the old sports ground. I was a 'South Ender' and proud of the territory. I stood just to the left behind the goal. This was a favoured spot that I had watched from for over 20 years. I had a great view and elevated perspective from this position until it rained. When it did, I moved towards the back of the stand and huddled in with everyone else under the roof. There I could still get a good view of the pitch, but with the added dribble of water down my neck from the leaking gutter! How and why supporters of cash-strapped clubs in the lower divisions have tolerated such poor conditions for so long remains a testament to our supporter loyalty.

For the Newport match the sun shone brightly high in the summer sky. I surveyed the stadium and reflected on the possibilities of what might take place in the old arena this season. Dean Court 1986 had been given another summer makeover – gleaming new advertising boards, a fresh coat of cherry red paint on all metallic surfaces, and something never seen before. Yellow paint marked passageways on the concrete steps and sections of the terrace area enclosure. These yellow sections now indicated a no-standing area designated as clearways and were to be kept free at all times. My match day programme notes explained under the heading 'KEEP OFF THE YELLOWS' that this safety innovation was not a drive to put the local public transport (Yellow Buses) out of business, but the club's positive action to manage crowd control and operate within the Safety of Sports Grounds Act (1975).

The Dean Court pitch looked superb. John Harriss, the groundsman, had been busy all summer tending the hallowed turf. His efforts had produced a lush thick green velvet carpet tightly mowed in 2 metre-wide sections in either direction to give it a polished two-tone green effect.

As I studied the content of my 50 pence official match day magazine I was a little bemused and failed to understand why the front cover featured three separate action shots of Bournemouth players Brown, Beck and Clarke. In fact, Beck and Clarke had left the club before the season start and Brown had hung up his boots and joined the management team, but the front cover feature remained in place throughout the entire season!

Newport County were the visitors for the first home League match and it turned out to be a good game, with Bournemouth winning 2-1. David Puckett opened his account for Cherries after five minutes, only for County forward Roy Carter to surprise and annoy everyone with a 40th-minute equaliser. Disappointment was turned into delight as rubber-legs Carl Richards netted the winner in the 71st minute, his first goal in League football. As he celebrated I heard someone behind me shout, 'Nice one, Bruno', an affectionate name that would stick throughout the season in view of his slight resemblance to boxer Frank Bruno.

On 75 minutes my heart sank and my head dropped. Newport striker Mick Vinter hit the back of the net with a shot from just outside the Bournemouth penalty box. The disappointment from the home fans at conceding a second equaliser was immediate and manifested itself as a deep groan. The small following from Newport located at the Brighton Beach away end of the ground were delighted. But as instant as the disappointment that hit me, there followed an immediate wave of joy. Murphy the linesman had his yellow flag raised. Referee John Moules consulted with him and agreed that a Newport player had strayed offside. The outcome – no goal. The two sets of supporters now swapped their original reactions to Vinter's strike and the bloke behind me who five minutes ago was praising 'Bruno' now yelled, 'well spotted, lino, you're not as stupid as you look'. Within moments of the decision the home crowd were in good voice – 'you thought you had scored, you were wrong, you were wrong' drifted across Dean Court.

Despite a number of goalmouth scrambles and a fair bit of nail biting on my part the final whistle eventually blew. Newport were a little unlucky as they struck the woodwork twice and had an effort disallowed for offside. But the points belonged to Cherries and I went home happy!

SEPTEMBER

Bristol City v. Bournemouth – Tuesday 2 September

Middlesbrough, in the hands of the Official Receiver, had to play their home match of the second leg of the Littlewoods Challenge Cup at Hartlepool because they were locked out of Ayresome Park. The club, on a life-support machine following a financial crisis, survived a traumatic battle when they were one hour from non-League obscurity, eventually being rescued when a new consortium agreed to pay all of their outstanding debts. Foolishly and naively I thought 'thank God, this terrible situation could never happen to Bournemouth' – words that would come back to haunt me in the future.

Football hooliganism remained at its peak and, if I'm honest, I did not fancy a midweek trip to Bristol. Having just returned from holiday, my cash flow situation had entered into crisis mode, and increased work commitments – poor excuses – prevented me from making the short trip to Ashton Gate for the second leg of the Littlewoods Cup match. Prior to kickoff I learned from a five-second television review of the match on BBC TV's 'South Today' that captain Mark Newson had been ruled out of the starting eleven, having aggravated a foot injury during the Newport home win. Much of this match remains a blur to me, but I do remember being very annoyed when I tuned into BBC Radio Solent only to find out that there was no 'sports special' that evening, just music and insignificant chat. By today's standards it may sound primitive, but Teletext was my lifeline and the only connection to the game. The first half was goalless, meaning that City still led 1-0 from the first leg.

On 60 minutes the screen flicked over and showed that Trevor Aylott had scored for Cherries. We were back in it. I stared at the screen for the remaining 30 minutes, but nothing changed. Then it updated and in green text displayed 'extra time being played'. On 97 minutes the screen refreshed again and recorded 1-1. Glyn Riley had equalised for City, making it 2-1 on aggregate, and that was the way it stayed. We were out of the Littlewoods Cup at the first hurdle, but I consoled myself with the view that we could now concentrate on the League! Talking next day to my colleague Peter Dodman, he mentioned that Bournemouth left back Paul Morrell had been stretchered off during the match. Later, when I read the 'Bournemouth Echo' report of the game, I was a little more relieved. Morrell had been in a heavy collision with David Moyes and as a result suffered a trapped nerve in the neck. Apparently it was not too serious and it was hoped that he would be fit for Saturday.

Notts County v. Bournemouth – Saturday 6 September

Notts County, the oldest club in the Football League, were due to host Cherries next. The Magpies were founded in 1862 during the reign of Queen Victoria at a time when Bournemouth was only a fledgling town. Meadow Lane had not been a particularly happy hunting ground for Bournemouth teams in the past and, with further reports in the media regarding incidents of violence at many League grounds, I remained concerned for my safety and chose to stay at home. At this point you could question my loyalty as a genuine supporter and describe my decision as cowardly. Confidence was at the heart of the matter and, looking back, I now blame the popular media in Britain at that time, with their unique penchant for hysteria and sensationalism, branding some supporters as 'mindless thugs' and 'scum'. I eventually learned that they tarred all supporters with the same brush.

I had travelled to away games in my late teens and early twenties and had already run the gauntlet of fear, meeting examples of this 'scum' at Exeter, Reading, Bristol Rovers and Windsor and Eton. Even Bournemouth had their warriors, one of whom I remember meeting on the way to Exeter two seasons earlier. A friend of a friend had hired a 12-seat Ford Transit minibus and we had stopped on the road at Dorchester to pick up a character known as 'Axe-Head'. Boarding the bus with cans of Stella in each hand I could see how he got his name as he had an ugly seven-inch scar on his face running vertically from his forehead down to his lower jaw. Throughout the journey he talked about leading a charge against the Exeter supporters and the more he drank the louder he became. Thankfully he was in a minority, but he was an example of the disease that each club had. Axe-Head never made the bus ride back that day and I never knew what happened to him, although someone said that they had seen him legging it down a side street followed by a pack of Exeter nutters in hot pursuit. Experiences of this nature continued to make me nervous and, while I was desperate to travel to Nottingham and absorb the legend of the world's most famous outlaw, sadly I chose the comfort and wellbeing of 'Cherry Land' and the radio reports.

At the time BBC Radio Solent provided a good service for followers of Southampton, Portsmouth and Bournemouth with a Saturday afternoon sports programme presented by Grant Coleman. Each match would be previewed in depth before the kickoff, with interviews and analysis of each southern team's performance. I loved it, but it annoyed me that on most occasions Bournemouth were always last to be previewed behind Southampton and Portsmouth respectively. This is the price to pay for being the smallest club in the Solent area. This was in the broadcasting days before Solent provided live commentary at a match and technological advancements had developed sufficiently to facilitate the capability of split-frequency broadcasting. As matches kicked off, Grant and his team would play some great music, interspersed with reports from the three southern games. If a goal was scored the music broadcast at that precise moment would be abruptly interrupted, with a crowd cheering sound immediately indicating that there had been a goal in one of the three games. As the cheering halted the music the suspense was incredible as I waited to hear where the goal was.

For 45 minutes the music played and was twice interrupted with the cheering jingle. Each time the goal was at Southampton's match, so at half-time the Bournemouth game was goalless. Eleven minutes after the restart the cheering interrupted Abba's 'Mamma Mia'. Presenter Grant Coleman said, 'There's a penalty in our featured Third Division game at Meadow Lane.' My heart raced as reporter Tony Mitchener excitedly yelled, 'It was for Notts County, but Cherries keeper Gerry Peyton has saved it.' Phew! That was close, I thought, as we were taken back to the last 30 seconds of 'Mamma Mia'. Four minutes later the cheering sound came again. Grant followed with the words, 'This time there has been a goal in our featured Third Division game at Meadow Lane.' Reporter Tony Mitchener excitedly announced that David Puckett had fired Bournemouth in front after being set up by Newson. I did a little jig in the kitchen to celebrate the news.

If anyone had asked me at the time what my dream job would be, it would have been Mitchener's. What a life, paid to watch and report on the Cherries home and away in complete safety. Oh how I envied him. It was only some years later through my connections with Hospital Radio Bedside when I acted as 'sports reporter' for a handful of games at Dean Court that I met him and witnessed at first hand the broadcasting discomforts that are experienced when reporting from lower-Division grounds and exposed to the elements. It transpired not to be the job of glamour that I had anticipated and I respected him for his professionalism in such challenging environments.

On 73 minutes the cheering radio jingle rudely interrupted a Beach Boys number and I learned that Notts County had equalised. Mitchener explained the detail, but I felt numb. 'Bugger' was the first word I uttered and my thoughts were only of Robin Hood and how he had successfully robbed again.

The final quarter of an hour was tense and frantic. In that time Southampton pulled a goal back at home to Nottingham Forest and Portsmouth cemented their lead at Barnsley, before Southampton conceded a late third goal. Each time the cheering jingle sounded my heart stopped, only to breathe a sigh of relief when I heard that the goals were not at Meadow Lane. The game ended 1-1 and, considering County had missed a penalty, I thought that was a reasonable result. Later that evening the boys and I headed for Sinatra's to sink a few pints of the amber nectar and eye the local talent.

On Monday the 'Bournemouth Evening Echo' ran a back-page headline, 'Old Pals Act pays off with point'. Apparently, a couple of days before the match Redknapp had spoken to his football friend John Rudge, who was manager at Port Vale. Rudge, the former Cherries forward, had given Harry some advice on County's style of play. That included a tip about Ian McParland's penalties. In the same report, but under a brief but new section headed 'Harry's View', Redknapp was quoted saying, 'John tipped me off about McParland's penalty kicks. I had a word with Gerry Peyton before the game and it worked!'

Bournemouth v. Bolton Wanderers – Saturday 13 September

This was Bournemouth's 2,500th match since joining the football league in 1923. Ironically that was the same year that visitors Bolton had won the first FA Cup final at Wembley, remembered as the famous 'white horse' final when PC George Storey, with the help of his white horse Billy, helped clear the Wembley pitch of spectators to allow the game to start. Sixty-three years later the glory days were a distant memory for Bolton and their 1986 encounter with the Cherries turned out to be a Dean Court thriller that ended with Bournemouth's 937th league victory.

To celebrate the club's milestone it had been planned that the Army would be literally dropping in on the match. The occasion was meant to have been marked by the Silver Stars, the Royal Corps of Transport free fall parachute club, led by Sergeant Jeff Chandler, landing in the centre circle at half-time and then announcing the winner of a holiday draw. Disappointingly, the spectacle had to be postponed due to unfavourable weather conditions.

Standing in my usual South End spot I saw a courageous fightback by my team. Bolton took the lead in the 36th minute when Tony Caldwell met a header from Elliot with a first-time shot that easily beat Peyton and flew into the top right-hand corner. Three minutes later it all turned rather ugly as Bournemouth captain Mark Newson was on the receiving end of a vicious kick by Bolton's Mark Gavin. Referee Ron Groves had no hesitation in sending the culprit off, to the great delight of the home fans. Gavin strolled to the touchline with head down and pulled his shirt off in disgust as I joined the vocal home fans in the South End stand and delivered a barrage of, 'You dirty northern bastard!' – and we frantically waved him 'cheerio' as he left the pitch. He replied to us with a brief two finger salute before heading off down the tunnel for an early bath.

In the second half Bolton were struck another blow when Mark Winstanley was carried off following a challenge with 'Bruno' on 68 minutes. Any player who challenged Bruno usually came off worse. With eleven minutes remaining and with the team attacking their favoured home end, David Puckett was brought down in the penalty area by Bolton defender Dave Sutton. Bob Savage drove home the resulting spot kick, and I punched the air and jumped for joy. The celebrations in the ground were boisterous, with the exception of the Bolton players and fans. Savage had a mean left foot and I have never seen anyone to this day hit a football harder than he could, and he rarely missed from the penalty spot. He hit the ball so hard that he made Leeds star Peter Lorimer, the Brazilian Rivelino and Liverpool hero Jimmy Case look like girls!

With just five minutes remaining, Cherries' Paul Morrell found himself in acres of space on the left, following a beautifully timed pass from Aylott. I willed him to deliver a good cross into the box, but he just looked up and hammered the ball with his left foot. I thought, 'selfish bastard', shooting from there. My apology was almost instantaneous as Morrell spectacularly curled a left foot shot into the roof of the Bolton net. The angle from where I stood made it appear for one bizarre moment as if the ball had gone through the side netting, but there were no complaints from Bolton and the referee signalled a goal while Morrell and the rest of us all celebrated.

Morrell or Mossie, as he was affectionately called, also had a habit of popping up with crucial goals during the season. He was well liked by supporters and I think we had special affection for him as he was the only local lad in the team.

There was still time for Steve Elliott to be dismissed for dissent as Bolton finished the game with nine players and the Dean Court choir once again burst into song. As the final whistle blew I stood and applauded the team as they left the pitch, then pushed my way out of the ground through the happy crowd and back to the car. Once in the car I tuned into Solent to hear Grant Coleman announce that Bournemouth occupied fourth place in the table and were now in a play-off place!

Elsewhere, Aston Villa had been thrashed 6-0 by Nottingham Forest, with their reserve side being walloped 7-0 by Manchester City. The following day manager Graham Turner was sacked and became the season's first managerial casualty from Division One. The Heysel stadium tragedy continued to haunt English football as the case involving 26 Liverpool fans dragged through the courts. The fans appeared before magistrates, but the proceedings against them were adjourned twice. Finally, the presiding magistrate said that there was a case to answer and that they should be extradited to Belgium to face charges of involuntary manslaughter.

Bournemouth v. Chester City – Tuesday 16 September

The halogen filaments pierced the darkness across King's Park as I made my way to Dean Court for the evening encounter with Chester. Night games feel different and have a 'Je ne sais quoi' about them. I have always loved their atmosphere. In typical routine for an evening game I had raced home from work, gulped down my tea and raced out again to get to the match. Because of a 'long hours' office culture and valuable double-time overtime rewards, the 7.30pm kick off was too early for my lifestyle and now I could feel mild indigestion in my stomach.

Having drawn their first four matches of the season, Chester had developed a reputation for being a difficult side to beat. Checking off the team line up on the match programme I noticed that ex-Cherries' striker Milton Graham was in the Chester starting eleven. I remembered his goal in the cup-tie against Manchester United on 7 January 1984, a date etched in my memory forever. United keeper Gary Bailey had spilled the ball from a corner and Graham hooked it into the net as Bournemouth shocked the football world, dumping holders Manchester United out of the FA Cup 2-0.

Milton Graham was a useful player on his day, but he was a lightweight who never really cut the mustard at Bournemouth. However, I knew our defence would need to watch him closely. It has always intrigued me how past players

53

from a club always seem to have a knack of scoring against their old clubs. No doubt they have a point to prove and go all out to inflict it. Graham would be no exception.

As it turned out Milton Graham never got a look in on the night as he was well marshalled by the Cherries' defence. Bournemouth midfielder Gary Howlett opened the scoring in sensational style in the 49th minute with an unstoppable shot that screamed into the roof of the Chester net. That man Puckett scored a second goal on 70 minutes to give Cherries a comfortable lead as they cruised to a 2-0 victory. As the final whistle blew a disappointing, but vocal, crowd of 3,027 gave a huge cheer and the latest Dean Court anthem erupted, 'Here we go, here we go, here we go.'

When their team is victorious supporters are overwhelmed by the adrenalin of the occasion and it leads them instantly down a path of optimism. Outside the stadium, as the crowd made their way home, I heard a small group of home fans break into a brief, but very excited, chorus of 'The Reds are going up!' A tad premature, I thought.

Top of the UK singles chart on this night was the Communards cover version of 'Don't leave me this way'. Five games into the season and Bournemouth were also number one, top of Division Three and remained unbeaten along with Gillingham, Bristol City and Middlesbrough. Who needed the play-offs? Redknapp said, 'We must not get carried away just because we have gone top of the division because it's early days yet.' He was right, of course – Harry usually was – but nonetheless it was quite an achievement, and I was feeling a little dizzy myself with Bournemouth at this League altitude.

Mansfield v. Bournemouth – Saturday 20 September

As League leaders the Cherries travelled to Mansfield without me. The insurance business had entered into a busy period, overtime was in abundance and my cash flow desperately required replenishment. I sat at my desk and processed another dull motor insurance file. Working on a Saturday severely shortened my weekend, but double overtime pay was sufficient compensation.

Despite not making the physical journey to Nottingham, I was there in spirit as the clock passed 3.00pm. The Stags were mid-table; they had won only one of their opening five matches, drawn three, but only lost one. Bournemouth had taken a point from all of their away games to date, so there were no surprises really when this match finished honours even at 1-1. At 3.45pm I sprinted down to the car park to hear the half-time scores on the car radio. Once again I had to wait patiently for Solent to report on Southampton and Portsmouth first, before Bournemouth, which continued to annoy me. Eventually they reached the Cherries game and at half-time the score was 0-0.

It sounded a drab affair and, worryingly, striker Trevor Aylott had been carried off with suspected ankle-ligament damage, Carl Richards taking his place. Richards had adapted quickly following his step up into professional football and was well liked by both players and fans. He passed his initiation test earlier in the season when some of the players, led by Newson, cut off the ends of his socks during a routine training session. He saw the funny side of it and had clearly begun to settle in the squad. I strolled back to the office letting those interested know that it was goalless after 45 minutes before I sat down and opened the next customer insurance file.

I telephoned Mr P. Jenkins to explain that it would cost a further £146.12 to comprehensively insure his new Volvo estate in Accrington. While politely discussing the detail of this transaction I was blissfully unaware that Cherries' midfielder Mark O'Connor had just given Bournemouth the lead, his first goal for the club. Had I known, I would have leapt to my feet with a great shout of excitement, probably causing Mr Jenkins to suffer a perforated eardrum, but the moment passed calmly and I continued with my work. As the clock ticked on, unbeknown to me Mansfield stepped up a gear, applying pressure to the Bournemouth goal. Keeper Peyton stood firm, made two excellent saves and Bob Savage rode his luck as he cleared the ball off his own goal line by slicing it onto the crossbar and out. If I had been aware of this desperate defending my nails would no doubt have suffered with a severe biting. Twelve minutes from the end Mansfield equalised, following a corner from which Neville Chamberlain rose unmarked to head his first goal for the home side. Thank goodness that I was no longer on the telephone to Mr Jenkins at this point – if I had known of this setback I think customer relations may have become strained and he would have been shocked at the language that could be spouted from an insurance professional from 'down south'.

Just before 5.00pm I said goodnight to my colleagues and took the stairway to the car park. I switched on the radio just as Grant Coleman uttered 'and Bournemouth come away with a point after a 1-1 draw with Mansfield'.

A point away from home is always a good result, but the shine was taken off as other results came in. Middlesbrough had won 2-0 at home to Chesterfield and were top of the Division, York were second after beating Bury 1-0. Despite Bournemouth's endeavour they had dropped to third place; a play-off spot. Driving home and listening to the radio report, it was concerning to hear that Cherries had been forced to field Youth Team Coach Keith Williams in midfield because of an injury to Tony Pulis. This was the juggling challenge that Redknapp, like all managers operating with a limited resource pool, continually had to face.

Elsewhere, there had been another fire at Bradford City when Leeds fans overturned a fish and chip stall, which caught alight.

Bournemouth v. Bristol City – Saturday 27 September

Recovering from a hangover on Saturday morning was a regular occurrence and one that I had become quite proficient at. This particular Saturday morning hangover, though, was somewhat persistent. The day before had been my 24th birthday and the boys and I had celebrated in style at Sinatra's on Friday night. Volumes of amber nectar had been consumed and recycled; now all that remained was a vague memory of events and a blistering headache. Two more Paracetamol with lunch and gradually my senses returned in time for the big game with rivals Bristol City; a third meeting in a month.

This was a day to celebrate the milestone of Bournemouth's recent achievement of playing their 2,500th League game. To mark the occasion the Silver Stars, the display team of the Royal Corps of Transport Free Fall Parachute Club descended from the sunny September skies to the cheers of spectators from both sides. I was still feeling queasy and the thought of jumping out of an aeroplane almost made me vomit on the steps of the Dean Court South End terrace. The 'Bournemouth Echo' grandly supported this League milestone by sponsoring the match and offering the prize of a weekend for two in Paris, which would be drawn at half-time.

City were a strong side and brought with them a large travelling support that filled much of the Brighton Beach terrace away end of the ground. The match started in good humour, with home fans making fun of the Bristolian accent by singing in an exaggerated West Country style 'ooh-arr ooh-arr, ooh-arr ooh-arr', which I found mildly amusing.

As the taunting between supporters continued, however, I could feel the tension in the air, which was only relieved when referee Dennis Hedges blew his whistle to start the game. The first 45 minutes was disappointing mediocre stalemate and not worthy of note.

In the second half the pace quickened and the urgency from the Bournemouth players to take the game to City was apparent. On 56 minutes Sean O'Driscoll sprinted through into the City penalty area, only to be held back by Brian Williams. Hedges pointed to the spot and there were no complaints from City. Bob Savage stepped up to blast the spot kick into the back of the net and Cherries were in front. Looking confident, Bournemouth held on to their slender lead and I gradually demolished my fingernails one by one until a flashpoint in the dying minutes distracted my nervous munching.

Referee Hedges gave a second penalty to Bournemouth as David Moyes brought down Carl Richards and then sent off the City defender for the way he protested. I have always believed that shouting at an official and aggressively pointing a finger has never been a good strategy to adopt. His dismissal sparked an ugly reaction from the visiting supporters and from City manager Terry Cooper, who now sprinted onto the pitch to remonstrate with the referee. The former England and Leeds fullback soon left again, sent off for foul and abusive language. It was a rather embarrassing outburst from one of my '70s boyhood heroes, but Cooper clearly was upset at the decision.

A small number of City and Bournemouth idiots ran onto the pitch to taunt one another and both sets of players ushered them back onto the terraces while, to the great delight of the home fans, two policemen unceremoniously carried out a rather angry Bristol fan. As calm was restored, Savage stepped up and blasted home his second penalty kick of the game to give Bournemouth a 2-0 lead. It was the last kick of the game as referee Hedges blew his whistle early and sprinted for the safety of the dressing rooms. In the South End we were quite content. However, City fans were angry and a few minor isolated scuffles took place outside the ground.

Such aggressive behaviour appalled me and I wanted no part in it. I valued my head and wanted to keep it attached to my neck! As a police siren wailed in the distance I made a quick exit across King's Park and back to my car. Solent reported that Middlesbrough had also won, but that Bournemouth were equal top, with both sides on 15 points, Middlesbrough having scored more goals.

On Sunday morning I played for Lloyd's Bank in the Bournemouth league and scored the second goal in a rare 4-2 victory against local rivals White Heather Reserves. In the pub afterwards with the boys we boisterously relived the Friday night celebrations and debated intensely whether Cherries could get a midweek result at York on Tuesday. On reflection, it was a great weekend and a very pleasurable way to round off my birthday celebrations.

York City v. Bournemouth – Tuesday 30 September

The main local football talking points of the week were a match postponement and court appearances. The much-anticipated Dean Court clash scheduled with Gillingham the following month had been postponed again. The original 11 October date for the game had already been dropped as it clashed with Margaret Thatcher and the Conservative Party Conference visit and police cover could not be provided for the match. The second postponement was agreed when Cherries keeper Gerry Peyton was called up for International duty with the Republic of Ireland for their European Championship match with Scotland. If the Football League had refused the postponement request then Bournemouth would have stopped Peyton playing in the international. Redknapp explained, 'We have not got cover for him and to stop him playing would have been a great shame.' I remained concerned that, as Cherries pushed for a promotion place, they did so with only one first-team squad goalkeeper, a reflection of the difficult times and a situation that today might be unthinkable. New dates had been offered to the Kent club and the rearranged fixture would soon be confirmed. The second news item reinforced my concern regarding travelling to away matches. Following the incidents in the home match with Bristol City, three Bristol fans had appeared at Bournemouth Magistrates Court and been fined a total of £700. Among their collective offences were abusive gestures, threatening behaviour and striking a police officer. The court report indicated that much of the trouble had started when many people objected to a Bristol City National Front flag.

I continued to feel uneasy and made the following entry in my diary: 'supporters travelling away from home in limited numbers were exposed to a higher risk of violence, but now it had occurred in the relative safety of my football club'.

Bournemouth travelled midweek to Bootham Crescent as joint League leaders and remained unbeaten after seven games. Manager Denis Smith had assembled a useful York team, which included striker Keith Walwyn, the Third Division current leading scorer with seven goals. It turned out to be his night as he increased his personal tally to nine by scoring twice to inflict Cherries' first defeat of the season. I watched the final result unfold on Teletext while simultaneously listening to a Radio Solent sports special broadcast. Listening to a music programme with intermittent reports from the ground is a very isolating experience and I felt so helpless.

Each time Solent reverted their broadcast live to the ground their reporter described what appeared to be a personal duel between Keith Walwyn and keeper Gerry Peyton. At first Peyton had come off best, pulling off a string of fine saves, but then came Walwyn's first successful strike on 33 minutes. Peyton palmed a powerful header onto the post, but could not avoid the rebounding ball, which struck his knee and nestled in the back of the net.

The half-time report confirmed that Cherries still trailed by a single goal. My remote frustration exasperated me as I learned that Savage, Newson and O'Connor had all wasted good opportunities to level the game.

With the restart came a surge of renewed optimism as our man at the game excitedly described Cherries' applying pressure on the York goal with Howlett, Puckett and Richards all going close to equalising. Then, on 67 minutes – another goal – that man Walwyn again getting the better of Peyton, who had made a stunning save from Banton's forceful shot only to see the ball fall right into the path of the oncoming Walwyn, who buried it in the net.

To console myself I made another cup of tea and tucked into a packet of chocolate digestives; I needed comfort food to alleviate my disappointment. As the digestives disappeared so did any hope of a Cherries' comeback. Bournemouth had succumbed to their first defeat of the season.

Redknapp lifted my spirits in a brief post-match interview, stating: 'It was a pity our unbeaten spell ended, but I was pleased with the performance as York are a strong side.' With other results not going in Bournemouth's favour, the Cherries slipped to fourth place below Middlesbrough, York and Blackpool.

Defeat at York ended a nervous month on the financial markets, which had seen seven billion pounds wiped off share values in London following a record fall in Tokyo and Wall Street. This global uncertainty was further confounded when a bomb was hurled from a speeding BMW into a busy Paris department store killing four and wounding 44. It was the fifth bomb in a week-long Arab terrorist campaign.

OCTOBER

Darlington v. Bournemouth – Saturday 4 October

Bournemouth took to the road again for the second of their three away games in the North. Cyril Knowles was manager of the Quakers and his name instantly brought back vivid memories of February 1973 as I pictured the Cockerel Chorus on 'Top of the Pops' singing, 'Nice one, Cyril'. In his programme notes Knowles invited home supporters to give the Cherries a big Quaker welcome, which I imagine was quite timid as only 2,006 spectators turned up at the Feethams Ground, including a handful of Cherries' diehards.

Once again the desire to travel was strong, but more isolated crowd trouble in the media deterred me. Anyway the overtime rewards were too good to be missed, so I worked all day and followed Bournemouth's progress sporadically on my Ford Capri car radio whenever I could sneak out of the office. Pre-match reports indicated that Pulis was back in place of Youth Team Coach Williams, but Aylott had failed a fitness test, so rubber-legs Carl Richards kept his place. By the time I returned to the car for the half-time report the match was as good as over.

Darlington keeper Mike Astbury had been putting on a one-man show, spending the first 45 minutes desperately diving at Cherries' feet. Despite his efforts he could not stop O'Driscoll breaking the deadlock after 15 minutes as he slipped the ball under the advancing keeper and into the corner of the net. O'Driscoll was a subdued individual, not a player to overtly voice his opinions and feelings. In fact, he was so quiet, especially in the dressing room that the rest of the team nicknamed him 'Noisy'.

Puckett and Richards had been causing panic in the Darlington defence and it was Puckett who scored a second for Bournemouth in the 33rd minute, driving a low 20-yard shot in off the bottom of the post. Puckett was a clinical finisher and gave Bournemouth a cutting edge, but, like many players, he was superstitious and would always be the last player to put his shirt on in the dressing room.

It was a convincing first-half performance and, beaming from ear to ear, I walked back to my desk via the vending machine, stopping to punch in the number 24 for 'white coffee no sugar'. It tasted consistently bland, but at only five pence a cup it was drinkable, though only just! I exuded confidence; I knew we would go on to win easily. My intuition was correct – Bournemouth relaxed a little in the second half and captain Mark Newson put the result beyond doubt by heading a third goal in the 73rd minute. I drove home at 5.00pm to hear the full match report and Harry Redknapp extol Bournemouth's performance claiming, 'This was our best performance away from home this season. We have 18 points out of nine games with just one defeat. I couldn't have asked for more than that.'

Following Redknapp was an interview with Southampton striker Colin Clarke, who had bagged his second hat-trick of the season in a 4-1 home win against Newcastle, bringing his season's tally to ten goals in ten games. My diary entry remained consistent: 'Bollocks!'.

Bury v. Bournemouth – Saturday 11 October

Having crushed the Quakers, it was now time to see off the Shakers. The northern tour continued with a visit to Gigg Lane after a fortnight's break because of the rearrangement of the Bournemouth v. Gillingham home game. Cliff Richard was top of the charts with 'Travellin' Light' the last and only time Bournemouth had won at Bury – that was 21 November in season 1959/60 when goals from Tommy Southren and Ray Bumstead gave the Cherries both points in the days of two points for a win. Some 26 years later, Madonna was now queen of the musical charts with 'True Blue', not a good omen as Cherries prepared to take on the white and blue of the Shakers.

In his pre-match interview Redknapp hinted that as part of his standard pre-match preparation he had had Bury watched and they looked a useful side.

The Shakers had recently signed Liam Robinson from Huddersfield and he had scored twice on his debut in the previous week's 2-0 home victory over Doncaster.

I continued to dig for gold with the Saturday overtime while the Cherries did battle in the north with Bury. By now I nearly had enough savings to put down a deposit on a skiing holiday with my friends planned for mid March 1987. It continued to be a heart-wrenching decision to either support the bank balance with overtime or travel away with the Cherries. Up until now I had regularly plumped for personal safety and financial stability, but as the results continued my decision became harder.

Under the disguise of the coffee run, the same routine continued with regular visits to the car to listen to BBC Solent reports on the radio. Aylott was back after injury, but the weather in Lancashire was atrocious with heavy

61

rain making the playing surface treacherous. Bournemouth teams have always liked to play football on a good surface and I have seen many a Cherries side make a good start to the season only to falter in the winter weather that often produced a heavy muddy quagmire of a pitch. Today both goals were to be guarded by International keepers; Peyton for Bournemouth, and Phil Hughes for Bury, who three days previously had made his international debut at Wembley for Northern Ireland.

Four coffees later the half-time score came through – 0-0. At 4.20pm and 4.35pm it was still goalless, the tension unbearable as I switched off the radio and sprinted back upstairs to finish my work. At 4.50pm, unable to concentrate, I left early, jumping down the stairs three at a time to the basement. Reaching the bottom I suddenly realised that I had left my car keys on my desk. 'Sh*t' was my only word as I matched Linford Christie's time over 100 metres to return to my desk then back to the car. Solent were broadcasting the last few minutes of Southampton v. Everton and the Saints were trailing 0-2. 'Stuff Saints, what about Bournemouth?' I impatiently blurted at the radio.

It was worth the wait. Despite Bury dictating much of the game, Aylott had set up David Puckett who had swept home a splendid shot to beat Phil Hughes in the 83rd minute. As Solent went live to the ground, reporter Tony Mitchener excitedly confirmed that Cherries had achieved their second away win of the season to take maximum points.

The last five minutes sounded frantic as Peyton came to the rescue and in the dying seconds denied Bury newcomer Liam Robinson with a point-blank save. Turning the key in the ignition I shouted, 'Nice one, Gerry!'

At home I watched the League tables on BBC Grandstand 'Final Score', having correctly set the timer on our new VHS video cassette recorder to capture the football round-up. Cherries sat in third place behind Blackpool and leaders Middlesbrough, a position I was content with for now. In the evening I celebrated in the usual fashion with one too many beers in Bournemouth town centre, knowing that I had the luxury of a Sunday sleep-in as there was no local Sunday match for Lloyd's Bank the following day.

Bournemouth v. Doncaster – Tuesday 21 October
The first of two consecutive home games began with another almighty rush to get to Dean Court for the 7.30pm kickoff. Still breathing heavily from the dash across King's Park, both my father and I pushed our way through the tightly

packed South End spectators towards the left of the goal and leaned on the end of a unoccupied crush barrier – a comfortable perch, we both agreed.

The public address system confirmed the line-up of the two teams, with a cheer for each Bournemouth player named followed by the customary muted boo after each Doncaster name. A special hostile Dean Court welcome, however, was saved for ex-Cherry Colin (Jack) Russell, now playing up front for the visitors. At a cost of £700, this evening's match was sponsored by Gresham Life who had a head office located at Marler House in nearby Westbourne. Some years later I worked in the top-floor office of this building before it was sold and converted into private flats.

In his programme notes Redknapp predicted a hard game and summarised Cherries' early season success with the comment, 'The league is a marathon not a sprint and has been proved over the years, but we are doing the right things at the moment.'

Newson won the toss and chose to attack the Brighton Beach 'away' end terrace for the first half. Newson's decision, applauded by the crowd, meant Bournemouth would be attacking the South 'home' End terrace in the second half. The crowd always seemed to lift the team as they attacked the goal in front of them, even more so in the second half. Referee Roger Gifford looked at both linesmen, blew his pealess Fox 40 whistle and the 'Today' League Division Three game started.

The first quarter of an hour of action remained even, with a brief series of half chances for both teams. If a side is to be successful it needs a bit of luck and the Cherries received a slice in the 17th minute. As Trevor Aylott moved towards Mark O'Connor's centre, referee Gifford ruled that Doncaster fullback Mickey Stead had handled. Stead, along with everyone else in the ground, was surprised by the decision and he was cautioned for his protests. Bob Savage, in customary style, blasted Bournemouth into the lead from the penalty spot, firing a cannon ball into the net.

Ten minutes later I squirmed as Doncaster equalised with a Gary Clayton header. Before my father and I had finished debating the defensive lapse that led to the equaliser, Doncaster's other fullback, Dave Rushby, won possession in his own half. Sprinting down the touchline, he delivered a powerful cross that Bournemouth centre half Mark Whitlock intercepted with his head, but diverted the ball across goal and inside the far corner of the Bournemouth net. Whitlock, hands on hips, and keeper Gerry Peyton looked at each other in disgust. If looks could kill! An elderly, thinly grey-haired man behind me bellowed, 'Whitlock – you've got a head like a bloody threepenny bit.' At the break Cherries trailed 1-2.

The teams came out for the second half, with visiting goalkeeper Andy Rhodes making his way to the goal in front of the home fans and we all sportingly applauded his arrival. A little surprised, he acknowledged our welcome only for some of the home fans to unanimously change their greeting to that of the wanker sign and to guffaws of great amusement. Rhodes had been duped; he knew it and he laughed too. His reaction earned him genuine applause for being such a good sport.

Attacking the 'favoured end', Bournemouth were sharper after the interval and wasted two good chances to equalise, with Puckett guilty on both occasions. The crowd sensed a goal was imminent and burst into a chorus of 'Score in a minute, we're going to score in a minute'. Literally within a minute the prediction was delivered. Newson and Whitlock engaged on a series of quick passes that set up Puckett, who executed the move with a rasping shot for his sixth goal of the season. On a cool autumn night Dad and I warmed our hands applauding a fine equaliser and a superbly executed strike.

With tails up, Bournemouth pushed forward and stepped up a gear, applying pressure for the winning goal. Our patience was rewarded on 84 minutes when, following a throw-in from the industrious midfielder Mark O'Connor, Cherries' fullback Paul Morrell, once again went on another of his weaving runs. Head down, he beat three defenders before rounding off his solo charge with a left-foot winner. The South End went berserk, ecstatic with proceedings, and Dad and I applauded vigorously.

In the final stages as Doncaster attempted one final assault on the Cherries' goal we whistled furiously to encourage Mr Gifford to signal the end of the game. In a moment of distraction the public address system announced, 'Would Stan Sloggit go to reception immediately!' This always led to amusement and laughter amongst the crowd as it was such a stupid name. I imagined it could only be a character name befitting an Australian outback cricketer. The announcement became a regular occurrence towards the end of every home match and later I learned that it was a recognised signal for match stewards to prepare for their end-of-game duties. Finally, Mr Gifford blew his whistle and a combined sigh of relief and a huge cheer erupted from inside the ground. Despite this seesaw spectacle, Bournemouth had secured their fifth successive home win of the campaign. As the players were applauded off the pitch the public address announced, 'Notts County 1, Middlesbrough 0', to the great delight of the home support.

Although they had lost, Middlesbrough still remained League leaders with 24 points, and hot on their heels came Bournemouth with now the same number of points but having scored one goal less. It was tight.

Bournemouth v. Wigan Athletic – Saturday 25 October

Cutting it fine, I sprinted across King's Park and pushed my way towards the South End entrance to Dean Court. It was 2.50pm as I handed over my £3.00 admission fee, the turnstile clicked and I was inside.

As I passed through the turnstile gate I was given a small postcard-sized colour photograph of the Bournemouth squad, given free to all supporters in recognition of the match being sponsored by the 'Evening Echo' and Coopers of Wessex. It was a mild autumn afternoon and the sun shone brightly on the very small band of Wigan supporters who stood on the Brighton Beach away terrace. Cherries' fans were in a jovial mood and making fun at the Wigan supporters' expense. To the tune of 'Bread of Heaven' a chorus of 'What's it like to, what's it like to, what's it like to see the sun?' wafted across Dean Court followed by a vociferous cry of 'You must have come in a taxi.'

Sponsored by Heinz, Wigan had recently been flexing their small, but developing, financial muscle in the transfer market. Recent signings included Northern Ireland International Bobby Campbell, the scruffy unshaven striker with the penchant for cigarettes and alcohol from Bradford City for £25,000 and ex-Chester defender Andy Holden for £40,000. Fortunately for Bournemouth, Holden was unavailable and so was striker Paul Jewell, sidelined through injury. Cherries remained unchanged from the Doncaster game. Before kickoff a special announcement was made to thank AFC Away Travellers who, via a series of social evenings and raffles, had raised £200 as kit sponsorship for Cherries' midfielder Tony Pulis. A polite ripple of applause followed.

Newson lost the toss and the teams changed ends with the Cherries attacking the South End goal for the first 45 minutes. Bournemouth started the better side and on 9 minutes took the lead following a beautifully weighted centre from Howlett that was met with a glancing header from Carl Richards. Instant cries from the South End of 'Bruno, Bruno' rang out. From my spectator perspective Richards was an infuriating player. His raw power gave him pace and the advantage over most defenders. At times he was agile and quick,

65

panicking defenders when on the ball. But at other times he was too clever for his own good and would regularly either fall over the ball or his own long athletic legs that appeared to stretch like rubber! I had to be patient with him, it was his first season in professional football, but it was exasperating. Half chances came and went for both sides as the 45 minutes ticked by. Cautions were given to Hamilton for the visitors, who clipped Aylott's heels on 19 minutes, then on 44 minutes Aylott got his revenge, but also suffered a caution before referee Keith Miller brought the first half to a close.

Before Wigan had settled in the second half, Howlett crowned his outstanding midfield contribution by steering the ball past Wigan keeper Roy Tunks for Bournemouth's second goal following a neat pass from Puckett. Further trouble for Wigan came on 62 minutes when new boy Bobby Campbell received his marching orders following an innocuous challenge on Paul Morrell, who had Campbell in his back pocket throughout the game. Campbell was shocked at the decision and trooped off the pitch for an early bath, to the great amusement of the home fans: 'You dirty northern bastard'.

Bournemouth sealed victory against their ten-man opponents in the 81st minute, when David Puckett scored his seventh goal of the season, driving a low cross into the near corner of the Wigan net. In the closing moments Cherries lost their concentration, allowing Wigan to snatch a late consolation through Chris Thompson – a soft and unnecessary goal, which took the gloss off a buoyant and dominating display from Bournemouth. Two minutes of injury time were completed before referee Miller blew the final whistle.

BBC radio 'Sports Report' entertained me on the drive home as James Alexander Gordon read the full classified football results. At Ashton Gate Bristol City had held Middlesbrough to a 2-2 draw, Gillingham had won at Port Vale 2-1, but Blackpool had no game. This combination meant that Bournemouth were top of the League with 27 points, having a two-point lead over Middlesbrough and Gillingham in second and third place, respectively.

The 3-1 victory over Wigan was significant. It meant that Bournemouth had taken maximum points from their October fixtures and had treated the Dean Court faithful to six straight home League victories. My copy of the 'Evening Echo' speculated that Redknapp must surely win the manager of the month award for October. This was deserved, but I shook my head disapprovingly as the award was universally recognised as the ultimate 'kiss of death' for any football manager.

The stage was set for a superb mouthwatering confrontation the following week at Ayresome Park between Cherries and arch-rivals Middlesbrough. It was a game too good to miss and, although I still wrestled with my fear of travelling to away matches, I decided to put this aside and use the official AFC Bournemouth Travel Club service, which I felt would be a sensible and secure option. I planned to purchase my travel and match ticket from Dean Court during my lunch break on Monday.

As I sat in front of the TV to watch 'Only Fools and Horses' further thought of my proposed journey north had added personal interest for me. My grandfather, who had died before I was born, lived in Skipton, North Yorkshire, and I had learned that my very unusual surname with Scandinavian origins was prevalent around the Middlesbrough area. It seemed that my ancestors may have been Vikings! I had never met another Neesam outside my family and the thought of a friendly and sporting encounter with a fellow Neesam 'Boro' fan briefly, but nervously, excited me.

FA Cup First Round Draw – Monday 27 October

Off the pitch, Bournemouth became involved in a bizarre incident on this day as the FA Cup First Round draw was made. The draw was regionalised, with northern and southern clubs separated in an attempt to boost attendance at matches and create exciting local derby opportunities. The draw had progressed as expected and was going well until Darlington came out of the bag with a home draw against Bournemouth! With embarrassed faces at the FA, the draw was abandoned and a new draw made. For the record Darlington were second time around drawn at home to Mansfield and Bournemouth were given a local home tie with Southern League Premier side Fareham, an example of the kind of local derby the regional draw hoped to produce. All ties were due to be played on Saturday 15 November.

I visited the travel club on Monday at lunchtime as planned – 'Sorry, sold out'. The cruel response came in a short sharp moment of devastation. In a pathetic reply I mumbled, 'What? You're joking?' By 1.30pm Monday all available coach and allocated match tickets for the Middlesbrough encounter had been sold. I had seriously underestimated the interest in this match and had now paid the price, resulting in my bitter disappointment.

The one consolation came in the form of a travel and match ticket to the following midweek away visit to Walsall. I worked flex-time and was due time off following a number of additional hours that I had accumulated. To alleviate the disappointment of not being able to get to the Middlesbrough game, I decided there and then to split the time owed into two half days. That would allow me sufficient time to travel to the midlands for the next match with Walsall and have the following morning to catch up on sleep. Determined to crack my fear of away travel, I paid my £7.50 to the Travel Club and left Dean Court in bitter disappointment, resigned to the fact that I would not be travelling north on Saturday.

Elsewhere, despite concerns over the cost of the event, the Conservative Party conference opened at the Bournemouth International Centre and a suspected bomb was removed from a shop front in Old Christchurch Road.

NOVEMBER

Middlesbrough v. Bournemouth – Saturday 1 November

If I had been able to travel to the match I would have been scrutinising the 'Boro' match day magazine as kickoff approached. Bruce Rioch, Middlesbrough manager, in his 'Bruce's Page' notes welcomed Cherries to Ayresome Park. He highlighted that, 'The game with Bournemouth gives us an opportunity to measure our abilities against strong leading contenders.' Rioch gave a special welcome to Cherries' Managing Director Brian Tiler and reminisced on their days together at Aston Villa where they were both players and next-door neighbours. He also expressed his sadness at still not seeing any English clubs participating in the previous week's European competitions due to the indefinite ban imposed by UEFA on English clubs following the tragedy at the Heysel stadium where 39 people lost their lives on 29 May 1985.

It was a bitterly cold afternoon and the wind chill factor added to the severity of the temperature drop across the United Kingdom. Like a true southern softy I chose to sit beside the warm fire at home and listen to proceedings via the frequent reports on BBC Radio Solent. Just before kickoff it had been confirmed that Harry Redknapp had won the 'Today' League Division Three manager of the month award for October. It was appropriate recognition for a series of great results, but the award had the habit of bringing to an end the recipient's fine run of success.

Ian Gibson, the former Middlesbrough and one-time Cherries player in the '70s, met up with his former team-mate Redknapp at this game. Gibson coached a youth side in the north east and his lads were on duty as ball boys as his old clubs came into opposition. In front of 10,710 spectators, the second biggest crowd of the season at Ayresome Park, Bournemouth started confidently taking the game to their hosts with positive and precise play. With the game a mere two minutes old Puckett and Richards combined passes, with Puckett striking a venomous shot that smacked against the Middlesbrough post and bounced out.

The mould was set – it was not to be Cherries' day. On 23 minutes and against the run of play 'The Boro' took the lead when a back pass from Bournemouth defender Paul Morrell was intercepted by Stuart Ripley and, despite Peyton blocking his shot, Archie Stevens was on hand to bury the rebounding ball in the net. An equaliser looked likely as Aylott's through ball was struck firmly by Puckett, but Stephen Pears in the home goal pulled off a fine save.

On 43 minutes disaster struck when, from their first corner, Middlesbrough scored again. Stevens rose above the Bournemouth defence and nodded the ball on for Bernie Slaven to score at the far post. At half-time I consoled myself with another cup of tea and half a packet of McVities chocolate digestives for comfort.

The second half started slowly, but 12 minutes after the restart Solent reported another goal at Ayresome Park. It had to be a Bournemouth goal, surely? No, Peyton had again blocked a shot from Slaven, only for Gary Hamilton to slot home Middlesbrough's third goal. More digestives were consumed and at an alarming rate. Worse was to follow in the 71st minute as Bournemouth pushed forward, leaving gaps that were soon exploited by the home side. Hamilton provided the pass as Ripley raced away unchallenged to shoot past a stranded Gerry Peyton. Solent broke the news and I realised it was game over.

I felt numb, the curse of the manager of the month award had struck again and Middlesbrough had regained the top spot in Division Three at Cherries' expense. In his post-match interview Redknapp stressed, 'Middlesbrough were never four goals better, but things went their way on this occasion. We expect to bounce back at Walsall on Tuesday.' 'Bloody better do,' I thought as I turned off the radio in disgust. Later that evening the boys and I debated the result in Sinatra's over several rounds of beer. The unanimous verdict – quite simply, a crap result.

Walsall v. Bournemouth – Tuesday 4 November

At 2.20pm, with sandwiches in one hand and travel ticket in the other, I boarded the single 52-seater coach and took my window seat for the journey to the Midlands. It was a bright, but chilly, autumnal afternoon as the coach headed up the A34 to Newbury, then joined the M5 motorway to the Midlands and to Walsall. We arrived at Fellows Park just after 6.20pm because of congestion and heavy rush-hour traffic around Halesowen. Fellows Park had been something of a bogey ground in recent seasons.

The last time Bournemouth won there was in September 1973, when Donny Osmond was at number one in the singles chart with 'Young Love'. On that occasion two goals from Phil Boyer gave Cherries a rare 2-1 victory. Walsall had struggled since the start of the current season and were third from bottom with 13 points. Despite their lowly position they had just embarked on an unbeaten run of form, collecting seven points from their last three games, scoring nine and conceding three. I stood on the open terrace in the cold night air and surveyed the stadium. Where the floodlight beams could not penetrate dark shadows eerily covered large parts of the stands.

Like Dean Court, this old historic ground set in the dismal industrial heart of the Midlands had seen better days and now looked tired and grubby. As the atmosphere grew with the expanding crowd anticipating the kickoff at 7.30pm, Cherries went through their pre-match warm-up routine in their all pale blue away strip. Defender Tom Heffernan was put through his paces as he underwent a fitness test before being selected to play, and the air was filled with the clinical smell of muscle-warming 'Deep Heat'. Many Bournemouth supporters had driven to the match and to my right and behind me a number of fans had gathered to maximise their vocal impact. Like a well-rehearsed choir they sang through the usual routine before falling silent. After only a few seconds of the silence a solo voice somewhere behind me bellowed, 'Up the Cherries!' – to which the remaining Bournemouth supporters collectively replied, 'In all departments!' I have always found football songs amusing, yet basic in their content. Somehow, though, this unusual and coordinated outburst seemed to have been given some limited intellectual thought in its creation. I smiled and continued with my programme reading.

Again Newson lost the toss, and Walsall chose to attack towards the Bournemouth supporters in the first half and their own fans in the second. From the outset the Saddlers looked lively, with top scorer David Kelly up front supported by the experienced Trevor Christie and David Cross. Bournemouth seemed comfortable just sitting back and let Walsall control the game, and I became increasingly concerned at these tactics. The action was all at our end of the ground and it unnerved me.

On 25 minutes Kelly showed his capability by striking a hard low shot against the Bournemouth upright just in front of me. It produced a dull thud that was followed by a two-second delayed cry of disappointment from the home fans watching on the other three sides of the ground. As Walsall dominated, Peyton came to the rescue on several occasions before the interval whistle blew.

The clear night sky meant that the temperature had dropped considerably, so I made my way to the small kiosk to my left for a half-time cuppa. Twenty-five pence bought me a lukewarm watery grey liquid served in a polystyrene cup, easily the worst cup of tea I had ever tasted in my life. It tasted similar to what I imagined warm dishwater might taste like, but I drank it in an attempt to keep out the chill air.

Newson led the Cherries back out and my fellow supporters and I encouraged the team as they kicked off the second half. Most of the play was in the Bournemouth half at the far end of the ground. The floodlight illumination was appalling and in the dim light it was becoming difficult to clearly see the action at the far end. I winced as a number of 'oohs' and 'aahs' from the home crowd followed two near misses on the Bournemouth goal.

On 56 minutes the near misses became a successful strike on goal. In the murk at the far end, Gary Childs successfully connected with a low centre from Kelly and fired in at the far post. Cherries kicked off to some disgruntled noises from supporters around me, who vented their frustration while the more optimistic amongst us encouraged the team by singing a few choruses of 'Come on you Reds!' which we then hastily changed to 'Come on you Blues!' having quickly remembered that our team was wearing the away blue-coloured kit! Somehow, though, blue just didn't sound right; it was alien to me.

Mark O'Connor joined proceedings as substitute for Bob Savage as Redknapp tried to take control of the midfield. With eleven minutes remaining, Walsall sealed their victory when Nicky Cross drove a wonderfully angled cross-shot into the far corner of the Bournemouth net. Peyton didn't move for the ball. He was either beaten by the sheer velocity of the strike, or perhaps just didn't see it in the Fellows Park gloom.

I was grateful when referee Burge ended my suffering by bringing the game to a close with three sharp blows of his whistle. It was a disappointing performance from Bournemouth and the players left the pitch to a mixed reaction of mild applause and shouts of 'Rubbish Boscombe!'.

In a deep West Midlands accent the announcer on the public address system confirmed that Middlesbrough had been held to a goalless draw at home to Bolton, but Gillingham had leapfrogged to the top of the Division Three table by defeating Blackpool 2-1. I boarded the coach glad to be out of the cold night air and fell into a deep sleep.

Two days later Thursday 6 November marked the most expensive sacking to date in British football. Manchester United parted company with Ron Atkinson after a run of dismal results that had left United nineteenth in Division One. Atkinson walked away with £100,000 compensation and his successor was immediately announced as Aberdeen manager Alex Ferguson, who had secured a £400,000 contract.

Bournemouth v. Carlisle – Saturday 8 November

As I approached the South End turnstile a policeman beckoned me towards him, pulling me out of the line. He asked if he could check my pockets. I complied and asked him what he was looking for. To my surprise he replied, 'We are searching for offending vegetables.' I could not help but laugh – the police were searching home supporters for sticks of celery that they might have upon their person. I had heard the celery song on the terraces and seen the celery sticks thrown onto the pitch, but I had no idea that they were being targeted by the law as an offensive weapon. Oh well, this was 1986.

My travelling demons appeared to have been successfully exorcised and the dreadful fear of travelling away was now replaced with a cautionary fresh confidence. I reflected upon what the fuss was about and my attention drifted to the plight of Carlisle supporters. They had earned my respect and I realised that they must have clocked up some serious mileage. A small band of faithful followers had made the trip from Cumbria to Dorset; a mere 340-mile, six and a half hours journey – roughly the same number of hours it takes to fly between London and New York, albeit by a different mode of transport. I applauded them for their marathon effort and grimaced as my brief mental arithmetic calculated a round trip of 680 miles and thirteen hours! Pure loyalty.

Studying the match day magazine, it was heartening to read Bournemouth Chairman Rodney Barton talk about the excellent and ongoing work to re-establish the Youth Team and the development of a new youth policy for the club after it was abandoned ten years earlier.

The programme notes covered a number of reports on the Middlesbrough game, with the common theme that Cherries were unlucky and the scoreline flattered Middlesbrough. Today's Player Profile featured midfielder Mark O'Connor, who had the nickname of Des for obvious reasons. I also noticed that Cherries' keeper Gerry Peyton currently led the Pound-Stretcher Sheraton Hotel 'Player of the Year' league table sponsored by John Plank Travel, which surely had to be the longest sponsorship title of the season.

My reading was interrupted just before kickoff as cheers (no pun intended) were forthcoming for Harry Redknapp. He was presented with the Third Division Manager of the Month award and the associated prize of a 4.5 litre bottle of Bells Scotch Whisky. In the South End we burst into our favourite song, 'We've got Harry, Harry, Harry Redknapp on the bench, on the bench'.

As the game got underway Bournemouth started the better side and Trevor Aylott was close to scoring twice in two minutes as he caused former Southampton fullback Mike McCartney problems. The crowd took full advantage of this and each time McCartney touched the ball he was booed.

Carlisle looked a useful side and I spotted their number ten, who looked every bit the confident midfield maestro who could win and hold the ball and also create opportunities. The player concerned tussled for the ball and elegantly sprayed passes across the Dean Court turf to dangerous and creative effect. I looked at my programme team list to find his name was Ian Bishop, signed from Everton. At half-time there was no score in what was a keenly fought contest.

After the restart the game continued to be even and my heart rate quickened in the 58th minute when Bournemouth had a let-off as Malcolm Poskett glanced a header past Peyton, only to see it bounce off the foot of the post and out. With 30 minutes remaining, Harry brought on substitute Carl Richards to great cheers of 'Bruno, Bruno'. His pace injected new life into the game and each time he had the ball I sensed that something was possible. Two dazzling runs saw him first strike the ball just wide of the post and the second saw him trip over the ball and fall flat on his face. A series of Bournemouth corners followed, with Cherries continuing to apply pressure. The Dean Court faithful and I were convinced that it was only a matter of time before a goal was delivered. I joined in with the singing, 'Score in a minute, we're gonna score in a minute'.

With time rapidly running out, Richards won another corner at the South End, O'Connor swung in the corner kick and Aylott rose majestically to place a header towards the bottom corner. As I jumped in anticipation of a goal, Carlisle keeper Scott Endersby leapt 'cat-like' through the air to parry the ball out and disappoint us, but Newson slammed home a half-volley into the net to finally send us all wild with delight. Relief had come at last, 1-0 after 85 minutes, so Cherries just needed to shut up shop for the last five minutes. That is not something that Bournemouth teams have historically been good at – my experiences have revealed that we seem to prefer to make it difficult for ourselves.

I need not have worried; within a minute Bournemouth had scored again. Aylott won a tussle with ex-Birmingham defender Billy Wright and centred for Bruno to score at the far post. It was the knock-out punch for Carlisle. I punched the air, cheered and chanted the name of my rubber-legged hero, 'Bruno, Bruno'.

Carlisle kicked off again as the crowd settled down. Having fought determinedly for 84 minutes I thought it was a little cruel for their supporters to witness two late strikes, but few around me really cared about that. But two minutes later that man Bishop struck back to make it 2-1, with two minutes to go. 'That's typical,' I thought to myself, 'why do Bournemouth always have to make hard work of it?' Bournemouth then played possession football, holding the ball for the majority of the final minutes as Carlisle chased in vain. After 90 seconds of frantic whistling from home supporters, referee Darryl Reeves from Uxbridge blew the final whistle and the 4,284 Dean Court faithful let out a roar of delight as Cherries secured their seventh straight home win of the campaign.

Middlesbrough had beaten Darlington 1-0 at Feethams to go back to the top of the Division with 32 points, while Gillingham dropped into second place with 31 points, having been defeated the previous evening 2-0 at Doncaster. Cherries remained in third place with 30 points. Still early days, but the promotion race was becoming competitive and tighter after each set of results. We were in the leading pack and that was important at this stage of the season.

As Cherries returned to winning ways, I'm sure that Harry Redknapp enjoyed his Scotch whisky that night, especially as his old pal Jimmy Gabriel was back in town.

As for that man Bishop, Redknapp must have made a mental note of him because he went on to secure his signature two seasons later, paying Carlisle just £35,000 at a transfer tribunal. This proved to be another example of the shrewd Redknapp ability to identify and secure a gifted talent for a bargain fee. Nice one, Harry!

Bournemouth v. Fareham – Saturday 15 November

The FA Cup is a wonderful competition dating back to 1871/72, and the envy of the world when it comes to football prizes. For football pundits it is a competition for romantics, with the possibility of David slaying Goliath. For supporters like me it is a dream to draw a top side in the country and see the nation's heroes in action against my team, while for players it is about performing against the best in a magnificent arena. For the Club Manager it is a scalp to add to the CV and for Chairmen it is a much-needed cash windfall to ease liquidity and boost investment. In this tie Fareham were the underdog with nothing to lose and for Bournemouth it was the proverbial banana skin.

Fareham, who attracted on average 200 supporters for their regular home League matches, reached the FA Cup for the third time in their history by beating Trowbridge 4-1 in the fourth qualifying round of the competition, after a 0-0 draw at Trowbridge. For the midweek home replay 870 fans turned out to watch the local side's success.

Before entering Dean Court I visited the 'Cherry Bees' club shop. New merchandise included the AFC Bournemouth apron and tea towel, but I bought a replica home shirt for £16.50 and a ski hat for £1.95, and wore both immediately. It was a chilly and overcast November afternoon. 4,758 others and I paid to watch step one on the road to Wembley. I took my usual standing position in the South End just to the left of the goal and leaned against a cherry red crush barrier. The bloke next to me lit a fag and his smoke blew right in my face. It was disgusting and so I moved further along the barrier up wind of him to enjoy the match smoke free. For a non-League club Fareham had brought quite a following to Dean Court, their numbers probably boosted by the fact that Portsmouth were playing away at Shrewsbury and so a few Pompey fans no doubt had made the short journey down the M27 motorway in the hope of seeing a cup shock. It was a carnival-type atmosphere as both sets of fans were in good voice and contributing to the pre-match atmosphere.

Three firecrackers were let off with a startling shotgun bang as both teams ran out onto the pitch with ex-Cherry Kevin Dawtry featuring in the Fareham line-up and back on his old stomping ground.

The opening exchanges of the tie were pretty equal until on 14 minutes the unthinkable happened. Fareham midfielder Malcolm Wilkes, a draughtsman during the week, put the non-League side in front to a series of gasps and groans from those around me. I imagined the video-printer on BBC TV's 'Grandstand' flashing up 'Bournemouth 0 v. Fareham 1' and the nation laughing at Cherries' expense. The guy to my left lit up another fag; he looked pale and tense. I watched him as he inhaled, then exhaled a barrage of smoke onto unsuspecting victims downwind to his left. Their reaction was similar to mine.

It took Cherries a while to settle, but on 25 minutes Tom Heffernan sprinted down the right touchline towards me on the South End terrace and delivered a perfect centre for Trevor Aylott to head home. The cheers that followed the goal were pure relief for the home fans. Five minutes later I relaxed further when Carl Richards capitalised on a mix-up in the Fareham defence to score Bournemouth's second goal and he then proceeded to milk the 'Bruno, Bruno' acknowledgement of his efforts. Bournemouth maintained the pressure and, when David Puckett's shot rebounded off the post, Richards buried the rebound to the delight of all Cherries' fans and we responded again with the now customary chant. Minutes later referee Roger Wiseman blew his whistle for half-time. With all the frantic action, tension and excitement the first 45 minutes had appeared to pass in a flash and I was pleased to be able to pause for breath and envisaged with a smile the vidi-printer half-time score on the TV screen.

More firecrackers and bangers greeted the return of the players for the second half, with Cherries' fans applauding the arrival of home keeper Gerry Peyton between the sticks at the South End. Despite the 3-1 advantage I felt this contest was not over and early in the second half draughtsman Wilkes confirmed this when he took a return pass from Kevin Dawtry to make it 3-2, notching his second goal of the game. Moments later I had a further fright when Kevin Moody let fly with a 25-yard strike that clipped the outside of the post, with Peyton helpless. The smoker to my left exhaled a cloud of grey fog and muttered, 'Well left, Gerry.'

The tension was immense and despite the cool late afternoon air the palms of my hands felt clammy.

In the space of seven minutes Cherries' and my own anxiety was alleviated. Bruno and Sean O'Driscoll combined to set up David Puckett to score on 62 minutes. Five minutes later a hesitant back pass provided Puckett with his second goal, steering the ball past the advancing Paul Grant in the Fareham goal.

Just two minutes later Puckett was again causing havoc in the Fareham defence and, when Grant only parried his shot, defender Russell Davies accidentally turned the ball into his own net to give Cherries a 6-2 lead. The game was all but over and I relaxed, knowing that Cherries would be in the hat for the second-round draw. Fareham continued to battle, but Puckett finally killed them off as he pounced again in the 88th minute to score Cherries' seventh and his third of the match. As the final minutes drifted away, the attention of the home fans centred with great delight on a small number of Fareham fans who were being ejected by a group of Day-Glo yellow-jacketed police officers for their part in a small ruckus.

The score flattered Bournemouth. It was, however, their biggest home win in the competition since 20 November 1971 when Cherries legend Ted MacDougall scored nine goals in Bournemouth's 11-0 annihilation of Margate. Redknapp's cup view of Fareham was praising: 'This was a cracking cup-tie! Full credit to Fareham for making such a good game of it. Their approach did not really surprise me – but their early goal certainly did!'

Elsewhere in the FA Cup first round there were stories to be told. Caernarfon beat bottom of Division Four Stockport County 1-0. Chorley held the once mighty Wolves to a 1-1 draw and little Bishop's Stortford gave Colchester a scare, drawing 1-1. Swansea only just managed a replay at Wealdstone in another 1-1 encounter and Whitby held Doncaster 2-2. The best non-League performance was undoubtedly Telford's 3-0 victory over Burnley; their tenth Football League scalp in five years.

Bournemouth v. Chesterfield – Saturday 22 November

Earlier in the week, on Monday 17 November, the draw for the FA Cup Second Round had been made, this time without any hiccups. Bournemouth were drawn at home to Fourth Division Orient, but the home draw triggered concerns of chaos in the town on 6 December. That day in the town calendar was marked for the annual Bournemouth Christmas parade. Its route ran through Holdenhurst Road, and the fear was that its procession of 2,000 participants, with many more thousands lining the roadside, would run into trainloads of Orient fans arriving at the station.

While Orient supporters had no previous reputation that gave rise for concern, the local police advised that the clash would cause congestion and chaos, so the parade start time was sensibly brought forward to avoid any overcrowding. This was an obvious and sensible solution, but what surprised, though did not shock, me was the mind-set and perception that others had of football supporters. I was staggered at parade organiser Ernest Merrifield's public comments, especially when he said: 'It would be like the battle of Hastings or Waterloo with the two armies meeting.' What a terrible image of the beautiful game. It appeared as though the reputation of football had succumbed to its lowest ebb and returned to its primitive medieval character.

On a far more positive note Chairman Rodney Barton unveiled his bold dream for Cherries' future with ideas for a multi-purpose sports stadium to be discussed at a public meeting called by the club at the Town Hall on Thursday 27 November at 8pm. Quoted in the 'Bournemouth Echo' he said: 'It is decision time for the future of AFC Bournemouth. To survive over the next couple of generations we must be part of an overall leisure complex where we are just part of the sporting activities available to the public.' Elsewhere it was sad to hear Southampton reported a goalkeeping crisis with Peter Shilton out of training and reserve keeper Tim Flowers also out with a fractured cheek-bone!

I am not superstitious, but I bought my match day magazine for the Third Division Chesterfield game from the usual seller near the entrance to Thistlebarrow Road. This had now become a ritual since the start of the season and this dumpy balding vendor was my lucky talisman. Looking at the programme front cover I could not believe my eyes. There it was in black and white 'Today League Division **Two** – Bournemouth v. Chesterfield'. I blinked again to check that it read Division Two, not Three. I was not sure if it was a premonition or maybe wishful thinking, but it appeared that Bournemouth had been promoted to the next league above and it was only November! Sadly it was just a simple printing error. AFC Bournemouth still remained in Division Three.

In his programme notes under 'Harry's Line' Redknapp applauded the Bournemouth players on their fitness and for keeping themselves in shape, revealing that the players were regularly weighed and if they had increased their weight from that stipulated they were fined for the offence. I wondered if this was one of Redknapp's schemes to fund his gambling exploits?

With Bournemouth holding a one hundred per cent home record it was no surprise that Chesterfield kickedoff this match with five defenders protecting their goal from the start. They appeared to have come for a point and were content with only being adventurous on the counterattack. Bournemouth dominated from the start and home striker Trevor Aylott thought he had scored his first League goal for the club with a curling shot that was destined for the top corner of the net, only for Chesterfield keeper Chris Marples to make a spectacular one-handed save, similar to that Wembley save made by Peter Shilton from Scotland's Kenny Dalglish. Cherries' keeper Peyton applauded his opposite number. Aylott was disappointed; by now we were twelve weeks into the season and big Trev had yet to score a League goal. However, his contribution was never in question and in matches so far his participation had been significant, so I had no axe to grind. Peyton remained a spectator for the first 30 minutes before being called into action, tipping over the bar an in-swinging corner from the visitors. This demonstrated another of Peyton's great strengths, his ability to remain focused and concentrate despite not seeing the ball for long periods during a match. He was confident and as steady as a rock and, although I am not a gambling man, I would have put my mortgage on him stopping a shot. The half-time whistle blew to a mixed reception of applause and the usual moaning from some segments of the crowd.

The second half had to be better and, thankfully, it was. On 55 minutes the Chesterfield defensive wall cracked under further Bournemouth pressure. Puckett pounced to notch his 11th goal of the season and I relaxed. I finally got behind my team one hundred per cent and shouted as loud as I could. The visitors reorganised and substituted Reid for Scrimgeour, but it had little impact and, with seven minutes remaining, Bournemouth sealed the game thanks to an Aylott cross that was turned in by Mark O'Connor. In the closing minutes there was time for the home fans to relax and we sang 'Harry, give us a wave, Harry, Harry give us a wave' and he duly replied from the bench just as referee Downey brought the game to a close.

In anticipation that Bournemouth might have gone top of the League after beating Chesterfield I sprinted back to my car to hear other results only to be disappointed by the news on BBC Radio Solent. Middlesbrough had won away at Newport County 1-0 and Gillingham had beaten Notts County at home 3-1. There was no change at the top, but it did set up a mouthwatering encounter for next Tuesday evening as the Cherries were to play hosts to Gillingham.

Port Vale v. Bournemouth – Saturday 29 November
Cherries were unable to continue their promotion battle in the Potteries at Vale Park on Saturday 29th as their opponents Port Vale were suffering from a player crisis due to illness, injury and suspensions. From a squad of 15 they

only had four fit men available for the match. Personally I failed to see what the problem was, but following a report from a local doctor the Football League had agreed to postpone the match.

Scanning the sport pages of the 'Bournemouth Evening Echo' I spotted a small item under the heading 'Redknapp Rescues Russell'. Intrigued that this might be a potential new signing I continued to read further. A young woman had been walking her dog on St Catherine's Hill when her Jack Russell pup had been spooked by the sight and sound of a panting posse of AFC Bournemouth players pounding by on a training run. The frightened dog had run off and despite the Cherries' training session being halted while the players searched for the pup, there was no sight of him. Never short of ideas, Redknapp instructed the players to continue their run while he went straight to the house where the dog lived. His intuition was correct; the dog had returned to the house where its owner lived and the pup was sitting on the doorstep. Redknapp waited with it until its tearful mistress arrived.

Prior to the news of the postponement it had been a good week. I had managed to dodge responsibility for organising the office department Christmas party and it looked like Cherries might get a new stadium within the next two years. The 'Bournemouth Echo' headline on Friday 28 November read 'New stadium by summer 1988?'

The previous evening's Public Meeting at the Town Hall was attended by almost a thousand people and I squeezed my way in to the crammed hall to hear plans for Bournemouth's bright future, for which nearly all present gave unanimous backing to the AFC board's vision.

The event was chaired by TVS Sports presenter David Bobin and during the meeting Club Chairman Rodney Barton indicated that the cost of a new stadium would be somewhere in the region of two and a half million pounds, stating: 'I see no reason why within 18 months, Bournemouth should not be playing in a new stadium if all the red tape can be negotiated and if we can get the right financial backing.' I considered this statement to contain two very important 'ifs'.

Drawings of the proposed new stadium were placed on display for supporters to peruse and there were guest appearances from Sir Walter Winterbottom, who was the former England manager and one of the world's leading experts on artificial pitches. Graham Mackerell, former secretary of Luton Town, pacesetters in the world of all-weather surfaces and community involvement with professional football, was also present. What surprised and impressed me was that the players were also knowledgeable advocates of a new stadium and artificial surface. Redknapp and Peyton both gave their endorsement, as did Sean O'Driscoll, who had studied the Luton Town surface. He said that the squad were one hundred per cent in favour of playing on a good artificial pitch.

The club appeared to be in no doubt; without a new ground it would fold. Towards the end of the meeting Cherries' Managing Director and Secretary Brian Tiler summarised, 'In ten years time, there will only be 70 clubs playing full-time football. We aim to be in that elite.' After we observed an overwhelming show of hands in favour of the scheme, Rodney Barton concluded: 'This has given us a mandate to look to the future.' My mind drifted for a while. My humble opinion, although not offered, was that the new stadium was a must for the future, but I remained unconvinced about the plastic pitch. My personal experiences of synthetic surfaces had been tarnished when playing five-a-side on a similar-type surface. I had fallen heavily on my outstretched hands and scorched my palms as they broke my fall. The blisters and burn marks were tender for weeks afterwards.

The meeting was then thrown open to questions and one of the most controversial points raised was obscene chanting at matches. Brian Tiler told the audience: 'We want to put a stop to obscene chanting. It is people like that who are keeping the public away from football matches. People don't want to hear that.'

The guy to my left, who reeked of stale tobacco, had 'AFCB' tattooed across his left knuckle and was wearing a tatty denim jacket, then leaned towards me and whispered 'Bollocks!', got up and strolled out. I thought that perhaps he had just popped out to get some celery!

One other interesting football news item this weekend was that the FA had refused to allow the Bristol Rovers versus Brentford first-round FA Cup-tie to be put back to 6 December (second-round day). The tie had already been postponed six times because of a waterlogged pitch at Twerton Park.

On a more serious note, President Ronald Reagan confirmed he had sanctioned the sales of arms to Iran, the Australian High Court backed ex-MI5 officer Peter Wright in his bid to publish his 'Spycatcher' memoirs and boxer Mike Tyson became the youngest world heavy-weight champion. Closer to home in the local news County planners slammed the rejection of a major travel interchange at Bournemouth station, dubbing the current site an eyesore.

DECEMBER

Bournemouth v. Gillingham – Tuesday 2 December

'Christmas is coming and the pace is hotting up!' was the first football entry in my diary for the new month. The Cherries entered December facing a hectic period of eight games during the month. The winner of tonight's game would go top of the table, which added extra spice to an already exciting encounter. I hated Gillingham, an abhorrence that only dated back to October 1985 when I foolishly stood at the Brighton Beach away end of the ground and watched Bournemouth lose 2-3 to the Kent side. I chose to stand with the visiting supporters purely so that I could say that I had watched football in all parts of the ground, but got threatened in the process. It was a stupid error of judgement on my part and I was lucky to get out of the ground without injury. Maybe this was another self-inflicted source fuelling my fear about football hooliganism.

To arrive on time Dad and I had undertaken the now normal ritual of gulping down our evening meal and then rushing to the ground; burping and wheezing all the way to Dean Court. On this evening parking proved more difficult than usual and with an impatient queue of traffic heading for Dean Court we abandoned the car in Cecil Road and sprinted towards King's Park for the 7.30pm kickoff.

As we approached the South End of the ground the queue from the turnstiles snaked back to the King's Park entrance. Dad kept my place in the line while I dashed in and out of the milling people looking for my lucky programme seller, but he was nowhere to be found. Despite this setback it looked like being a healthy sized crowd.

We entered the stadium at 7.26pm, just as both teams jogged onto the pitch to a great cheer from both sets of supporters. The atmosphere in the stadium was electric, carnival-like as both team line-ups were announced via the public address. As I scanned my match day programme I was intrigued by Redknapp's notes inside: 'Let me make it clear once and for all for the small minority of people who are still in doubt. AFC Bournemouth want promotion.' He stated further, 'After our excellent win against Chesterfield five people asked me if the Cherries really wanted to go up.' Then added: 'They have heard some old wives' tale that the club does not want to go up. It is as if we are close to promotion all the time yet we've had only two real chances of going into the Second Division since the club was formed in 1899. If we don't get promotion this time it is because we are not good enough.'

Handshakes, pleasantries and photographs were exchanged in the centre circle before Newson lost the toss (again) and the teams changed ends. The realisation of the change of ends produced some disgruntled moaning from the home fans – in particular from those in the New Stand who had chosen the wrong end to watch their heroes for the first 45 minutes and were now packed in like sardines, unable to move. Due to the houses behind, the New Stand had been erected close to the pitch and ran alongside the touchline opposite the Main Stand. When only filled to half capacity home supporters would move towards the end that Cherries were attacking to get a better view of the action. From where I stood at the South End of the ground I could witness the regular half-time migration of supporters from one end to another. For tonight's first half Cherries would be attacking towards the South 'home' End of the ground. Referee Mike James from Horsham blew his whistle and the game got underway.

The first 20 minutes were tense, neither side wanting to make an early slip. The turning point of the match occurred when Cherries team-mates Mark Whitlock and Trevor Aylott collided when challenging for the same ball in the 23rd minute.

Both players needed attention following the clash and it was one of the rare times I have witnessed both trainers on the field of play at the same time attending to players on the same side. Gillingham trainer Bill Collins helped Whitlock to his feet and departed the field to a small ripple of applause from the home fans. Aylott looked in some trouble, but eventually got to his feet to continue. 'Sort it out Boscombe' came a shout from behind me. Before either player had fully recovered, Gillingham scored. Gills striker Tony Cascarino, being watched by Arsenal manager George Graham in the Main Stand, headed down a Graham Pearce centre for Martin Robinson to fire a crisp shot just inside the post to send the visiting fans from Kent wild with delight. Oh, how I hated Gillingham!

The Dean Court faithful attempted to rally Cherries as they resumed the match and I shouted and yelled for all I was worth. The injured Aylott hobbled on for a while longer before being replaced by midfielder Bob Savage, while Whitlock struggled, but played through his discomfort. As half-time approached, Howlett lofted the ball over the visitors' defence to put Puckett clear on goal. As he raced towards the home fans and the penalty box he slid the ball under the advancing Ron Hilyard and the ball rolled towards the empty Gillingham net. Cherries' fans in front of me anticipating a goal jumped up and raised their hands in preparation to celebrate the equaliser. At this point and in all the excitement I lost sight of the ball as it entered the six-yard area. Blindly expecting a goal myself, I too raised my hands and began to jump and shout, but instead of a great cheer what followed was a desperate communal moan of disappointment. The ball had rolled agonisingly just inches wide of the far post. Supporters looked at each other in disbelief and shook their heads. I looked at Puckett, who held his head in his hands; he could not believe it either.

Cherries came out for the second half with renewed determination. Gillingham, though, stood firm; they were a strong side and fancied by many to be among the final promotion contenders. Time ticked by as the night grew colder and the game became bogged down in a midfield struggle with Cherries' passes going astray far too frequently. Eight minutes from time Gillingham inflicted another cruel blow as substitute Howard Pritchard claimed a second goal that was assisted by a deflection off the boot of home skipper Mark Newson. It was not to be Cherries' night; their system had been upset by the injury to Aylott and despite much toiling it was to be in vain.

As the final whistle blew the majority of the 7,756 spectators, the best home attendance of the season so far, let out a despairing sigh, with mine being louder than most. After eight successive home victories, Cherries had succumbed to their promotion rivals and had once again failed to rise to the big occasion in front of a bumper crowd. This was a familiar old story that had repeated itself throughout the years. The result and performance served as a timely reminder that there was still much hard work ahead on the promotion trail.

Redknapp, gracious in defeat, stated: 'We were all disappointed that it did not go right for us tonight – especially with such a big crowd to see the side. The players worked hard enough, but as a team, could not find their best form. Full credit to Gillingham, who played well and took advantage of the circumstances.' Gillingham manager Keith Peacock was delighted: 'We worked hard for this win and thoroughly deserved it with a good all-round performance.' Gillingham leapfrogged over Cherries and Middlesbrough to sit proudly on top of Division Three. My unfounded and biased hatred towards Gillingham grew ever greater after this result, but I was confident that we would exert revenge at their place later in the season.

By now you must have realised that I am a bit of a statistics nut, so one more interesting statistic was produced the following day. After six postponements of their 1st round FA Cup tie, Bristol Rovers and Brentford finally played their much delayed cup-tie. Between them, as though it were a deliberate act, they produced a goalless draw and had to meet again. The FA later rescinded their earlier decision and agreed to allow them to play the 1st round replay on 2nd round day.

Bournemouth v. Orient – Saturday 6 December

Subsequently I learned that Colin Clarke had been in the crowd for the Gillingham game. Living nearby in the beautiful area of the New Forest, he still had many friends at the club and came to watch Bournemouth play whenever he could. Oh how we could have used him on the night I thought and I drifted into a daydream featuring Clarke scoring a double hat-trick in a 6-0 rerun of the Gillingham game.

Attention now conveniently moved away temporarily from the promotion race and to the FA Cup. The Cup began in season 1871/72 and, while the world had significantly moved on, the buzz, excitement and tradition of the competition remained. By the 2nd round stage it meant that a draw or victory for teams competing could produce a money-spinning tie against First Division opponents in the third round of the competition. Following the postponement of the Port Vale game, Harry had given the players the weekend off and he had travelled to Brisbane Road to take a look at Cherries' cup opposition Orient as they drew 2-2 at home to Tranmere. The 'O's were sitting mid-table in Division Four and, with 38 rungs on the current League ladder separating the two teams, I felt quietly confident that Bournemouth would be in the hat for the third-round draw scheduled for Sunday afternoon. Add Cherries' strong home record into the equation, together with the fact that Orient had only managed to collect two points on their last eight League trips, I had already begun dreaming of a trip to Highbury or Old Trafford. Even my hero Cherries' skipper Mark Newson had gone public in his 'Captain's Corner' section of the match day magazine and was already talking about round three and how he would very much like to be drawn against Arsenal or West Ham. 'I've always wanted to play at Arsenal. When I was a young kid our football team had a walk around Highbury when Arsenal won the double. I picked up the League trophy and the FA Cup and have wanted to play since.'

85

The last time Cherries were paired against Orient in the FA Cup was back in January 1974 when the 'O's won a third-round tie 2-1 at Brisbane Road. The Cherries side on that day included Phil Boyer, Micky Cave, Jimmy Gabriel and the nippy winger Harry Redknapp. The visitors' current manager was Frank Clarke and he had used his playing experience to great influence and the 'O's were capable of raising their game and playing good football. 'We won't be getting any favours,' Redknapp added.

Aylott remained injured following the clash with Whitlock in the Gillingham game, so Bob Savage was restored to the starting line-up. Newson won the toss and, as always, chose to defend the South End for the first half. Orient in their all-white away strip began brightly creating neat triangles as they exchanged passes and held possession.

The visitors' key man was midfielder Sean Brooks, who conducted the orchestra by continually weaving graciously in and out of Cherries' defenders, hopping over tackles and fooling his marker with a gentle drop of the shoulder. Brooks was an ex-England amateur and he looked a class act. The following season Redknapp would snap him up for £10,000.

Puckett came close for Cherries, just slicing the ball wide following an O'Connor in-swinging corner that was only punched out by Orient keeper Peter Wells. 'Put some chalk on your boots,' I shouted politely. At the other end Peyton collected two speculative crosses before the half-time whistle brought proceedings to a close. To beat the stampede, I sprinted to the tea bar for some refreshment and warmth. As I queued for my brew the supporter in front of me turned and, briskly rubbing his hands to keep them warm, muttered, 'That was pretty dire wasn't it? Something's not right.' We exchanged observations until he was served. We both agreed that Cherries were struggling and then parted company to watch the second half.

The winter sun began to set and transform the late afternoon sky into an eerie red all above Dean Court. Was this an omen of what was to come? The players trotted back out for the second half and for a place in the third-round draw. Cherries kicked off and, with the crowd still settling down, Morrell produced a fine run down the left flank, delivering a perfect centre that was plucked out of the air by Wells. 'Come on you Reds!' came a shout from behind me. In the centre circle Brooks exchanged a neat series of passes with Lee Harvey, who sprinted clear towards the Bournemouth goal with Morrell chasing. He skipped over the defender's lunge and from an acute angle just inside the penalty area surprisingly beat Gerry Peyton with an angled shot. As the ball nestled in the far corner of the net, Harvey ran to the visiting fans behind Peyton's goal at the Brighton Beach End and disappeared under a mob of back-slapping celebrations from colleagues and supporters. Three minutes into the second half and Orient had struck a killer blow.

'Come on Boscombe!' shouted the trilby hat behind me as the Cherries picked up the tempo with a series of five consecutive corner kicks at the South End, O'Connor jogging across the field each time to take the kicks as the ball went out left, right and then left again for yet another corner kick. Despite this pressure all were well defended by the 11-man Orient defence. Cherries were now beginning to buzz and O'Driscoll worked tirelessly in midfield. Yet again O'Driscoll tackled and dispossessed Kevin Hales and he turned to set up Bob Savage 30 yards out. Savage, head down running forward, looked up and with his left foot unleashed an Exocet missile, which fizzed through the air faster than the speed of sound.

As it closed on goal it swerved and dipped viciously in the air and thudded into the crossbar and back out again into play. For several minutes after, the crossbar shook violently as it absorbed and recovered from the full impact of such a powerful strike. Some fifteen years later when the stadium was rebuilt I heard that when Barr, the construction company, removed the goal frame, the crossbar was still quivering from that Bob Savage rocket!

We began to rally our heroes. 'Score in a minute, we're gonna score in a minute' came the cry from the South End and, as if on cue, Puckett obliged, only for it to be ruled out for offside. The South End vehemented its disapproval of the decision: 'Who's the wanker in the black?' Then, on 70 minutes, Puckett jinked through a maze of Orient defenders and fell under a heavy challenge from 'O's Colin Foster. 'Penalty,' cried the Dean Court faithful, but referee Bob Harmer from Bristol ignored the pleas and I joined the chorus of 'Who's the wanker in the black?' Who would be a referee?

Cherries were running out of time. Orient continued to panic. Another scintillating Paul Morrell run and cross fell to the feet of Newson just on the penalty spot but, surrounded by defenders, he fired over from close range and with that went Bournemouth's last chance. Two minutes of injury time expired before referee Harmer blew his whistle to signal Cherries' exit from the FA Cup. Orient players and fans were delighted and joined one another, with Frank Clarke leading the celebrations at the Brighton Beach End of the ground. I turned for home, surrounded by much moaning and head shaking.

David had slain Goliath on his own turf and Orient would be in the draw for the third round. Arsenal, Liverpool or Manchester United would not be lubricating Cherries cash flow this season and would have to wait for another year. Elsewhere there were further unexpected results, but no major cup upset. Bath, Caernarfon and Chorley all earned replays after drawing against League opposition, with Telford the only non-League side guaranteed a place in round three after beating Altrincham 1-0. The biggest shock came when Brentford and Bristol Rovers finally settled their first round tie at the eighth attempt, Brentford winning 2-0 in the replay. Brentford would travel to Cardiff to play round two, probably when everyone else was playing round three!

Next day FA Cup romance was once again in evidence as non-League Maidstone United defeated Fourth Division Cambridge United 1-0. In the afternoon the draw was also made for the third round. Telford got a home tie against Leeds and Maidstone an away tie at Watford. As for Orient, they drew an East End derby home tie against First Division West Ham, Redknapp's old club. The phrase 'Sick as a parrot' sprang to my mind!

Bournemouth v. Cardiff City – Tuesday 9 December

New this season for the Freight Rover Trophy (FRT) calendar was that games had been scheduled slightly earlier and that two teams would qualify from the groupings at the start of the competition. The previous season only one team won a place in the next round, which proved a disaster as in some cases a team could already have been out of the competition and still had a game to play. The teams from Division Three and Four had been divided into sixteen groups of three, giving eight groups in the North and eight in the South of the country. The North and South split would continue through to the Area Final, which would provide a North and South Wembley final on Sunday 24 May. In the Southern section group one preliminary round, Bournemouth had been drawn with Cardiff City and Wolverhampton Wanderers.

Cherries were unable to continue their cup action as the scheduled FRT preliminary round match against Cardiff was postponed. This time there were no pitch problems, or viruses, but taking priority over the encounter was the delayed FA Cup second-round game between Cardiff and Brentford. For the record, Cardiff won 2-0. In the evening FA Cup replays Caernarfon bagged a League scalp, winning 2-1 at York City, but Bath City and Chorley went out at

Bristol City and Preston respectively. Bournemouth's FRT match with Cardiff was rescheduled to Tuesday 6 January.

At least it would be back to League action at the weekend, but not before further disappointing midweek news. On Thursday 11 December it was announced that Cherries' tough little Liverpudlian midfielder Robbie Savage who had been at Dean Court for three years had signed for Bradford City for a fee of £35,000. In the office we argued and debated the logic of this decision at great length. The question of why would Harry sell a key member of the squad at a crucial time in the season was uppermost in our minds and my colleague Peter Dodman was the first to raise it.

We all had one hundred per cent faith in Harry and his decisions. After protracted heated discussion the consensus was that since Savage broke his leg in a Hampshire Professional Cup game against Portsmouth at the beginning of the previous season, missing the whole of last season, he had been unable to compete to the same high standards. It was a good price and sell decision providing the vacuum he left would be filled. Our speculation was incorrect and clearly we knew nothing. The truth was that Savage and his family favoured a move back to the north as neither his wife nor he had settled in the area.

A giant would soon occupy the void. Redknapp had been searching for a commanding centre half to help sustain Cherries' promotion drive. Standing at six foot two inches, John Williams was playing for Port Vale and was invited to join the club following a recommendation from former Bournemouth striker Colin Clarke, who had teamed up with Williams at Tranmere. It's a small world. After negotiations with Port Vale, Williams signed for Cherries at a fee of £30,000. The Liverpudlian had appeared in 173 games for Tranmere before moving to Port Vale last season. Vale manager John Rudge, reluctant to release his centre half, told Redknapp that Williams would win the championship for Bournemouth.

Rotherham United v. Bournemouth – Saturday 13 December

For once I briefly forgot Cherries as I became occupied and concerned with the forthcoming festivities and Christmas. With no Sunday shopping and working all week, there now remained only two Saturdays to buy my Christmas presents. Those words of an old school friend regarding piss poor planning would come back to haunt me. Next Saturday Blackpool visited Dean Court, so that meant that Saturday 13 December was my one main opportunity to purchase my seasonal gifts. I made the decision to forfeit the long trip to Millmoor and sacrificed pleasure for festive necessity.

Under manager Norman Hunter Rotherham had been struggling since the start of the season and just one point kept them off the foot of the Division Three table. They had amassed a mere 15 points from 17 games, scoring a paltry seven goals in eight home games all season. Even without Savage, I was confident that Cherries could comfortably complete a successful Yorkshire raid while I shopped on the south coast.

After working in the morning until 2.00pm I prepared to battle my way through the town-centre festive chaos. Driving into town I listened to BBC Radio Solent and their pre-match review of Cherries' trip to Millmoor. Injuries were a problem. Aylott and Pulis remained sidelined, as did new signing John Williams. Despite being desperate to play, Williams had been recovering from a knock on his ankle that had not responded to treatment in time. With a small squad hit by injuries Redknapp had drafted in the services of both club coaches Keith Williams and Roger Brown for the game. Williams would start in place of the departed Savage and Brown would be on the bench. It was a grey overcast day as I parked the car in Meyrick Park, strolled past the Town Hall and then crossed into the Upper Gardens to John Menzies store. Glancing at my watch, it was 2.58pm and I whispered to myself, 'Come on you Reds!'

In 45 minutes I had already made good progress with my Christmas shopping and, with carrier bags in hand, I made my way to Debenhams TV department for the half-time scores and the anticipation of a Cherries lead. There were five other guys crowded around a 26-inch Ferguson colour TV, the only one tuned into BBC 'Grandstand', but with sound muted. 'Have Bournemouth come up yet?' I asked. 'Not yet, but Arsenal are winning!' came a reply that was partly irrelevant. For two minutes we all stared silently at the screen until there it was in black and white on the tele-printer 'D3: Rotherham 1 Bournemouth 0. With the exception of the Gunners fan we groaned our disappointment in unison and turned away.

Outside it was now getting dark. It was only half-time and so I put on a brave face and continued with my Christmas shopping, still confident that Cherries could turn the situation around. M&S, Boots, C&A, WH Smith and House of Fraser bags hung all around my feet by 4.45pm as I made my way to Beales TV department for the final results. Spoilt for choice, with nine TVs tuned into 'Grandstand' I settled my bags down in front of a colour Grundig. The BBC were broadcasting the last few minutes of a London Irish rugby match, but the tele-printer sat at the foot of the screen flashing late goals and final scores. At 4.50pm the Scottish results appeared and true to form Celtic and Rangers had both won easily.

English League results began to filter through as my stomach tightened and my palms perspired. The tele-printer flashed 'D3:', then paused for several seconds, my heart skipped a beat and I held my breath. It continued 'Middlesbrough 1 Doncaster 0'.

'Shit,' I blurted, looking around in case anyone had heard my outburst. I stared intently at the screen 'D3: Bolton Wanderers 3 Gillingham 0'. This was an unexpected surprise and I smiled with pleasure at the score line. The results continued to appear on the now full screen as the rugby match had ended. 'D3: Rotherham 4 Bournemouth 2'. My heart sank to my boots. It had to be a mistake. Surely Rotherham could not have delivered a 60 per cent increase in their home goal tally at Cherries' expense? I waited for the classified results read by James Alexander Gordon. He confirmed the nightmare, 'Rotherham 4 Bournemouth 2'. I stared at the screen in shock and disbelief. My attention re-engaged as the League table was displayed. Middlesbrough were back on top with 38 points, Gillingham had dropped to 2nd position with 37 and Notts County, who had walloped York City 5-1, had now moved into 3rd place with 34. Bournemouth dropped below them five points adrift of the League leaders with 33 points and had yet to gain a point in December.

I trudged out of Beales with my shopping and back to the car in Meyrick Park. As I drove home I listened to Solent and their match report. Defensive errors had contributed to Cherries' downfall as Douglas, Trusson and Campbell had taken advantage to give Rotherham a 3-0 lead after 70 minutes. David Puckett then spearheaded a spirited Cherries comeback to make it 3-2 before Gooding settled it for Rotherham with a spectacular 25-yard pile driver. It could have been worse as the report added that keeper Peyton saved Cherries from conceding five for the first time this season with a brilliant last-minute save from Daral Pugh. There had been further injury misery, too, as Cherries' midfielder Gary Howlett had failed to recover from a 35th-minute 'Norman Hunter bites your legs' style crunching tackle on his right ankle and he had limped off at half-time to be replaced by Cherries' coach Roger Brown. Such a move highlighted the limited resources available to Redknapp at this time.

Christmas shopping duties may well have kept many fans away from this match as only 2,092 turned up to record the lowest attendance of the season at Millmoor.

That evening I went out and got hammered. Woke up and played with a murderous hangover next morning for Lloyd's Bank and we lost 2-6 against Blue Star, who had now completed the double over us.

Wolverhampton Wanderers v. Bournemouth – Tuesday 13 December

Now in its third season the Freight Rover Trophy (FRT) appeared to be proving a successful partnership between the Football League and the Freight Rover company, but the competition had been dubbed the 'Mickey Mouse' cup because of its lack of glamour until the Wembley final was reached. It had failed to attract supporters.

A cup clash with Wolves inevitably resurrected memories of the Cherries' 1-0 fourth-round FA Cup victory at Molineaux, a famous result in the glorious cup run during season 1956/57 when Boscombe defeated Tottenham in round five before losing at home to Manchester United in the quarter-finals. At that time Wolves were third in Division One and 42,011 watched in amusement as Cherries' winger Reg Cutler collided with and knocked the goal post down, with play held up for several minutes while repairs were made. Undeterred he went on to score the only goal of the match. On numerous occasions my father recounted the cup run in great detail and it sounded magical.

Thirty years later times had changed. The once mighty Wolves had experienced two receiverships in the last seven years and plummeted from Division One to Division Four. Following his sacking from Aston Villa, new manager Graham Turner was quoted in the first week after he took over hard-up Wolves as saying: 'I have to count the practice balls after training because we can't afford to lose any. What we need is a bag to keep them in, but somebody pinched it.' To add insult to injury, in the current season's FA Cup competition Wolves had suffered a humiliating defeat, dumped out unceremoniously by Chorley 3-0 in a first-round second replay.

The FRT did not have the prestige of the FA Cup and, in contrast to the 1957 encounter between Wolves and Cherries, a mere 1,923 had turned out on a chilly December night. Unable to travel midweek because of work commitments, I listened to a very brief sports review on Radio Solent.

Hit by injuries, Bournemouth fielded young Adrian Randall and Morgan Lewis in midfield, with David Coleman and Tommy Keane on the bench. The

Wolves' attack was spearheaded by new £50,000 signing, Andy Thompson, together with Andy Mutch and a young Steve Bull who had scored in his last two previous matches. The game kicked off and Solent reverted back to their music programme, so I wrapped Christmas presents.

With no commentary available, I tuned back in at half-time. The two-minute report from Molineaux was delivered by a local Wolverhampton sports journalist in a colloquial, but sophisticated, BBC accent. Wolves led 2-1, thanks to goals by Dougherty and Bull. Puckett had replied for Cherries. The report ended and the station output reverted back to the music.

At 9.40pm Solent reconnected with the Molineaux reporter. It had been close, but Wolves had won 4-3. Bull and Dougherty had both scored again for the home side, while Puckett had struck twice more to produce his second cup hat-trick of the season.

Just as the bad news was delivered on the radio, my father popped his head around the door and asked, 'What do you want for Christmas son?' Looking at him dejectedly, I replied, 'A win and three points would be nice!'

The 'Bournemouth Evening Echo' headline the following day summed up the performance with the appalling, but expected, headline 'Sad Cherries get mauled by Wolves'. Redknapp was disappointed: 'We have got to tighten up in defence again! It is especially frustrating to know that we have scored a total of five goals in the last two away games and got beaten both times. We defended badly but we looked great going forward with David Puckett taking his three goals in brilliant style.'

Despite another defeat the one consolation was the form of Cherries' striker David Puckett. He sat on top of the Division Three 'hot shots' list as leading marksman with 16 goals, the same total held by Saints' Colin Clarke. Ironically, at this point he had scored more goals than Clarke had at the same point in the season before. At this rate Puckett was expected to pass the 30-goal mark with ease by season end. It briefly crossed my mind that if he topped 30 goals we might be able to sell him to Real Madrid for a cool £1 million!

Bournemouth v. Blackpool – Saturday 20 December
As the busy Christmas fixture period approached the bookmakers Mecca offered the following odds for the Division Three Championship: 2-1 Middlesbrough, 4-1 Gillingham, 6-1 Notts County, Walsall, 8-1 Bristol City, 10-1 Swindon, 12-1 Blackpool and 14-1 Bournemouth. Harry Redknapp, who

enjoyed the occasional flutter commented: 'That's a good bet! At those prices I would rate us as a better bet than the favourites!'

On Friday 19 December the match with Blackpool was postponed because of a Dean Court epidemic, which had decimated the Cherries squad. I was devastated – my careful and cunning plan to complete the Christmas shopping the previous weekend had backfired. The brief TV report stated that thirteen squad members, including nine first-team players, had been hit by the virus and it had also spread to include administrative and lottery staff. Redknapp explained, 'We wanted to play but there was no way that we could raise a team.' Provision to call off a match under these circumstances had been made under regulation 17 of the League.

Weekend results did not go in Cherries' favour as Gillingham, Wigan, Notts County and Middlesbrough all won and only Swindon dropped points away at Doncaster with a 2-2 draw. Sunday morning I played for Lloyd's Bank and scored a peach of a volley in a 5-1 demolition of 2CI Strollers at Duck Lane public playing fields. My celebrations were tarnished though and none of my team-mates came close to congratulate me as I had fallen in a small pile of dog shit just inside the penalty area. For the remaining fifteen minutes no-one came near me, including the opposition, and I roamed the pitch freely. Oh, the joys of playing amateur football! In the evening the family gathered and we celebrated my mother's birthday.

Bristol Rovers v. Bournemouth – Friday 26 December

Professional footballers get a raw deal at Christmas as they are unable to indulge in merrymaking like the rest of us. The Bournemouth players were no exception and Redknapp had them all undertake light training on Christmas morning. I had a lazy Christmas Day and after excessive eating it was good to be out of the house and in the car on route to Bath via the A36. Munching on cold turkey sandwiches, the boys and I sang 'Jingle bells, jingle bells, jingle all the way, oh what fun it is to see Bournemouth win away oh!'. Despite zero points in December our mood was optimistic and, anyway, it was the season of goodwill.

I had visited Eastville the previous season, but for various reasons Rovers had been forced to leave their old Eastville ground at the end of the previous season and had signed a seven-year lease as part of a ground-sharing scheme with Bath City at Twerton Park, some ten miles away from their previous

Eastville home. The forced move to a smaller stadium had caused problems. There were only 600 seats in the grandstand and season tickets were limited, so revenue and attendances were down on the previous season.

While queueing to enter at the visitor turnstile I noticed that the Bath police were searching Bournemouth fans before allowing us to approach the turnstile gates. I was beckoned towards a tall bearded officer who ordered me to empty my pockets. I showed him the contents, a set of car keys and an apple. Pointing to the fruit he asked, 'What's that for?' Somewhat bemused by the question, I responded with 'It's an apple for eating.' His eyes narrowed and he raised a pointed finger at me, then barked, 'Don't get cheeky with me son, or you won't see the match!' He followed that statement with an ultimatum, 'Eat it or throw it away.' I chose to spend the next five minutes chomping on my half-time vitamin C before I was allowed to rejoin the queue of Cherries fans. It was a pathetic moment of defiance on my part and I could only think that he thought I might use my Golden Delicious as a threatening terrace weapon.

I paid my £2.50 and entered the visitors open terrace. It was a compact stadium with basic facilities. The away supporters enclosure had been rebuilt before the start of the season with new terracing and sturdy steel crush barriers painted white. The pitch was appalling. It had suffered serious drainage problems, which had caused the postponement of several games. Standing behind the goal I looked out upon a carpet of flat mud interjected with tufts of grass. The goal area was mainly mud and sand, and a strong icy cold wind blew in my face.

Just over 600 Bournemouth supporters had travelled to Twerton Park and between us we were armed with a festive selection of red and white balloons and ticker tape, which would be released as a tidal wave of colour as the Cherries ran out. Football supporters are tribal in their nature and we proved that by all standing compactly on the sloping terrace and singing our peculiar tribal songs. It was bizarre and it reminded me of a scene from the film 'Zulu'!

At 2.55pm Newson led the team out onto the pitch to rapturous applause from the visiting fans. As if well rehearsed, the sea of red and white was released by supporters, but instead of a massive wave of colour ascending skywards the balloons and ticker tape were immediately swept away by the strong wind, sending the concoction behind the Bournemouth fans and into the car park behind. An unsuspecting motorist was the only one to benefit from the colourful shower. Hours of preparation lost in seconds.

95

I noticed a new face on the pitch. New signing John Williams jogged towards the Bournemouth fans and applauded us. In return we acknowledged his arrival with chants of 'Willo, Willo'. Reflecting now, I think this was the defining moment when both Willo and Cherries fans united in a long loyal relationship. He came close to where I stood, he looked big and strong and turned and jogged back towards the centre circle passing ex-Cherry striker Trevor Morgan on the way. I thought it seemed odd to see one of my old favourites 'Chesty' Morgan in a blue and white quartered shirt.

The Pirates, managed by Bobby Gould, kicked off towards the Bath end terrace with Cherries attacking towards us in the first half. The early exchanges were even as both teams began to settle on the treacherous surface. As the ball was played to Rovers' striker Morgan, Bournemouth fans began to boo. Then, just as a statement of intent, Cherries' hard man Tony Pulis thundered in and clattered him to the ground. The boos turned to cheers. Morgan ignored the outstretched hand of apology and a smirking Pulis patted him on the head as the Rovers star sat on the deck. Moments later Puckett turned and picked up a loose pass 35 yards out. As he controlled the bobbling ball Rovers defender Darren Carr clattered him from behind and Puckett gave out a sickening shriek as he fell. Carr was lectured and subsequently booked by referee Brian Stevens while Puckett lay in agony in the mud. The extent of the injury looked severe when the St John Ambulance stretcher bearers were summoned onto the pitch. The volunteers in their luminous orange Day-Glo jackets attended to Puckett. Eventually he was carried off the field to sympathetic applause. I was sickened, Cherries' leading goal scorer stretchered off in considerable pain and probably out of action for several weeks. If ever there was a low point during the season, this for me was it. I began to think that our season had begun to fall apart.

Tom Heffernan replaced him and, in a tactical change, Heffernan went to right back and fullback Newson moved forward to play as striker alongside Carl Richards. It was Newson leading by example and playing in an unaccustomed role who had a hand in the first goal. He headed on a Sean O'Driscoll chip for Mark O'Connor playing against his old club to finish in style. Behind the goal we jumped for joy. I had my camera ready to capture the goal on film, but I had been ball watching; distracted by following the play I missed the opportunity, an event of regular occurrence, to my frustration. Cherries led 1-0 at the interval.

In the second half Bournemouth took a grip on the game. Paul Morrell played a long ball over a static Rovers' defence and Carl Richards raced away towards the

Colin Clarke rises above the Swansea defence to score one of his 35 goals during the season of 1985/86.

Above: Divine intervention! Club Chaplain Alan Fisher leads a Cherries prayer for promotion at the beginning of the season. Left to right: Mark Newson, Robbie Savage, Gary Howlett, Mark O'Connor, Sean O'Driscoll, Tom Heffernan, Mark Whitlock, Alan Fisher, Tony Pulis, David Puckett, Trevor Aylott, Gerry Peyton.

Above: 'Big Trev' keeps a
Newport County defender at
arm's length.

Right: Captain Mark Newson
makes a note of tactics from
the boss during a training
session.

Left: David Puckett swivels
neatly to complete his hat-
trick against Fareham Town
in the FA Cup.

Left: Delighted Cherries fans in the South End clebrate another successful Robbie Savage 'bullet' from the penalty spot against Bristol City.

Below left: Carl Richards and David Puckett wait patiently for a corner kick at Twerton Park, moments before Puckett's injury.

Right: The famous 'Willo' flick-on gave Cherries a new attack weapon that proved highly successful during the second half of the season.

Below: A goalmouth scramble causes panic in the Chester defence at Sealand Road.

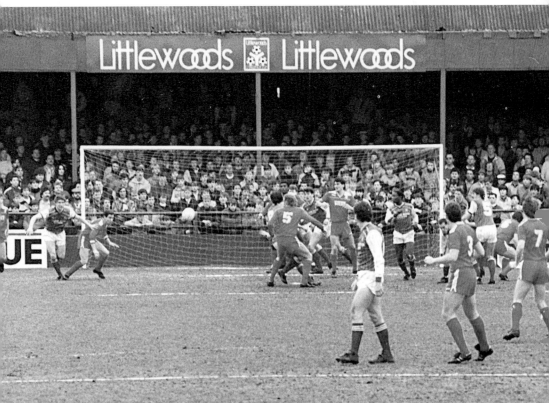

Above: 'Little Richard' – Richard Cooke reveals his blistering pace as he accelerates past another unsuspecting defender.

Below: Oh what a night! Captain Mark Newson powers home Cherries' first goal against Middlesbrough.

Above: One of the goals of the season. Sean O'Driscoll fires home Bournemouth's second goal against Middlesbrough.

Below: 'We're going up!' Cherries' supporters at Craven Cottage.

Harry Redknapp proudly presents the Championship trophy to the Dean Court faithful.

Yellow Buses parade the Champions on a tour of Bournemouth before a civic reception at the Town Hall.

far end of the ground to score his sixth goal of the season. In the away supporters enclosure I jumped for joy and along with my fellow supporters from Dorset made a fantastic noise, hailing our hero 'Bruno, Bruno'. Seven minutes later new boy John Williams made it 3-0 after heading Howlett's cross onto the post and netting the rebound. For the third time I punched the air with both fists and jumped for joy, this time singing 'Willo, Willo'.

The makeshift forward partnership between Richards and Newson had paid dividends, but in the 80th minute Richards limped off with a thigh strain and Bournemouth ended the game with only ten men, but the joyous celebrations of 'Jingle bells, jingle bells, jingle all the way, oh what fun it is to see Bournemouth win away oh!' drifted across Twerton Park. The journey home was quick and much discussion took place in the car regarding whether our season was a disaster about to happen, or one that was very much back on track.

Bournemouth v. Fulham – Saturday 27 December

In the cold light of dawn the next day I realised that the victory against the Pirates had come at a high cost. Both Puckett and Richards had joined fellow striker Trevor Aylott on the treatment table and would not be available to play 24 hours later against a useful Fulham side that included Paul Parker, Dean Coney and Gordon Davies.

At 2.55pm the noise in Dean Court was one of vibrant expectancy as 6,670 turned up for Cherries' and Fulham's second game in 24 hours. With Redknapp failing to secure the loan of Joe Jordan from neighbours Southampton, it meant Captain Marvel, Mark Newson, would lead the Cherries' attack. Youngster Morgan Lewis would replace the injured Richards and coach Keith Williams would be on the bench. No disrespect is intended here, but we were scraping the bottom of the barrel.

Newson lost the toss again! and Fulham chose to swap ends, attacking the goal towards their large band of travelling supporters behind the Brighton Beach End goal. Bournemouth drew first blood on 21 minutes as Mark O'Connor fired the home side into the lead with a deflected shot that squeezed past keeper Vaughan despite the narrowest of angles.

Fulham came back strong and, just five minutes later, equalised through a well-rehearsed free kick taken by Wayne Kerrins. Cherries battled hard, but lacked penetration up front despite Newson's efforts. Six minutes before half-time Fulham went ahead with another well-worked goal executed by Gary

Barnett to lead 2-1 at the interval. The promotion challenge looked like it was about to be derailed.

Newson led the team back out for the second half and kicked off with Mark O'Connor. 'Come on you Reds,' I screamed in the ear of the bloke next to me. Supporters in the Main Stand had still not taken their seats as O'Driscoll and O'Connor exchanged a series of passes before O'Connor found Newson on the edge of the Fulham penalty area and he struck a low shot past the static Vaughan. With Captain Marvel to the rescue, Cherries had equalised just 30 seconds after the restart. We were back in it.

Both sides began to tire, although Bournemouth maintained the edge over Fulham despite the visitors' dangerous counterattacks. The game looked to be drifting towards a draw, but then O'Connor was fouled just outside the Fulham penalty area and the home crowd won the free kick. Heffernan swung in the kick and John Williams rose majestically at the far post to head in. Dean Court erupted to a now familiar chorus of 'Willo, Willo'. Moments later the final whistle blew to another huge cheer and sigh of relief. Exhausted and elated, the Bournemouth players hugged each other in recognition of their battling team victory ground out in difficult circumstances. I left Dean Court drained of energy and emotion.

Redknapp was delighted and summed up the result in two words: 'Absolutely fantastic!' Beaming, he added: 'In the circumstances, it was the best performance I have seen from a Bournemouth side since I've been in charge.' I had to agree it had been a remarkable team effort and a gruelling test of endurance only 24 hours after a tough scrap in the Bristol mud.

Considering the awful start to December, since the arrival of John Williams Cherries had obtained a maximum six points from the two festive games. Middlesbrough remained top at the end of the year with 45 points, a clear six points ahead of Bournemouth in fourth place. Notts County and Gillingham remained two points ahead of Cherries. Swindon, one point behind Cherries in sixth place, were next on the Dean Court agenda scheduled for New Year's Day.

8.
Season 1986/87
(Part 2: January to
May 1987)

JANUARY

Bournemouth v. Swindon – Thursday 1 January

Two days earlier news broke regarding the seriousness of David Puckett's injury during the Bristol Rovers mud fight on Boxing Day. Puckett was on the operating table at the Lansdowne private hospital as surgeons attempted to sort out the cartilage and ligament injury he had suffered. The victim of a vicious tackle, his sensational debut season for Bournemouth had been abruptly halted and he was expected to miss much of the remaining season. A dejected Redknapp explained the loss: 'He (Puckett) is having his best ever season and would have got 30 goals this year. Some people may not realise it, but he has scored more goals at this stage of the season than Colin Clarke did last year.' The loss of Cherries' star forward meant that Redknapp now faced a long-term striker problem. Aylott was still recovering from ligament problems, but would not be available for the clash with Swindon. Richards should be fit again and the circulating rumours that Joe Jordan might cover short-term were finally squashed when he declined to make the temporary move to 'Cherry Land'. Bournemouth would face Swindon with another depleted forward line, but which had surprisingly so far delivered six goals over the holiday period.

I spent New Year's Eve at the Mariners Wharf nightclub in Poole. Fancy dress was traditional for the night, so I hired an outfit and dressed as the 'Mad Hatter' character from 'Alice in Wonderland' with long lime-green coat tails, pink checked trousers and an oversized top hat. I looked a complete berk, but somehow still managed to maintain my dignity throughout the evening, getting served regularly at the bar and chatting to many girls. Perhaps they felt sorry for me.

New Year's resolutions made, I took my father as a treat to the promotion clash and local derby with Swindon. Dean Court was heaving and for the second time we queued at the South End turnstile to enter the stadium. Once inside I bought a programme and we both shuffled along the yellows to the usual spot. The Robins were managed by Lou Macari and had successfully fended off an approach for their young manager during the summer months from Glasgow Celtic. In his programme notes under 'Harry's Line' Redknapp welcomed Swindon and praised Macari for his success to date. Redknapp's wish for the New Year was quite simple – promotion from the Third. He added a cautionary note regarding the frailness of the squad and that injuries had begun to concern him and he still had no cover for goalkeeper Gerry Peyton.

For once we actually arrived at Dean Court early. The atmosphere was tense, but the game had been delayed by fourteen minutes as supporters from both teams continued to push through the turnstiles; just my luck! Cherries kicked off attacking towards the South End home supporters in the first half after Newson had lost the toss again and the visitors had chosen ends. How and why he lost the toss so many times I will never know. The first 15 minutes belonged to Bournemouth as they attempted to kill the game early. O'Connor and O'Driscoll exchanged passes neatly and O'Connor swept the ball into the Swindon penalty area for Carl Richards to connect superbly, but his header struck the post and bounced out. Moments later it was Richards again in the thick of the action as his shot was kicked off the line by the visitors' defender Alan McLoughlin. For a third time Richards went through, but fell over the ball attempting a neat piece of trickery. Swindon began to recover their composure and I became concerned as they forced a series of corners that were easily dealt with by the home defence, John Williams mastering the back four. Bournemouth had the better of the first 45 minutes, but had failed to assert their superiority and at half-time it was goalless.

As the team jogged out for the second half I realised that Cherries' central defender Mark Whitlock had failed to reappear, following a knock on his ankle. Morrell switched to the centre of defence and substitute Morgan Lewis moved to left back. Chances to break the deadlock came at each end and were wasted to disgust and relief of both sets of supporters. Five minutes from time I began to clock watch as Bournemouth midfielder Howlett played a long ball towards the centre circle, where acting striker Newson nodded it on into the path of the sprightly Richards. 'Bruno', with our encouragement, brought the ball under control and accelerated away from two chasing Swindon defenders, then slid the ball past the advancing Fraser Digby in the Swindon goal and the ball nestled in the back of the net. Dean Court erupted in an explosion of shouting, cheers and singing. I revelled in a chorus of '1-0, 1-0, 1-0, 1-0, 1-0, 1-0' as we all taunted our visitors.

Three minutes from time Swindon broke down the left flank and Mark Jones centred towards Steve White on the edge of the six-yard area. 'Catch it, Gerry!' I shouted as the Bournemouth keeper came off his line to collect. In the aerial challenge with White, Peyton appeared to fumble, and expensive new signing Jimmy Quinn smashed the loose ball into the roof of the Bournemouth net. 'Bollocks,' I shouted as Swindon began to celebrate. The celebrations were, however, premature as referee Lester Shapter from Torquay ruled the goal out for a foul on Peyton. Jones, who had delivered the perfect centre, was livid and let fly a torrent of abuse at the referee, who subsequently gave him his marching orders for continuing to protest. In the South End we waved goodbye to him as he left the pitch.

Disappointed Swindon supporters had suffered enough torture and began to exit the Brighton Beach terrace in their droves. Streaming out, they were serenaded by Bournemouth fans in the South End, 'We can see you sneaking out!' My eyes moved from the Swindon fans back to the action, which was now right in front of me. Ten-man Swindon were back on the attack and Cherries' fullback Tom Heffernan cleared the danger at the back post, hoofing the ball high into the night sky and over the New Stand into one of the gardens in Thistlebarrow Road. Heffernan was a tough, committed and no-nonsense player who knew when not to fanny about with the ball.

A new ball entered the field of play from the dug-out, its slow arrival wasting precious seconds as catcalls and whistles echoed all around Dean Court. Finally, to a crescendo of cheers, referee Shapter blew his whistle and Bournemouth had won this critical promotion derby 1-0.

10,537 people – the best home attendance of the season – had witnessed Cherries complete a hat-trick of wins in the space of seven days, a truly remarkable feat with a depleted forward line. The Swindon victory had also come at a cost, though. Defender Whitlock was unable to play in the second half, tough tackling midfielder Tony Pulis left the field with his wrist strapped after suffering a fracture, and both Newson and Heffernan limped off at the end of the match with leg injuries.

Redknapp was delighted: 'Taking everything into account those three wins

101

have been a fantastic spell. Because of the injuries it has been something of a patched up side, short of key players.' When pushed on the injury crisis, he added, 'I'm hoping to bring in another player soon.'

The following day Redknapp was given the go-ahead to sign a new player on a permanent basis, thanks to the generosity of Swindon. Let me explain. This was possible due to the New Year's Day bumper gate; Swindon had brought 3,500 travelling fans and on top of the splendid support from Bournemouth fans this had helped find funds for a new signing.

To cap a wonderful New Year's Day, League leaders Middlesbrough lost away at York 1-3 and Southampton lost by the same score at Oxford United. Unfortunately, Gillingham continued their good run by thumping Walsall at home 4-0, a result made even more impressive by the fact that Walsall had spent £300,000 on new signings just before the Christmas period.

The New Year news headlines were dominated by the disappearance of Terry Waite, who was feared kidnapped in Beirut, and Mikhail Gorbachev, who outlined his plans to modernise the Soviet Union through perestroika (restructuring) and glasnost (openness).

Chesterfield v. Bournemouth – Saturday 3 January

The back of my throat throbbed constantly; it felt like I had gargled with, then swallowed, a coil of barbed wire. Laid low by a virus and too sick to work, I had spent the previous day in bed feeling extremely sorry for myself and desperate for a dose of sympathy. Saturday arrived and I still felt as stiff as a skinhead's boot, so wisely decided to remain at home rather than travel to The Recreation Ground in Chesterfield. My lifeline to the Cherries' action was again BBC Radio Solent.

Bournemouth had reached the halfway point in the season. With the exception of the postponed Blackpool and Port Vale matches, Cherries had played every team in Division Three and Chesterfield were the first club where Cherries could attempt to complete their first 'double' of the season. Bournemouth continued to be injury jinxed and so youngster Morgan Lewis once again found himself in the starting line-up with fellow youth David Coleman on the bench. The character of the side shone through as Newson had also been patched up to take part and Cherries' tough midfielder Tony Pulis, nicknamed 'Iron Man' would also play despite having a fractured wrist, six stitches in his knee and a slight groin strain. Ron Greenwood in his book

'Yours Sincerely' described character as the 'courage that takes him into the heat of the action and the determination that makes the apparently impossible possible. It comes from within a man and it so often separates winners from losers.' The whole team oozed character and Pulis was an exemplary figure. He paid the price with injuries because of his wholeheartedness and commitment in the tackle, but he never took prisoners.

Chesterfield did not rate Bournemouth highly. Programme editor Phil Tooley in his 'Who's Going Up?' column predicted that Bournemouth would end the season in 7th place, stating 'They've not quite got what it takes this term. Maybe next season.' His money was firmly on Middlesbrough for the title, followed by Walsall and Swindon.

I remember the Solent pre-match review of the encounter. Reporter Tony Mitchener described a cold blustery afternoon with a difficult pitch frozen at one end, soft and spongy at the other.

I must have drifted in and out of consciousness because I have minimal recollection of this game, only waking from slumberland to hear the final result. Honours even, a 1-1 draw and a well-earned point away from home, the tenth point earned in nine days of action. Mitchener described the key moments. Mick Henderson had given the hosts the lead on 25 minutes, with Gary Howlett securing a point for Bournemouth with three minutes remaining – apparently a brilliant looping shot over the keeper. On reflection I decided that I had been pleased that I had slept through the tension.

However, it could have been so different. On 12 minutes Cherries' keeper Peyton saved Bellamy's spot kick, his second penalty stop of the season. 'Play anywhere' Newson missed a good opportunity and Cherries had dominated with 13 corners during the match. With centre half Williams pushing up, and Coleman replacing the flagging Pulis, Cherries had a five-man attack for the remaining 25 minutes of the match, but still failed to penetrate sufficiently to win the game.

Middlesbrough, as expected, had beaten relegation candidates Newport County 2-0, but Gillingham had lost at Notts County 1-3. I smiled and suddenly I felt so much better.

Bournemouth v. Cardiff City – Tuesday 6 January
Revealed this week was the announcement that AFC Bournemouth made a profit last year of £188,000. This was made possible following the sale of Colin

Clarke for a club record fee and largely due to the sale of 17 houses built by the club on the land at the back of the Brighton Beach End of the ground, which brought in £1.4 million. Bournemouth were also beneficiaries of a £105,297 safety work grant made by the Football Grounds Improvement Trust. I am sure there were plenty, but I could not recall any obvious signs of physical ground improvement apart from the 'Keep off the yellows' initiative. Was yellow paint really that expensive?

Since the weekend result at Chesterfield the main talking point was the speculation that Redknapp was about to sign a new striker. On Monday 5 January the 'Bournemouth Echo' ran the headline 'Spurs striker is the target', revealing that promising young winger Richard Cooke was the subject of the speculation and the player Redknapp wanted to strengthen his squad. Cooke had gained England Under 21 recognition and First Division experience with Tottenham. The price tag was £20,000 plus, but Redknapp refused to rush into a quick signing on the basis that the squad needed strengthening in a number of areas.

Back to nearly full health I stood in the usual Dean Court spot on a bitterly cold night. As I blew my nose to ease the dripping congestion I thought to myself that I must be mad to be out in the bitter cold after being so ill and it was only an FRT game.

To progress beyond the preliminary round of the Freight Rover Trophy Bournemouth had to win against Fourth Division Cardiff, who had only lost once in their last six matches. Ex-Cherry defender Phil Brignull stood at the heart of the City defence and blocking the route to goal. The game was a poor spectacle watched by 1,482 frozen spectators, the lowest turnout of the season. I shivered through the first 45 minutes of stalemate. The second half had to be better. I jumped up and down and clapped my hands vigorously in an attempt to keep warm. I had anticipated the cold and it had given me a first opportunity to test out my newly acquired ski clobber. I was most impressed with the moon boots, even though I looked a prat in them.

The game restarted and followed a similar pattern until midway through the half, when Bournemouth stepped up a gear. Coleman, industrious down the left flank, brought a fine save from City keeper Graham Moseley as he pushed his shot against a post and out for a corner. Teenager Tommy Keane, playing his first full game for Bournemouth, also went close before Newson rattled the crossbar on 72 minutes and knocked off the hanging icicles. Cherries' perseverance and my patience were rewarded on 83 minutes with another late strike. Heffernan pushed forward, catching the City defence square and found O'Driscoll in the penalty area, who snapped up the opportunity with his left foot.

Eighteen more minutes of shivering were relieved when the final whistle blew. My feet, now numb with the cold, slowly broke free from their virtual ice-block mooring and I headed home. Bournemouth were now one of the remaining 32 teams in the competition. 'This might be the win to set us on the road to Wembley!' quipped Redknapp.

Bournemouth v. Brentford – Saturday 10 January

The Cherries squashed by Orient and the Bees stung by Cardiff City had both been victims of lower Division cup upsets and so ironically met on the day that the calendar hosted the FA Cup Third Round.

Despite Newson's valiant efforts temporarily leading the forward line, Redknapp admitted that he couldn't expect his captain to continue in that role indefinitely. Injured striker Trevor Aylott had missed the last nine matches and was still struggling to regain fitness. Even a run out in the reserves during midweek saw the damaged knee trouble flare up again, resulting in the necessity for a series of further injections and treatment. Redknapp continued to trail Tottenham winger Richard Cooke with renewed interest as the England Under-21 International turned down an offer to join Dutch club Groningen. The obstacle to the deal remained the sum of £5,000, the difference between Tottenham's asking price and Bournemouth's initial bid of £25,000. Redknapp considered the offer fair and was not prepared to budge from this figure. The stalemate continued. Other options were being considered, with Cherries coaches Roger Brown and Keith Williams scouting throughout the Leagues studying other possible transfer targets. I cleaned my boots just in case I got the call.

Bournemouth had, however, completed the paperwork on one new signing just in time for the Brentford game. Jimmy Gabriel had rejoined the Cherries in the role of Assistant Manager. An old friend of Redknapp and a key figure in AFC Bournemouth's 1972/73 promotion challenge that, like all the others, ended in another near miss, Gabriel had returned to the UK from America where he had recently been coaching San Jose Earthquakes, ending a 12-year involvement with American soccer. His insight and vast experience would be a considerable asset to Redknapp and his coaching staff.

Brentford had experienced a mediocre season with points hard to come by despite the efforts of manager Frank McLintock, who was now in his third season with the club, and coach Terry Mancini. The Bees languished in 18th place, hovering just above the relegation zone. The Brentford danger man was forward Robbie Cooke. He had top scored the previous season with a total of 18 goals and in the current campaign had already notched up 16 to his name.

In the centre circle the coin was tossed and Newson guessed correctly, choosing to defend the South End. Brentford kicked off, Francis Joseph nudged the ball forward to Cooke, who turned and laid it back to ex-Tottenham star Steve Perryman. As a 'welcome to Dean Court' gesture Pulis steamed in and flattened him. Free kick Brentford, caution for Pulis.

The first 45 minutes was a docile affair as Bournemouth attempted in vain to open up a stubborn Brentford rearguard where they were stifled by a five-man defence marshalled superbly by the experienced Perryman. Behind the South End goal a selection of Bournemouth supporters amused themselves at the expense of the visitors' keeper Gary Phillips. Each time he took a goal kick in front of them they attempted to distract his concentration by holding a vocal tone that grew faster and louder as he ran forward to take each goal kick. Upon connection with the ball the hanging vocal tone was replaced by a collective shout of 'You're shit aaagh!' followed by loud guffaws. The ritual continued for all goal kicks and on one occasion it appeared to have worked as Phillips sliced the ball into the Main Stand for a Bournemouth throw. The volume of cheering and laughing increased each time.

Francis Joseph was a well-built, bustling black centre forward who had always been a handful for defenders at this level. He was causing the Cherries' defence a few concerns. Three times he outjumped Whitlock, Newson and Morrell in the air to win the ball and set up a Brentford opportunity. His persistence became annoying and the guy standing to my left, obviously frustrated, shouted, 'Come on Boscombe, you gotta turn the lights up to see him.' Redknapp ordered Williams to man-mark Joseph and the tactical change from the dug-out eliminated the danger.

The south-westerly wind swirling across the ground picked up speed, biting into cold flesh and blowing paper and empty crisp packets across the turf in short accelerating bursts. Coats, hats and scarves were adjusted as the teams were greeted for the second half. Within three minutes of the restart I had the perfect excuse to warm my cold hands.

Sean O'Driscoll took advantage of a dithering defensive mix-up to drive the ball into the Brentford net from just inside the penalty area. The crowd exploded into song: 'The Reds are going up!' The goal inspired Bournemouth, and O'Driscoll nearly made it a brace two minutes later, but shot narrowly wide. 'Unlucky Sean' came the cry to my right.

Bournemouth turned the screw. Mark O'Connor broke down the left flank, stepped inside his marker and entered the penalty area, drawing Brentford keeper Phillips towards him. As the keeper advanced O'Connor squared the ball to the unmarked Richards, who tapped it into the empty net. No goal – referee Malcolm Cotton ruled that Richards had strayed offside. The Dean Court faithful were unsympathetic and we made our feelings public: 'Who's the wanker in the black!' Cherries were now rampant and attacked at will. O'Connor jinked and teased his marker before fooling him again and driving in a low centre that Newson smashed into the roof of the net. No goal – Newson was judged by the official to have pushed his marker. You can, no doubt, guess the crowd response.

Two minutes from the end Brentford counterattacked and Morrell, desperately chasing back, conceded the corner. From the resulting kick the ball swirled under the Cherries' crossbar and Brentford defender Keith Millen headed the equaliser. Having looked set for the three points that would have put them second in the table, the Cherries had been mugged at the death. Daylight robbery. Ask any football supporter and they will tell you that there is nothing better or worse than scoring or conceding in the last minutes of a match. I left Dean Court in disappointment.

Redknapp was melancholic: 'It was disappointing to concede that late goal when we looked like getting another win, but we've got vital goals in the same way recently and this time we were on the receiving end.'

Elsewhere the FA Cup Third Round produced the usual number of surprises. Fourth Division Aldershot embarrassed First Division Oxford United with a comfortable 3-0 win, but only 2,034 turned up to watch because of the large increase in admission prices, including £9.00 for terrace tickets instead of the usual £3.20.

The attendance was a new lowest record ever recorded for the Third Round. In contrast a crowd of 54,294 watched Manchester United beat Manchester City with a goal by Norman Whiteside. Third Division Walsall beat First Division Charlton 2-1 at Selhurst Park. The only non-League club that survived was Caernarfon, who held Barnsley to a goalless draw. The following day Telford

107

United's tie with Leeds at The Hawthorne ended in a 2-1 victory for the League side in front of 6,460 spectators. The price for providing more than 300 police was £20,000. It would have meant Telford losing money, but the FA did the fair thing and paid the bill. There was only one arrest!

The most bizarre story of the third round surfaced three days later when, because of heavy snow, Gillingham had to call in police assistance to gather their players together for the trip to Wigan. Skipper Mark Weather (how appropriately named), his telephone out of order, walked six miles through snowdrifts to get to the pick-up point, only to hear when he arrived that the game had been postponed.

Newport County v. Bournemouth – Sunday 18 January

At a fee of £27,500 a bargain was struck and Richard Cooke, the 21-year-old winger from Tottenham, signed for Bournemouth. With the London club's vast array of stars Cooke decided the time was right to move on. Securing the services of such a fine young player was a coup for the Cherries. In his first few days at Bournemouth he was a revelation, displaying all the skills, pace and character that had made him such a bright prospect at Spurs. In an interview with the 'Today' newspaper Tottenham and England star Glen Hoddle considered Cooke to be 'one of the best young products' he had seen at Spurs and always thought he had the talent to take him right to the top: 'I rate Richard highly and know he will do a great job for Bournemouth.' Weather permitting, it was expected that he would be in line to make his debut on Sunday against Newport County.

The UK had again been shrouded in a prolonged bout of bitter cold weather that had slowly crept across the whole country over the last few days. By Sunday morning the pitch at Newport was completely frozen and so the game was postponed, rearranged for Tuesday 24 February. The weekend sporting fixtures were decimated; even Poole Town's match with Ruislip at the Stadium was postponed. Only eight Football League and two Scottish League games could be played. The Pools Panel sat for the third consecutive week, the 53rd time since it was introduced during the Big Freeze winter of 1962/63.

Panel members included former International referee Arthur Ellis, ex-England stars Stan Mortensen and Roger Hunt, together with ex-Scotland players Tony Green and Ronnie Simpson. Chairman was Lord Bath of Longleat.

With no action this weekend, I revisited the Brentford match programme.

In the John Plank sponsored 'player of the year' points table Cherries' defender Mark Whitlock led the chasing pack after a number of sterling performances. John Williams had stormed into equal second place, level on points with captain Mark Newson. Williams had become the backbone of the defence. After only five games he had been voted best Cherries' player in the Chesterfield, Swindon and Fulham matches. Three out of five, not a bad start!

Bournemouth v. Notts County – Saturday 24 January

'Celery, celery and if she don't come I'll tickle her bum with a lump of celery,' echoed around Dean Court. Small sticks of celery flew through the air like arrows at the Battle of Hastings and landed on the turf. Back in action after the cold weather, Redknapp described the fixture against the Magpies as a 'cracker'. Notts County were the form team and had crept up to second place in the table behind Middlesbrough. Cherries occupied 4th place, both sides having accrued 44 points.

A little boy sprinted out onto the pitch with the Cherries team and proceeded to knock the ball around with forwards Carl Richards and Trevor Aylott. At first I thought it was the match mascot, but at five feet six inches tall Richard Cooke looked like a little child, resembling a schoolboy alongside six-footers Richards and Aylott. How could one so small be regarded as such a footballing talent amongst men? This was my first impression of new signing Richard Cooke. I had no idea how wrong my first impressions were.

Bournemouth charged out of the starting blocks at a furious pace and dominated the first half. Within the first five minutes Cooke had set the crowd buzzing. Picked out by fullback Newson with a long ball down the right flank, Cooke demonstrated his lightning pace as he outstripped the Notts County defence and centred, only for Aylott to head over. Five times Cooke duelled with the opposition defence, and on each occasion his explosive acceleration left the County defenders embarrassed and catching their breath. They needed to be on horseback to catch him.

The ex-Spurs winger was so quick that he could have given any prize greyhound a good run for its money over 50 yards. Every time Cooke ran at a defender the excitement buzzed throughout the crowd. Dean Court had a new supercharged hero and on 40 minutes Cooke capped an electric first-half display when he fired home Aylott's cross to give Cherries a half-time lead. Now I understood what Redknapp meant when he talked about 'Richard being a natural right-winger' and 'how much he reminded me of my own playing days.'

Cherries asserted their authority after the interval and Aylott, back after a nine-match absence through injury, scored on 52 minutes. Remarkably, this was the big striker's first League goal for the club. Carl Richards made it 3-0 after 64 minutes – 'Bruno, Bruno'. The third goal sparked the visitors into life where, in a hectic five-minute spell, the Cherries' goal lived a charmed life as County struck the woodwork on three occasions. With better luck on another day the Magpies could have pulled off an amazing comeback, but it was not to be as Bournemouth collected maximum points. Game over, the Cherries had moved into second place in the League table and I exited the stadium to a pulsating chorus of 'The Reds are going up!'

Swindon Town v. Bournemouth – Wednesday 28 January

I had originally planned to travel to watch this midweek match, but it had been postponed from its original date and rescheduled to the 28th.

Bournemouth Chairman Rodney Barton was still pontificating about a new stadium for the club. He revealed that the club were drawing up revised plans for a new £3 million stadium in King's Park. It would feature a grass pitch, all covered seating and a 15,000 capacity. The proposal was both ambitious and innovative. At one end of the ground there would be an artificial pitch enclosed in a mini stadium with a 6,000 capacity. The design of the stadium would allow both pitches to be viewed from the central stand. The new design would increase the cost and delay planning application by a month. Barton added that the grass pitch would have a sub-base, which would allow it to be turned into an artificial surface if such a playing surface were to be accepted in the future.

With Swindon entertaining Bournemouth in the first round of the Freight Rover Trophy there was an opportunity to introduce a new 7.45pm kickoff time for evening matches. The recent bad weather had thrown the competition into chaos and the Southern section had seen only one definite result so far. Robins versus Cherries was the tie of the Southern draw as both clubs were striving for promotion and the twin towers of Wembley would come a little closer for the victors at the County ground.

The rearranged date coincided with my midweek evening shift. The later kickoff was of little help either, as I left the office at 8.00pm and subsequently tuned into Radio Solent. At half-time it was goalless, with little to note in the report. At full time it remained 0-0 and so extra time became necessary.

Extra time in this lightheartedly branded Mickey Mouse cup was something I thought we could do without, especially with the impending long trip to Bolton in a couple of days' time.

On 94 minutes John Williams powered home a bullet header to give Cherries the advantage, and after 103 minutes Richard Cooke looked to have sewn it up for Bournemouth when he bundled the ball into the net following an Aylott header. First period of extra time completed and Bournemouth were in the driving seat. Just after the turnaround Peter Coyne netted for Swindon. Time slipped away and, as the home side charged forward for one more time, Heffernan was judged to have brought down Coyne in the area. The Swindon striker coolly picked himself up and converted the spot kick in the 118th minute in what was one of the most tense moments of the season so far at the County Ground.

Two hours of play and still no result meant sudden death. The Solent reporter commentated on the penalty shoot-out, describing in precise detail each spot kick and the tension associated with its execution. My hands were perspiring and my stomach churned violently. Coyne put Swindon ahead with the first kick, then Heffernan converted successfully to bring Cherries back on level terms. Wade made it 2-1 for the Robins and then Fraser Digby, with a 'catlike' leap, saved Mark O'Connor's kick – 2-1 Swindon. The tension was unbearable as Bamber stepped up to take the next Swindon kick, Peyton guessed correctly and blocked it. 'Nice one, Gerry!' I yelled in excitement. Disappointment followed one minute later as Digby saved Newson's kick. I put my head in my hands. Jimmy Quinn successfully converted for Swindon, which meant that Trevor Aylott had to score to keep Cherries in the competition. Cool as a cucumber he sent Digby the wrong way to make the score 3-2, but the advantage was now with Swindon. The vital penalty fell to Swindon's Charlie Henry.

All Henry had to do was convert the kick to send the Robins into the next round. As he stepped up the broadcast commentary paused, I heard a whistle and then silence fell at the County Ground, instantly followed by a huge cheer. Sitting in the kitchen I realised the outcome and the anguish hurt me. Henry had coolly stepped forward, kept his nerve and beaten Peyton with his kick. At the close Swindon proved to be more accurate, winning the penalty shoot out 4-2, a result that took them into the second round and cruelly ended any dreams of a first Wembley appearance for Cherries. Having exited all cup competitions it was now the League or nothing for Bournemouth.

111

The following day the Football League announced that there would be no new synthetic pitches for three years. The four clubs QPR, Luton, Preston and Oldham that already had plastic pitches would be allowed to continue to play on them, pending the whole matter being investigated by a new committee. Chairman Barton reacted with disappointment, but added that it was not the end of the world. He still believed that the First Division clubs were seeking to drive a wedge between them and the smaller clubs and create a super or premier league.

Bolton Wanderers v. Bournemouth – Saturday 31 January
Once again, because of my overtime shift, Bournemouth travelled to Burnden Park without me for what was the 12th Football League encounter between the sides, all of which had taken place in Division Three. The first League game between the clubs was at Burnden Park in August 1971 at a time when the AA claimed that it cost £8 a week to run a family car, Diana Ross topped the charts with 'I'm still waiting' and Edward Heath, skipper of 'Morning Cloud', led Britain to victory in the Admiral's Cup. That first game produced the only scoreless result so far and was the Wanderers' first ever Third Division game. The return match the following March was a much livelier affair, where Bolton recorded their only League win to date at Dean Court. Ex-England and Liverpool star Roger Hunt grabbed both goals for Bolton, while Ted MacDougall scored his 40th goal of the season with the last touch of the game.

The journey north was a fruitful one as Cherries snatched all three points from Bolton with an injury time winning goal. It was now 50 up for Bournemouth as they reached a half-century of League points, a distinction shared with First Division pacesetters Arsenal and Everton, Second Division leaders Portsmouth, and Middlesbrough and Northampton the leaders of Division Three and Four respectively. 'It was not much of a match, but the result turned out alright and what a time to score the winner!' chirped Redknapp at the post-match interview.

A minute from time Newson had taken a quick throw-in to Richard Cooke who crossed and, as the ball bobbled across the lumpy penalty area, Trevor Aylott popped up to prod the ball into the net off the post. It was Bournemouth's 40th League goal of the season and provided a satisfactory completion to a dull match that was generally devoid of incident. It was another team performance that ground out a result. Bournemouth captain Mark Newson put the shackles on Bolton danger man Mark Gavin and then summed up the 90 minutes – 'Hard work, a draw would have been a worthwhile result, but those extra points came as a bonus.'

The result, Bournemouth's 15th League win of the season, positioned the Cherries just one point behind leaders Middlesbrough. It opened up a five-point gap between second and third placed Notts County.

Elsewhere in the FA Cup fourth round, Third Division Wigan beat First Division Norwich City 1-0. Fourth Division Aldershot held Second Division Barnsley to a 1-1 draw. In the Scottish Cup Rangers were not only knocked out 1-0 by Hamilton Academical at Ibrox, but Adrian Sprott's 70th-minute goal ended goalkeeper Chris Woods' period of keeping his goal intact at a new British record total of 1,196 minutes.

FEBRUARY

Bournemouth v. Blackpool – Tuesday 3 February

The joint leading scorers in Division Three were currently Robbie Cooke of Brentford and Andy Jones of Port Vale, both having notched 18 goals each. In third place sat David Kelly with 17 to his credit, followed by Cherries' injured striker David Puckett with 16 goals. Owing to his serious injury Puckett had not played for six weeks, yet remarkably he was still in the leading marksman 'hot shot' list for the Division. His predecessor Colin Clarke had notched 17 goals in the First Division, but had played more games. The loss of such a talent was immense and a terrible blow to a small club like Bournemouth, which operated on limited resources.

Sam Ellis brought 'The Seasiders' to the seaside for the top six clash. As the pre-match anticipation grew to a climax Dean Court was unexpectedly plunged into complete darkness at 7.15pm. The floodlights and stadium lights had been expunged and the only illumination remaining came from brief flashes of ignited matches and cigarette lighters. The blackness was initially greeted with amusement and supporters around me joked, shouting 'put another 50 pence in the meter' and began to sing 'We want the lights on!' Over the public address system came an appeal for calm and patience while the problem was investigated, together with the amusing, yet bizarre, request for the electrician to make his way to main reception! Boredom soon set in,

113

manifesting itself with sharp whistles and the slow clapping of hands. A roll of toilet paper descended from the back of the South End stand, unravelling and trailing across the heads of supporters before striking the crossbar and falling into the goalmouth. The electrical problem was traced to a fuse that had blown, resulting in the ground lighting being knocked out. Twenty minutes later the lights were illuminated and I blinked and rubbed my eyes, dazed by the sudden brilliance that had caused my retina fatigue.

The game finally kicked off 15 minutes behind the planned schedule. The first half of the match was an equally contested dual, with the visitors breaking the deadlock after only 13 minutes. I had picked out striker Paul Stewart as the danger man as he had been trailed during recent weeks by Manchester City. I watched him turn elegantly on the corner of the penalty area, then jink his way along the 18-yard line before unleashing a fine left foot strike to beat Peyton. I politely applauded his perfect execution.

Minutes later Bournemouth bounced back. Fullback Paul Morrell found striker Trevor Aylott in space and he swivelled and struck a low shot that was blocked by veteran keeper Barry Siddall, but up popped my new petite hero Richard Cooke to place the ball in the back of the net. At 1-1 both sides shut up shop. Bournemouth's enterprise was marred by the repetitive Blackpool offside trap as strikers Aylott and Richards in particular were guilty of being caught out several times. 'Think about it' came a frustrated shout from behind me.

In the end I had to be content with just a point. Bournemouth drew level on 51 points with leaders Middlesbrough, but remained in second place due to an inferior goal difference and having conceded eight goals more than the watertight 'Boro defence. Harry Redknapp remained confident: 'We are still in an unbeaten run and sharing the leadership of the division.' He singled out Cherries' left-sided fullback for special mention: 'In defence we were given a test against lively opposition, but coped well. Paul Morrell was outstanding.'

Chester City v. Bournemouth – Saturday 7 February

Sharing top spot with Middlesbrough was exciting and inspired me to book my coach ticket and travel to Chester. My school history lessons taught me that Chester was a city rich in history. The name meant 'Roman fort' and was first recorded in the Domesday Book, interpreted as 'city or fortress of the legions'. In preparation for the laborious coach journey I took with me a selection of reading material ranging from the 'Today' newspaper to 'Cricketer

International'. Initially the countryside viewed from the A350 was pleasant on the eye as we passed Blandford Forum and Warminster. Then followed further greenery as I mentally ticked off Chippenham, Cirencester and Stroud before the M5 motorway haul began. Mile after mile of cold grey three-lane tarmac was endured before the monotony was broken with the excitement of joining the M6 to the north. By midday I had rapidly demolished my sandwiches. At junction 14 just past Stafford the coach overtook a Birmingham City supporters coach en route to Derby. Much shouting and gesticulating erupted from some of the lads at the back of our coach as we drew level with the City coach. Verbal 'nasties' were safely exchanged by both sets of supporters behind laminated tinted glass before a safe distance cooled the activity.

At 1.40pm we finally exited the M6 at junction 16, signposted Chester. Drawing closer to our final destination I scoured the horizon for the regular landmarks. At exactly 2.00pm I spotted them, the grey floodlight pylons of the stadium rising from the ground as we overlooked the city from the outskirts. I rubbed my hands in anticipation. A win for Cherries and a defeat for Middlesbrough would put Bournemouth back on top of Division Three.

Bournemouth's last and only previous visit to Sealand Road was on 24 October 1970. At that point in history BP had just recently struck oil in the North Sea, Freda Payne sat at the top of the music charts with the song 'Band of Gold' and closer to home the 'Bournemouth Evening Echo' ran a story regarding a local man who had been admitted to Boscombe Hospital after swallowing his own teeth in a town centre restaurant! In that first game between the two teams Chester were 4-2 victors, with Ted MacDougall and Tony Scott scoring for Bournemouth. Both sides were pushing for promotion during the 1970/71 season and at the end of the campaign Bournemouth were promoted back to Division Three and Chester missed out by just one point.

Sealand Road was a neat compact stadium covered on three sides and open at the away supporters' enclosure. The stadium carried the usual faded and tired advertising boards of local vendors together with the obligatory 'Today' League and 'Littlewoods' sponsor boards and logos displayed around the stadium. I stood on the exposed terrace with cold hands clasping my camera, hoping to snap some action for my scrapbook. The wind swept harshly across the pitch and I tightened the red scarf wrapped around my neck to combat the cold.

With 70/210 zoom lens in place, Sean O'Driscoll gave me my first goal action shot. At the far end of the ground he dispossessed Chester player-coach

Derek Fazackerley and, entering the penalty area, drove a low shot past home keeper Billy Stewart. I clicked with the shutter, then jumped for joy, delighted that Cherries had taken the lead and excited that I had captured the moment.

Several goalmouth scrambles ensued as the Chester defence desperately defended their goal. On 40 minutes and against the run of play, Chester replied with a pile-driver from John Kelly. It remained 1-1 at half-time. During the interval both sets of supporters were entertained with the current chart hits of Pepsi and Shirlie, Steve 'Silk' Hurley and Curiosity Killed the Cat over the public address.

It became colder. My thin jacket and scarf proved to be inadequate and I shivered as Chester kicked off the second half. The action was all at the far end as the home side applied pressure to the Bournemouth goal. Just five minutes after the restart the impressive and lively Gary Bennett struck a low drive that sneaked in at Peyton's far post. Chester held the advantage and looked very much in control. Disappointed, yet undeterred, I shouted encouragement for my team, confident that the situation could be redeemed. Bournemouth were a resilient side and would pick away tenaciously at the opposition, probing for a weakness and opportunity.

Time was running out and I was frozen in the biting wind. Cherries attacked down the left flank, and Morrell quickly took a long throw, which was nodded across the goal by giant John Williams, a rehearsed move that would later become known as the Willo 'flick-on'.

Three yards in front of me Richard Cooke bravely dived forward to score with a header at the far post. Though frozen like a fish finger, I still managed to leap in the air to celebrate Cooke's third goal in four League games. The pint-sized winger needed urgent attention. Just as his head connected with the ball, Chester defender Colin Woodthorpe's boot scraped across Cooke's face, the result being a very nasty mess.

As Cooke received attention off the pitch Aylott wasted a golden opening to win it for Bournemouth as Woodthorpe slid across the turf and thwarted the opportunity. Chester held on for their 14th draw in 24 League games and I sprinted back to the coach to get in the warm. Manager Redknapp was disappointed with just one point and felt that his side were the better team and should have won: 'The players will be working hard in training during the coming week as we try to sharpen up that finishing a little.'

Three days later, and with no connection with Bournemouth whatsoever, an extraordinary moment occurred, which is a worthy statistic to note. On 10 February Aldershot beat Fulham 11-10 in a record 22-penalty shoot-out after a 1-1 draw in the Freight Rover, Southern Area Quarter Final.

Bournemouth v. Mansfield – Saturday 14 February

As in previous years the postman again failed to deliver a surprise on this special day. I sent three cards, one each to girls that I had the 'hots' for, but received none in return. Life can be cruel and, as Rowan Atkinson once said (as 'Captain Blackadder' in the TV series 'Black Adder'), 'Baldrick, I think the phrase rhymes with clucking bell!'.

Working in the insurance industry, I spotted early on that having no reserve goalkeeper to cover Gerry Peyton in the event of injury was a high-risk strategy. As the season progressed I grew more concerned at this lack of insurance and obviously so did Harry Redknapp. With some relief the club announced that just like Arthur Daley in the TV series, Gerry would be getting a 'minder'. Although still to be confirmed, the likelihood of John Smeldeurs rejoining the Cherries for his third spell seemed likely. Goalkeeper Smeldeurs, currently with Torquay, had been second choice to Kenny Allen, another ex-Bournemouth player.

The atmosphere at Dean Court began to build about 2.30pm as the surrounding pubs emptied and the ground filled. The hardcore Cherries' supporters to my right were once again in good voice and worked their way through the usual repertoire that included 'Celery', 'Molly Malone' and the impromptu 'The Reds are Going Up!'. I joined in when they began to sing about the next away trip: 'If you're all going to Bristol clap your hands.' It was a simple visual sign of commitment.

In the Mansfield match day magazine the contrasting stories of football were in abundance. Redknapp praised the support and growing attendances, urging everyone to get behind the team and encourage them. Assistant Manager Jimmy Gabriel spoke of a League where 'the victorious are the ones who pool together all their resources for the common good'. Chairman Rodney Barton highlighted concern over the poor facilities for both spectators and players at the current Dean Court stadium and was afraid that Bournemouth could become the 'poor relations' of the Division. Featured in the 'player profile', Tony Pulis described his best goal scored as a 25-yard miss-hit against Chelsea, while off the pitch the Commercial department announced the launch of a new 25 pence lottery ticket to help generate additional funds for the push for promotion.

Bournemouth completely stunned visitors Mansfield with a dazzling display of football and they were outplayed from the start. Despite having a majority of possession throughout the first 45 minutes the teams were level at the interval. Neil Whatmore turned Mark Kearney's miscued shot past Peyton into the net after only five minutes and against the run of play, but Cherries' striker Trevor Aylott levelled on 16 minutes. The second half saw a Cherries' resurgence as they took control of the match by the scruff of the neck. Pulis was the heart of the engine. Industrious throughout, his work rate was phenomenal – chasing, tackling, crunching into tackles and never taking prisoners. Bournemouth won the day thanks to three second-half strikes, one from Aylott and a brace from 'Bruno'. A crowd of 5,261 saw Bournemouth regain the top place in Division Three as Middlesbrough lost 1-2 at Chesterfield.

On Monday 16 February the 'Bournemouth Evening Echo' back page headline read, 'We're back on top!' In his column 'Harry's View' Redknapp stated: 'It's great to be on top of the table again and the players deserve to be congratulated for their efforts.'

For injured striker David Puckett the week ahead brought the smallest of light flickering at the end of a long dark tunnel. David had taken the first step on the road to recovery from his crippling knee-ligament injury when he had the plaster removed from his left knee. He prepared to embark on a course of physiotherapy to strengthen the joint, but would not be back in action until the following season. Redknapp stated: 'With David out, I have emphasised to the other two lads (Aylott and Richards) that they need to score more goals and take on the main role. Trevor Aylott is a tremendous player, there is no one better in the Third Division.'

Keeper Gerry Peyton spent the week in Scotland preparing for Eire's International with Scotland at Hampden Park, while the search continued for a number two keeper who could act as cover in the remaining games. Redknapp remained anxious but still had a month to go before the transfer deadline. 'There is no rush yet,' he commented.

Bristol City v. Bournemouth – Saturday 21 February

As I drove through the local district of Wallisdown on my way to collect a colleague who was travelling to Ashton Gate with me, I was overtaken by a speeding jet-black Ford Escort XR3i. In the 'hot hatchback' were two guys, both wearing suits. Cherries' Captain Mark Newson and fullback Paul Morrell were obviously late for their team coach departure from Dean Court. I blasted my horn several times and waved my scarf in acknowledgement. In response both turned, then laughed and sped off into the distance.

City had played Bournemouth three times already this season, with honours reasonably even. There was added spice to this tie. City manager Terry Cooper had recently signed ex-Cherries' striker Trevor Morgan, who had migrated across the city from Bristol Rovers and ex-Leeds and Scotland legend Joe Jordan. Their pairing together had been an inspiration by Cooper, producing four goals (Jordan 3, Morgan 1) in the same number of games. It must have been frustrating for Harry Redknapp as he had trailed each of them and publicly admitted his interest in signing both players before they eventually plumped for City. He had also shown interest in City's Glyn Riley, but had drawn a blank with him too.

A healthy 14,539 filled a smart-looking and modern Ashton Gate as fifth place hosted the leaders. Bournemouth defended the Ashton Road goal for the first half , but though I had my camera set up to snap the action there was little opportunity as Cherries paid the price for poor finishing and their 12 match unbeaten run came to an end. Cherries, despite doing much right throughout the 90 minutes, were unlucky and it was not to be their day. It was a bitter, scrappy affair and two unfortunate moments of tragic luck suffered by Cherries' skipper Mark Newson were the cruel and deciding moments.

The first blow came on 29 minutes as City won a free kick 40 yards out and close by the right touchline. As Gordon Owen swung the ball into the Bournemouth penalty area it seemed harmless enough and keeper Peyton moved off his line to collect. In what appeared to then be an absence of communication between them, Newson rose in the crowd of players and headed the ball back to Peyton. The ball eluded the keeper in the icy goalmouth and bounced into the corner of the empty net. 'Sort it out Newson, you're useless,' came a harsh and unfair shout from behind me.

I recall one amusing spectator comment from this match and noted it verbatim in my diary. Both Jordan and Morgan had been well contained by Williams and Whitlock, but they were both a constant threat. There was a high ball played down the centre of the pitch, which was won in the air by Jordan, who neatly headed the ball forward for Morgan to run into the opening. The ex-Cherries' forward lumbered through the gap to chase the ball, but

Bournemouth fullback Paul Morrell accelerated past Morgan to instantly snuff out the danger. I responded with a small ripple of applause while the pensioner standing to my right shouted, 'Morgan, my granny's faster than you!'

The second and killer blow came 12 minutes from time when Owen was released into the penalty area and then went down under Newson's challenge. Referee Phillip Wright of Northwich pointed to the spot and Owen dusted himself off before coolly placing the ball past Peyton's dive. The voice from behind resurrected itself with more aggression. 'Newson you're f***ing rubbish!' I gave a stare in the direction of the obscenity and made it clear that such a comment was unwarranted. I'm sure it was vented out of frustration, but it was unnecessary and improper to inflict such abuse on Captain Marvel. There were also several kids close by. Newson et al. had just been unlucky and the game ended in a 0-2 reverse.

At the end of the game the Bristol police invoked the usual procedure of holding the away fans inside the ground to allow the home supporters to quietly disperse. It seemed a pointless exercise because those home fans who wanted to cause trouble just had more time to hide and gain an advantage. Bournemouth fans were held for ten minutes after the final whistle and we sang 'Let us out, let us out, let us out' before we were finally released and allowed to spill out into Ashton Road. My colleague and I sprinted ahead of the crowd, hoping to avoid the anticipated traffic congestion. In the quiet Ashton Drive side street en route back to the car my friend and I were cornered by ten or so City fans. We both froze and feared the worst. Clenching my fists in an attempt to prepare myself for the feeble defence I would muster, I thought, this is it. Unexpectedly they ran past us without any acknowledgement and stopped 20 yards behind us. The gang had greater mischief on their minds and, ignoring us, they congregated around a parked 12-seat white Ford Transit minibus. The vehicle had a Bournemouth hire company and telephone number on the bonnet and down each side, a red rag to a bull. Working as a team, the City fans lifted up the nearside of the vehicle and tipped the Transit on to its side into the middle of the road. The vehicle groaned as it toppled over and the glass on the driver's door mirror shattered as it was crushed under the weight of the body. One of the group urinated over the offside front wheel, while the others laughed and proceeded to kick at it and shout 'City, City'. A rapid exit from the crime scene followed swiftly. The incident lasted no longer than twenty seconds and was accomplished at lightning pace. It was a manoeuvre that I was sure had been practised before. While appalling and destructive, I had to admit that their interaction and effectiveness working together was superb. It was teamwork of the highest order with flawless execution. Shocked and relieved, we quietly walked away from the exposed underbelly of the vehicle and continued on to my car. Thankfully we found it where we had left it and in its upright position!

Reflecting on the pitch activity, positives could be taken from the game despite the defeat. Williams and Whitlock in the heart of the defence shackled the threat of Morgan and Jordan. Pulis, Aylott and Cooke all had opportunities and on another day it might have been a different story. Also Redknapp wisely articulated his view: 'We gave away two unfortunate goals and although there wasn't too much pressure on us, goals change games.' It was Bournemouth's first defeat in the league since 12 December 1986.

Middlesbrough had won 3-0 at home to Fulham to retake the Division Three leadership. Notts County and Swindon had also won, but Gillingham had lost 2-3 at Brentford. The race for promotion remained wide open. It was exciting, yet tense. The anxiety I felt was briefly reduced as I noticed that rivals Gillingham, Swindon and Notts County all had still to visit Ashton Gate before the season end. It occurred to me that City might end up being the team that would make a late final push for a promotion place and perhaps cruelly deny the Cherries.

Listening to Sports Report during the journey home we heard that in the FA Cup fifth round Third Division rivals Wigan Athletic and Walsall had gallantly flown the flag for Division Three football. Wigan had beaten Hull City 3-0 and reached the quarter-finals stage of the competition for the first time in their history and Walsall had held First Division Watford to a 1-1 draw at Fellows Park. Also an achievement worthy of note was that Clive Allen had scored from the penalty spot, his 35th goal of the season, as Spurs knocked Newcastle out of the competition 1-0 at White Hart Lane.

Newport County v. Bournemouth – Tuesday 24 February

Monday 23 February brought sobering off-pitch news. In the Bradford City fire disaster case at Leeds High Court, Sir Joseph Cantley ruled that the club were 'at fault' in the fire that killed 56 and injured 200 in May 1985. Under Government pressure in the campaign against hooliganism, the Football League agreed to a 50 per cent membership scheme in certain designated areas of the 91 League grounds next season. The third news item was truly bizarre. It was announced that Fulham would drop out of the League at the end of the season and merge with QPR at Loftus Road when the club would adopt the name Fulham Park Rangers. The QPR board would then quit and the property development company Marler Estates would take over, with Craven Cottage expected to be sold for a sum in the region of £15 million and developed for residential purposes. In the FA Cup Wigan police had asked for the Wigan v. Leeds FA Cup tie to be switched elsewhere. Wigan chairman Bill Kenyon had insisted on playing the tie at Springfield Park even if it had to be played behind closed doors.

On the Tuesday I picked up a copy of the 'Daily Telegraph' and proceeded to thumb my way through the sports pages. In the fixtures column showing that night's forthcoming matches Bournemouth were listed as playing twice! It was, of course, a printing error, but it clearly stated in black and white that on the same evening the Cherries were playing two games: one at Darlington, the other at Newport. An impossibility for a club like Bournemouth with limited resources, but I wondered if Harry Redknapp might appreciate a call from me with an offer to bring my boots!

Later that afternoon I left work at 4.00pm sharp, headed home and was picked up at 4.45pm by two of my Lloyd's Bank football team-mates, Steve Dean and Ian Harris. Steve drove a black Ford Escort RS2000 and was confident that he could chauffeur the three of us to South Wales in time for the 7.30pm kick-off. Despite the rush hour traffic we made good progress and took the short-cut toll bridge at Bathampton, paying the fee of twenty pence to cross at 6.00pm. Joining the M4 west we travelled over the Severn Estuary and remarked on the Severn Bridge eerily illuminated by passing vehicle headlights and its path ahead marked by a sequence of red low-aircraft warning markers at the top of the support pillars. By 6.20pm we had entered into Wales.

Despite a promising start, Newport had experienced a desperately disappointing season and just after Christmas the team had fallen apart. County's last home win was a 3-2 victory over Doncaster on 20 September and, although they had picked up odd points on their travels, the team had managed to accrue only six out of a possible 24 points since Christmas. Attendances had plummeted and the club were suffering a serious financial disaster. Following an application to the High Court on 16 February, Joint Administrators had been appointed to manage club affairs. With an estimated deficiency of £459,000 the administrator procedure was the last option to aid reorganisation and financial rescue of the club with a view to their ultimate survival.

Walking from side streets to the ground I was shocked at the sight of the surrounding area and bleak landscape. The adjacent streets were dark and narrow, with grubby façades disguising tiny houses stacked like small boxes in a row. Located in the distance, yet very visible and close to the stadium, stood an industrial coal-transporting railway yard. Dirty wagons lay empty under the towering black and grey peaks of coal and discarded slag heaps. It felt cold and reminded me of a scene from a science fiction film. It emerged as a dark and dismal alien world, the landscape devoid of colour and artificially illuminated only by poor quality floodlighting.

I paid my £3.00 admission fee and entered into Somerton Park and stood on the concrete stepped terrace behind the goal. Even the grass on the pitch looked noxious and it reflected a jaded green hue. The thin eight-page programme cost 40 pence and contained minimal reading material and mainly advertising. This was once a proud Welsh football club that had competed in European competitions and six years earlier had reached the quarter-final stage of the European Cup Winners' Cup. Now it was a football club in terminal decline, simply terrible and very distressing for its loyal supporters.

Newport, fighting for their very existence, competed ferociously from the outset as though it was a cup-tie. Cherries' keeper Gerry Peyton was the hero of the night as he stood firm on several occasions, blocking shots and diving at the Newport forwards' feet. My nails suffered badly as the play accelerated from end to end with near misses from both sides. Bruno found himself one on one with County keeper Roger Freestone, but failed to execute the opportunity given him as the ball became tangled up between his legs and the chance was lost. At half-time it was goalless. During the interval I stood in the gloom, straining my eyes reading the brief contents of the match day programme. Everything surrounding me was grim and depressing. Steve glanced across at me – 'depressing place, eh?' That sobering moment of half-time reflection enabled us to realise the joy of living in Bournemouth. I was lucky and very grateful for that.

The second half continued at the breakneck speed, with the first of my nails disappearing at the same rapid pace. The tension was finally broken in the 72nd minute as Bournemouth took the lead. Trevor Aylott picked up the loose ball in midfield and was given two options by the sprinting Cooke and

123

O'Driscoll. Choosing the latter, he placed an inch-perfect pass through to the advancing O'Driscoll, who calmly slotted the ball past the advancing Freestone from 12 yards. The relief felt by Steve, Ian and I plus our fellow supporters was immense. Even the players appeared relieved as they relaxed and began to assert their control on the game. Then, with three minutes remaining, the flawless John Williams sliced a clearance to put Newport substitute Steve Mardenborough clean through with only Peyton to beat. The big Irish keeper demonstrated his agility and international ability by diving low and blocking the shot. In my eyes it was the save of the season and thwarted the draw that Newport desperately wanted and probably deserved. To great relief the final whistle blew.

My Cherries were back on top of the Division Three table. In complete contrast Newport had hit rock bottom. I had no allegiance to County, but considering their plight and my observations, my heart went out to the club and supporters. Despite the victory I left Somerton Park in sadness. Although Bournemouth had won on the night it was clear that in the long run football would lose.

In any season there are defining moments. The victory at Newport was a tough hard-fought battle against a team that threw everything at Bournemouth. Despite a ferocious, and at times relentless, assault on the Bournemouth goal, the Cherries stood firm. With inspirational goalkeeping from Peyton and courageous leadership from O'Driscoll, the depth of character, determination and resilience of the team shone through. Confidence was now at a season high. This match was a pivotal moment for me in my thinking about the club achieving promotion. It was a shift in mind-set. For the first time in the season I began to believe that the Cherries might just have enough character and strength to sustain a promotion challenge with at least a play-off place now being a strong possibility. Wanting to burst with excitement, I kept my thoughts to myself and continued to dream of what might be.

Bournemouth v. York City – Saturday 28 February
Redknapp announced that he was looking for a striker to reinforce the promotion push and highlighted the need to fill the void left by injured leading marksman David Puckett, who would not be back in action until next season. Redknapp elaborated further: 'I have only got two front men. We do need competition for places up front. I don't want a youngster, I want an experienced player who can do a man's job. Someone with a goal scoring record.'

The Minstermen travelled south for the first of Cherries' two consecutive home games in a week. After much early promise, which included beating both Middlesbrough and Bournemouth at home, York had faded miserably and now languished near the foot of the table. Newson once again showed his courage and leadership as captain, taking the field with a pain-killing injection in his foot. A new pair of boots that he used at Newport had caused a problem in his right foot and it was expected that the injections would be a necessary requirement of his warm-up routine for the next couple of games.

In a moment of unprecedented madness I abandoned my obligatory standing position in the South End of the ground for a seat in the Main Stand. There was method in my madness, though. In previous weeks the attendances at Dean Court had increased by nearly 30 per cent and, while still a long way short of capacity, the average crowd of just over 6,000 spectators meant that clarity of view had become hindered. I also wanted to take action photographs, an exercise that would have been impossible from behind the goal in the South End. It cost £5.00 for a wooden bench seat in block B of the Main Stand enclosure and a further ten pence for a cushion to save your arse from numbness. From here I was guaranteed a clear view of the match without heads or arms popping up unexpectedly in front of me. I clicked my 70/210 zoom lens in place and waited anxiously for the game to begin.

A slightly lower crowd of 5,805 saw Bournemouth open up a six-point gap between themselves and third place. When the two sides met earlier in the season York inflicted on the Cherries their first defeat of the season. City striker Keith Walwyn was the hero as he took charge in that game with a personal duel with Bournemouth keeper Gerry Peyton. It was a different story at Dean Court, though, as both players had a quiet game and Walwyn seemed a little disturbed by the occasional monkey noises from the crowd. This was football behaviour at its worst and thankfully the majority correctly refrained from such shameful outbursts. Goals from 'Cookie' and 'Bruno' were captured on film as Bournemouth led 2-0 at half-time. In the second half the Cherries resumed their superiority as 'Bruno' slid across the turf at the Brighton Beach End to score again and secure maximum points.

Goal three was almost captured beautifully. I say 'almost' because the git sitting in front of me put both his hands in the air just as Richards connected with the ball and I clicked the shutter. The result produced a stunning record of the goal, but with Richards and the ball obscured by a great fat arm in the middle of the shot.

125

At the final whistle Bournemouth left the pitch to a standing ovation and a booming chorus of 'The Reds are going up!' Next to visit Dean Court were Middlesbrough, who had lost 0-1 at Swindon, allowing Cherries to regain the leadership of the Third Division, at least until Tuesday evening.

Elsewhere there were demonstrations in London against club mergers. QPR, Fulham, Crystal Palace and Wimbledon all experienced the wrath of their respective supporters. The kick-off at Loftus Road was delayed by 19 minutes, while the second half of the Fulham game was held up for police to clear the pitch of banner-waving fans. Days later the Football League moved to block the mergers.

MARCH

Bournemouth v. Middlesbrough – Tuesday 3 March
This was the big one, the game that every Bournemouth supporter had been waiting for. I felt the tension building throughout the day and I struggled to focus my concentration at work. I even misquoted a client for his car insurance, a rare error, writing-off the £15 discrepancy. I had good reason to be apprehensive about the outcome of the match. Twice during the current season when confronted with the big occasion Bournemouth had failed, first at Middlesbrough, then at home to Gillingham. Would it now be third time lucky or yet further disappointment? Long-standing Bournemouth fans can, no doubt, recount numerous occasions when the team over the years has failed to live up to expectations in a crucial match. This may have been the source behind the old wives' tale that Bournemouth never wanted promotion. Personally I think they always wanted promotion success, but when it came down to the big occasion the team regularly failed to cut the ice when it mattered.

A new kick-off time was scheduled for evening matches and by 7.45pm Dean Court was packed to the rafters. Match programmes had been snapped up by hungry supporters as though they were hot bargains in a January sale. Fifteen minutes before the start of the game several pleas were announced over the public address system for supporters already in the ground to move along the terracing to allow queues of eager home fans to gain access. The noise inside the ground was intense and both sets of supporters sang their anthems loudly in anticipation of the big showdown. Normally reserved for away supporters, the Brighton Beach End was opened to home supporters, who quickly filled it completely to bursting point with some travelling fans also present, but most Middlesbrough fans were located in a block of seats in the Main Stand.

Middlesbrough fielded a strong and mainly experienced side that included goalkeeper Stephen Pears, defender Tony Mowbray and forwards Archie Stephens, Bernie Slaven and Stuart Ripley in attack. Partnering Mowbray at the centre of the defence was a very young Gary Pallister, recognised by those within the game as a bright star of the future. Off the field the leadership team oozed even greater depths of experience. Football management was under the guidance of the talented Bruce Rioch, with the energetic Colin Todd as coach.

The teams emerged from the players' tunnel to a roar of excitement. Bournemouth, wearing their distinctive all cherry red kit, were led onto the pitch by skipper Mark Newson alongside visitors' captain Tony Mowbray. In contrast Middlesbrough wore their rather plain coloured away kit of pale blue and grey. In the centre circle the usual pleasantries and ceremonies were exchanged.

Newson won the toss, chose ends, so Middlesbrough would kick off. The players stood motionless like gladiators in a Roman arena, participants on both sides staring intensely at their opponents. It was the focus of battle in preparation for a clash of the titans, with the audience a heaving expectant mass slowly boiling inside a tightly packed cauldron. Newson and Mowbray rallied their respective troops and demanded success.

The first 45 minutes were a tense and frantic affair as both sides probed tentatively for a weakness. It was stalemate, but just before half-time Cherries' striker Trevor Aylott collided with the impressive Gary Pallister, who came off worse with a badly gashed leg. Unable to continue, he was replaced by Ripley who failed to touch the ball before referee Cooper blew his whistle for half-time.

The fingernails on my left hand were completely chewed away during the first period and the interval, but before I had time to start on the right hand the second half exploded into life. Attacking the South End, Bournemouth opened the scoring with a training-ground rehearsed and superbly executed move – Mark O'Connor's corner, John Williams familiar back header at the near post, met by Captain Marvel steaming in at the back post to head home a thunderbolt. Collectively we made a fabulous sound. 'The Reds are going up! The Reds are going up!' reverberated around Dean Court. Seconds later Middlesbrough were level as Newson and keeper Peyton left the ball for each other, allowing Bernie Slaven to sneak between them and prod the ball home from two yards out.

127

Boro' supporters spilled onto the Dean Court turf as they danced and celebrated their equaliser. In the South End we stood silent and stunned.

Middlesbrough now had the impetus, but as they searched for a second goal it was Bournemouth who rocked them with a stunning counterattack. Newson was the orchestrator, gliding past two challenges before finding Carl Richards, who then played a delicate ball into the penalty area for the accelerating Sean O'Driscoll, who let fly with a rasping shot 15 yards from goal. The ball struck the underside of the bar before burying itself in the back of the 'Boro net. 'The Reds are going up! The Reds are going up!' followed by 'You're not singing anymore! You're not singing anymore!'

The home crowd, still buzzing from O'Driscoll's fine strike, were euphoric five minutes later. Aylott and Mowbray collided in the penalty area and referee Cooper pointed to the spot. I looked towards heaven and whispered, 'Thank you, God'. Aylott picked himself up and coolly converted the spot kick. Dean Court rocked and heaved and in delight serenaded with a thunderous chorus of 'The Reds are going up! The Reds are going up! Cos' now you're gonna believe us, yes now you're gonna believe us, now you're gonna believe us, The Reds are going up!'

From that moment it was game over. Cherries' fans cheered each time a Bournemouth player touched the ball as the minutes slowly ticked away until the 90 were complete. Bournemouth had triumphed over their rivals and opened a six-point gap at the top of Division Three. On the night of the big occasion Bournemouth, under Redknapp's stewardship, had finally got it right.

The official attendance for the evening was 13,835, which smashed the nighttime capacity for Dean Court. It made for a marvellous atmosphere and produced record gate receipts of £38,500. The official recorded attendance included only those who paid to get in. Halfway through the first half, officials began to allow fans still queuing outside the ground to come in free. At the Brighton Beach End of the ground Bournemouth and Middlesbrough fans stood shoulder to shoulder, but there was no trouble. There were so many fans packed into the ground that Managing Director Brian Tiler had to stand behind the goal in the South End. His seat in the directors' box had been taken before the match started. He commented, 'What an atmosphere. It was terrific. We thought the days of crowds this size were over, but this was the impetus we needed.'

The unofficial attendance was put at over 14,000. Two fans were arrested, one for being in possession of a knife, and 15 were ejected from the ground for varying reasons. Superintendent Les Burns of Bournemouth police said, 'Generally speaking it was a reasonable night with the major problem being caused by the sheer volume of people that turned up.'

Wigan Athletic v. Bournemouth – Saturday 7 March

The day before this match brought tragic news of a terrible accident in the English Channel. Rescue divers had pulled 300 survivors out of the British ferry 'Herald of Free Enterprise'. At least twenty-six had died and nearly 200 passengers and crew remained trapped. They could not be rescued and died a terrible death. The car ferry capsized off the coast of Zebrugge, Belgium; the bow doors had not been properly closed.

Bournemouth's search for an additional striker was completed. Tony Sealy, a 28-year-old forward from Leicester City joined AFC Bournemouth in a loan move until the end of the season. Depending upon his performance the move might be made permanent at the season close. Redknapp was delighted with his acquisition: 'Tony's looked very sharp in training and it gives us some competition for places.'

Cherries' coach Roger Brown announced during the week that he had decided to leave the club to advance his managerial and coaching career. Although non-League Yeovil had shown a strong interest in him, within days of his departure he had joined local side Weymouth of the GM Vauxhall Conference League.

The Cherries launched a new scheme referred to as 'promotion tickets' at a price of £30. The idea was to offer supporters an opportunity to purchase a seat in the centre of the Main Stand for the remaining six home matches. Managing Director Brian Tiler pointed out that it not only gave supporters a guaranteed seat for the remaining home games, but gave them priority in the event of any of the games being made all-ticket.

At 6.30am I was rudely awoken from a deep sleep by my alarm clock, the start of what I expected to be a long, but rewarding, day. It was a bright sunny morning, but cold. I joined the official supporters' coach, which left Dean Court car park at 7.30am for the long trek north to Wigan.

The weather forecast indicated the strong possibility of snow in some regions above the Midlands and so I wore what I considered to be appropriate attire with an extra jumper and a coat. Just 30 minutes after commencing the journey I was already perspiring under my layers of clothing. My Sony

Walkman helped pass the hours as the coach travelled north via the M5 and M6. The sunshine and blue skies of the south coast were gradually replaced by grey cloud, and by Stafford the clouds were dark and heavy. At Knutsford, close to junction 19, it began to snow heavily. The adjacent fields either side of the M6 were soon covered in a thick white blanket and it looked beautiful. The severity of the weather quickly impeded progress and the final miles of the journey were completed at a snail's pace, the coach driver tentatively following the route through falling heavy snow. The poor conditions made it impossible for me to undertake my usual ritual of searching the horizon for the Springfield Park floodlight pylons. Visibility was so poor that even a scarlet-clad Father Christmas with reindeer could have slipped by unnoticed.

Wigan had been elected to the Football League in 1978 at the expense of unlucky Southport, who incidentally did not finish bottom of Division Four that year, but were not re-elected in the old voting system. Springfield Park remained a compact and uninviting stadium. Attempts had been made to upgrade and modernise the facilities from non-League days, but it continued to look like a relic from a previous era. Wigan were in the midst of an incredible cup run and were due to host Leeds United in the FA Cup sixth round the following Sunday – a potentially hazardous confrontation in this tired old stadium.

The coach parked and I prepared to face the elements of what was now a blizzard and biting cold wind. I felt uneasy and shivered at the thought of venturing outside. The coach doors opened and a red-faced rotund man climbed the steps and called for silence. He introduced himself as Bill Kenyon, Chairman of Wigan Football Club. He welcomed Bournemouth supporters to his club and in view of the weather conditions offered us sanctuary in the Wigan supporters' club bar. Normally a members' only facility, this was a kind, unexpected and welcome gesture. Inside I drank a pint and chatted to Wigan fans, some of the most genuine and friendliest football supporters I have ever had the pleasure to encounter. They universally praised Bournemouth for their achievement to date, but understandably were more interested in the forthcoming cup match. One Latics supporter kept muttering, 'We're goin' ta givit Leeds a reet tonkin' nex t'week.'

At 2.45pm I left the comfort of the supporters' club and proceeded to the turnstiles. The away supporters' terrace at Springfield Park was open to the elements, with only a small cowshed-style enclosure at the back to protect inhabitants from the blizzard. I chose to pay the extra £1.00 and bought a seat ticket with some other Bournemouth fans in the Main Stand, row D, seat 45. Here I would be under cover and somewhat protected from the severe elements. Both teams were attempting to warm up as the blizzard swirled snow across all corners of the ground. The pitch was a carpet of pure white covered in two inches of snow with lines cleared to just reveal the pitch markings. I looked around at my fellow travelling supporters huddled at the back of the stand. Faces blue, hands white, none had expected this or had prepared adequately for the conditions. The public address system blasted out the current number one hit, Boy George's awful version of the reggae classic 'Everything I own', but the northern soul hit 'Skiing in the snow' by the band Wigan's Ovation would have been a much more appropriate choice.

It was bitterly cold. In fact, I could not ever remember feeling so cold and numb in my life. Then I recalled one previous incident just over two years before. On Saturday 5 January 1985 I had travelled to Old Trafford to watch the third round FA Cup tie between Manchester United and Bournemouth on a British Rail 'football special' train. That day had long been logged as a special memory for me; it was an incredible experience to sit amongst the 32,080 crowd as United cruised to an easy 3-0 victory. But the journey back was terrible; it snowed all the way home until I reached Southampton – a six-hour journey on a bitterly cold night on a dilapidated rattling slam door train with no heating. My carriage was so packed with shivering bodies that the condensation on the windows inside turned to ice! My thoughts returned to the present and I pulled my Cherries ski hat tightly over my head in a feeble attempt to keep my head warm. Encouraged by the fact that I survived the United freezing experience I bellowed, 'Come on Bournemouth.'

After a few amusing seconds passed searching through the snow to find the fallen coin that had buried itself, it transpired that Newson had won the toss. He chose to attack the Springfield Road goal to my left, allowing Wigan to take advantage of a gale at their backs during the first half. Despite the orange coloured ball it was difficult to see the action through the snow as the players struggled to adjust to the poor conditions. Adding further confusion to proceedings were the white shirts of the home team. Peering through the blizzard the illusion appeared to suggest that Bournemouth in their cherry red kit were playing opponents without a head or torso between them! Cherries' keeper Gerry Peyton stood a lone figure in his penalty area facing head on into the blizzard. He wore a visor in what appeared to be an attempt to keep the snow out of his eyes.

131

Just eight minutes into the game Bournemouth took the lead. O'Driscoll found Richard Cooke on the right and he drilled a low shot across the white surface past Wigan keeper Roy Tunks. I jumped to my feet and clapped my hands in celebration, but exposure to the elements meant that they soon returned to my coat pockets for protection. The previous week I had bought a pair of ski gloves and was now cursing the fact that I had left them at home.

On 18 minutes Wigan equalised, Paul Jewell scoring against the run of play as the ball stuck in the snow. In the arctic conditions I sat motionless, head drooped in disappointment. Thank goodness for half-time and the opportunity to get a hot cup of tea, which I could barely hold in my hands as my fingers had seized up in the cold. Although concerned that I had begun to develop the early signs of hypothermia, I headed back to my seat for the second half.

The weather deteriorated further and as the second half got underway the game quickly developed into a farce. The pitch markings were no longer visible, the layer of snow covering the pitch had increased by another inch and the terracing had become icy. On 61 minutes referee George Courtney brought the game to a premature ending. The match abandoned, I left my seat and trooped discontentedly back to the coach. As I descended the steps from my seat Bournemouth players surrounded referee Courtney and Redknapp seemed to be remonstrating with the official, disapproving of the decision.

Back on the coach I stared out into the blizzard. Cherries' Managing Director Brian Tiler boarded the coach. Brushing the snow from his overcoat it was clear to see his anger and upset at the abandonment. He addressed supporters, stating that he thought it was a disgrace that the game was abandoned so late and apologised for a wasted journey. As a gesture of AFC Bournemouth's recognition to those on board the official supporters' club coach, Tiler offered all 52 fans a free return trip and ticket for the rescheduled game. It was a wonderful goodwill gesture from a man who recognised our disappointment and responded with rapid acknowledgement and reward for loyalty and commitment.

Heading back south, I learned that Notts County and Middlesbrough had both won to close the gap to three points at the top of the League table. At first the journey was painfully slow as the conditions caused traffic chaos. At Bromsgrove, just south of Birmingham, the snow eased and turned to sleet. By Stroud it had become rain and then drizzle by Warminster. Finally back at Dean Court it was dry. The day had been bizarre, but it was an ironic, yet useful, acclimatisation exercise for my skiing holiday in the French resort of Val d'Isère in nine days' time.

On Monday in the office I recounted the story several times over. Most thought I was mad to even have considered travelling to the match. That same day the 'Bournemouth Evening Echo' published an intriguing sports page headline 'Cherries' storm at snow-stopper'. I read the story and it transpired that Redknapp was furious that the game was abandoned and labelled the decision as a disgrace.

Bournemouth v. Bury – Saturday 14 March

On the Monday leading up to this game the Football Association's soccer headquarters at Lilleshall opened its new rehabilitation centre. The facility was designed to accelerate the recovery of players who had suffered long-term injury. Cherries' striker David Puckett, who had been sidelined since Boxing Day with a career-threatening knee ligament problem, would be one of the centre's first patients.

On the Tuesday evening after playing five-a-side football in the Frizzell internal office league I sat down and wrote two letters. The first was a letter of thanks to Wigan Football Club acknowledging their kindness and hospitality before the Wigan versus Bournemouth snow fiasco. It felt the right thing to do. With the letter I enclosed an article that I had exhumed from a 1968 copy of 'Charles Buchan Football Monthly' magazine. The item published described Wigan's ambitions to break out of non-League football with the dream of one day becoming a professional outfit in the Football League.

The second letter was addressed to captain Mark Newson, praising him and the team for their exploits against Middlesbrough. I also enclosed a copy of the Middlesbrough match programme and asked if he and the team would sign it as a souvenir to remember a wonderful night at Dean Court.

Midweek news broke confirming that Crystal Palace and Wimbledon had decided to finally call off their proposed merger after 90 per cent of Palace fans voted against it. At the same time former Fulham player Jimmy Hill announced progress with his efforts to form a consortium to save his old club.

Thursday 12 March recorded further transfer activity at Dean Court as 'The Bear' rejoined Cherries on loan until the end of the season. John Smeldeurs, a firm favourite between the sticks for most Bournemouth fans, arrived back from Torquay to provide goalkeeping cover for number one choice

Gerry Peyton. Smeldeurs, who once received a box of cigars from Redknapp for setting a club-record seven consecutive clean-sheets during the 1984/85 season, had wanted to make the move permanent, but a loan deal was all that he secured. The goalkeeping exposure I had been so concerned about had now been addressed and the risk alleviated. The squad for the final run-in of games was now complete with cover and strength in all areas.

It is often claimed that, 'Cometh the hour, cometh the man'. They say that timing is everything. Playing on his 26th birthday Cherries' stalwart defender Mark Whitlock chose to score his one and only goal of the season against a stubborn Bury side. Cricket commentators might compare Whitlock's scoring frequency with that of a tail-end batsman in that he rarely troubled the scorers. The facts confirm this. His last and only other goal was for Southampton against Stoke City during season 1980/81. Whitlock struck on 26 minutes when winger Richard Cooke floated a corner kick into the Bury penalty area. John Williams with his now trademark flick, nodded the ball on at the near post for striker Trevor Aylott to rise above the Bury defence and slam a powerful header against the underside of the visitors' crossbar. As the ball rebounded down, Whitlock was the first to react and he drove the ball home past bemused and stationary defenders from four yards out. Whitlock was as shocked as everyone else and clearly had no idea how to celebrate his strike, but was soon mobbed by his team-mates. I jumped for joy and thought to myself what a great time to score your first goal for the club and what a rare birthday gift.

Despite some tense moments, Bournemouth held their 1-0 lead until the end of the 90 minutes to secure three more valuable points. Harry Redknapp summed up the dour struggle: 'It is days like that, when you battle away and get the points, that win promotion. These points will be so vital.' I imagined that Whitlock celebrated his birthday in style in the evening after the match and toasted goal number two of his career. He no doubt raised a glass in expectation of the next goal that on current form was due in season 1992/93. What price for a hat-trick, I wondered?

My Saturday evening drinking plans were placed on hold for a fortnight because of my impending skiing holiday in France. I spent the evening packing the case with ski attire in preparation for an early Sunday morning flight from Gatwick. I would be away for one week and would miss the away trips to Doncaster and Gillingham. Excited at the prospect of the holiday I felt uneasy about leaving Cherries behind to cope with these two tough away matches alone.

In the FA Cup sixth round Coventry, Watford and Tottenham all made it safely through to the semi-final stage. The following day Third Division Wigan lost 0-2 to Leeds to exit their FA Cup dream. Also on the Sunday Cherries' giant centre half John Williams underwent an operation to relieve the pain he had been suffering due to an Achilles tendon infection, rather similar to an abscess. Williams would definitely miss the midweek trip to Doncaster. That was a concern.

Doncaster Rovers v. Bournemouth – Tuesday 17 March

My legs ached, my knees creaked and my calf muscles throbbed. The alarm clock began to clang annoyingly in my ears. It was 6.45am. I lay in bed and reflected on the previous day's skiing activity. For a brief moment I thought I might never walk again, until my room-mate Chris Gray dangled one of his used ski socks under my nose and I leapt out of bed and hurled a misshapen pillow at him. Morning ski lessons began on the slopes at 9.00am sharp and two hours were needed to shower, breakfast and don ski gear before ascending the lower slopes.

Our allotted ski instructor was Anna, an attractive, tall, tanned French woman. She wore an all-in-one cherry red ski suit that clung to every curve of her body. The ski class of 20, mainly men, showed no hesitation in following her every instruction.

Steadily I honed my skiing technique as I confidently traversed two green runs during the lesson, with only one mishap before Anna brought the session to a close. In the afternoon Chris and I repeated the morning course for ourselves. It was exhilarating exercise accompanied by breathtaking scenery. I built my confidence on the slopes, adjusting my technique from snowplough to the parallel turn. I tumbled several times, laughing raucously on each occasion. We had another fun, energy-sapping day and I wore my AFC Bournemouth ski hat with pride. The club crest received several looks – the stares came either from that or from the fact that I resembled a bright red-headed pixie.

That evening our ski group opted to watch the local ice hockey team play a national fixture that kicked off about the same time as Doncaster and Bournemouth prepared to engage each other at the Belle Vue stadium. Doncaster were comfortably placed in mid table and enjoying a season that marked their 60th year of Football League membership. This would be a tough fixture for Cherries and historically the odds of a victory were poor.

135

Bournemouth had made 12 previous visits to Belle Vue between the seasons 1958/59 and 1985/86. In that time Doncaster had won six and six had been drawn. Bournemouth had failed to win at Belle Vue and on the rare occasion when the Cherries had scored they had only ever managed one goal in any game. The omens did not look good for the thirteenth visit!

At the ice hockey match Chris and I supported the away team, who were getting hammered. As the puck flew into the net to record another successful strike for the home side my mind drifted to events at Belle Vue. I felt helpless, unable to connect in any way to the game.

Although I did not know it, Bournemouth did not need me and they buried the Belle Vue jinx in style. Two goals in the first half, one from O'Connor and a diving header from Aylott gave Cherries a commanding first-half lead. After the break Tony Sealy, making the second appearance of his loan spell, placed the result beyond doubt when he netted Cherries' third goal four minutes after the restart.

Walking back from the ice hockey game I spotted a public telephone box. In desperate need to know the Cherries' result, and unable to resist the temptation, I pumped the callbox meter with francs and dialled home. My father answered and delivered what I needed to hear – Doncaster 0 Bournemouth 3. I couldn't believe it. 'Three,' I hollered, as if to seek clarification!

It was thirteenth time lucky at Belle Vue. Bournemouth had now only conceded one goal in the last five games and once again opened up a six-point lead at the top of Division Three. In the other big game of the night Middlesbrough had beaten promotion rivals Notts County 2-0 to draw level with their defeated opponents on 64 points.

Gillingham v. Bournemouth – Saturday 21 March

As I perfected my Franz Klammer impression and whistled down the snow-crusted slopes for the last time before my holiday officially ended, back home in a damp corner of Kent Bournemouth prepared to clash with promotion rivals Gillingham at the Priestfield stadium. I hated Gillingham and so wanted to be at the game. The Ides of March had passed six days earlier, but I had an uncomfortable feeling about this match. John Williams had not yet fully recovered from his operation and that allowed Redknapp to name an unchanged side from the team that swept Doncaster aside. The big occasion once again appeared to be Cherries' Achilles heel as Gillingham completed a

Division Three double over Bournemouth, the only team to have achieved this success so far. I was unaware of the result until landing at Gatwick airport the following morning. Borrowing a scruffy copy of the 'Sunday Times' from a waiting traveller at baggage reclaim, I opened the sports section and scanned the weekend results. My heart sank as I read 'Gillingham 2 v. Bournemouth 1'. I uttered 'shit' and 'thank you' before returning the paper to its bemused owner and moved forward to collect my baggage from the conveyer belt.

Apparently it was a game that produced a remarkable second-half Cherries' display in a match that would eventually be remembered for the controversial refereeing by Noel Butler from East Moseley. The first period produced a tough but lively exchange, with the Gills taking full advantage of playing at home and experiencing the better of the encounter. Skipper Mark Weatherley led by example as he gave the hosts a 1-0 lead at half-time.

Midway through the second half the game exploded into life. Newson first came within a whisker of equalising before Aylott headed home from Cookie's inch-perfect cross. Butler said 'no goal' due to an infringement. There appeared to be no obvious reason for such a decision. Then on 81 minutes David Shearer, the unwieldy Gillingham striker, pounced to give the home side a comfortable lead. With five minutes remaining, Butler awarded a debatable free kick to Cherries 30 yards from the Gillingham goal.

Heffernan stepped up and fired a wind-assisted rocket into the top corner, 2-1. Bournemouth piled forward in search of the equaliser as the 90-minute mark rapidly approached, then passed. On 93 minutes Newson missed another opportunity to equalise. Gillingham fans whistled frantically for the end of the game, but still more time was added on. In the 10th minute, yes 10th minute of added time, Butler finally blew his whistle to end the 100-minute game. Gillingham fans were relieved, while Bournemouth supporters were dejected. As if to rub salt in the wound the broadcaster via the Priestfield public address system congratulated the Gillingham players and quickly declared that they had become the first team to achieve the 'double' over Bournemouth this season.

Redknapp was disappointed with the result and felt his side deserved a point, but was generally pleased with the display. He felt that referee Butler had been a little harsh with his decision and described being 'shocked' when Aylott's header was disallowed.

Tuesday 24 March marked a special day in my calendar. It was on this day back in 1973 that I made my one and only appearance on BBC TV's 'Match of the Day'. Bournemouth versus Grimsby was one of the televised matches and Bournemouth player Micky Cave had been injured at the South End of the ground just by the perimeter fence where I was standing. Aged ten years and dressed in a blue anorak, I turned and waved at the camera sited on an extended mechanical cherry-picker arm behind the South End goal, and the BBC kindly broadcast the moment.

Bournemouth v. Darlington – Saturday 28 March

With promotion in mind and the visit to Port Vale on 31 March, Bournemouth had contacted Eire manager Jack Charlton and asked to withdraw goalkeeper Gerry Peyton from the Irish squad that was due to play Bulgaria on 1 April. Charlton fully understood, duly obliged and the relationship remained intact.

Back in one piece from skiing, I came home to find a beige A4 envelope waiting for me. Excitedly I ripped it open to reveal the contents. Newson had returned my programme and the entire squad had signed it. I was thrilled. The last time I had been so excited at something so trivial was when I succeeded in obtaining the final outstanding Romanian player I needed to complete my 1970 Mexico World Cup sticker album collection.

Darlington travelled to Dean Court as bottom club of Division Three. On paper and on current form the result looked an easy home win. Bournemouth had won 15 out of 18 home matches while Darlington had failed to win away all season. Caretaker player-manager Paul Ward had succeeded as Quakers manager, replacing Cyril Knowles just two days before. Such an action usually kick-starts a change in form.

At 2.45pm I purchased my cushion, then proceeded to take my seat in the centre row of B block in the Main Stand. With the now customary 70/210 zoom lens fixed and ready for action, I thumbed through the match day magazine and scanned the content. As the team names were announced, each Darlington player was greeted with a short boo from the assembling crowd, while Bournemouth players were greeted with a loud cheer. The announcement 'Number 5 John Williams' received special acknowledgement with applause. 'Willo' gave the Cherries' defence a solid backbone and measure of confidence. Thankfully he had recovered from the injury that had kept him out of the previous two away trips. Injured Cherries' striker David Puckett sat in the centre section of the Main Stand and acknowledged well-wishers with a polite nod and wave of the hand. Across to my left the South End of the ground had filled up considerably and under the short protruding roof at the back came the song, 'We'll be top at five o'clock, we'll be top at five o'clock'. Three points were a dead cert.

Cherries started the match with all guns blazing and continued a fast-paced attack throughout. Darlington did not belie their position at the foot of the table; they were awful. However, there was one exception to the rule and on this occasion it was the Quakers' keeper Mike Astbury. He played the proverbial blinder, acrobatically diving left, right, then left again, to deny Bournemouth in the first 20 minutes of the match. Then, for the second time in as many minutes and in identical fashion, he sprinted out of his goal area to clear a poor back pass and hoof the ball skyward over the Main Stand roof and out into the car park. A bald head behind me bellowed, 'Steady on keep' we've only got three balls!' The comment provided great delight and amusement to those around him and the shaven head gave a broad grin in response to this acknowledgement of his quick wit.

Minutes later my shutter clicked and I thought I had captured the opening goal only to look up and see Williams' header come back off a post, with Astbury flapping, but well beaten. The lens clicked twice more before I finally got the result I wanted. Cookie took a long throw from the right where, wind-assisted, it drifted into the Darlington penalty area causing a panic. Quakers' defender Mark Hine was first to the ball and under pressure sliced it past keeper Astbury and into his own net. He looked sick and sat on the ground for a minute, very sorry for himself, ignored by disappointed colleagues. Meanwhile Bournemouth players were cock-a-hoop and laughed all the way as they jogged back to the centre circle.

At half-time I returned to my match day magazine. Club Chairman Rodney Barton highlighted the difficulties that the administrative staff had faced attempting to satisfy the demand for tickets at the recent Middlesbrough game. This was then followed by a poor crowd of only 6,806 for the visit of Bury. Barton openly criticised and shared his disappointment. He had anticipated a crowd in the region of 10,000. Assistant Manager Jimmy Gabriel in his 'Viewpoint from the Bench' column expanded on the recent challenges that Cherries had faced during the month of March. He described the month as 'One of the most testing times of the year for footballers'. He followed the statement with examples of Cherries playing Wigan in a blizzard, Doncaster in a gale force wind, Gillingham on a partly waterlogged field and then warm sunshine for home games at Dean Court. He summarised Bournemouth's performances as 'Magnificent in March'.

139

The teams ran out for the second half and on kicking off continued to follow the identical pattern of the first half. Bournemouth attacked at will, Darlington were awful, but Astbury continued to defy Cherries with a further series of one-man heroics. And so it continued until referee Ashby called a halt to proceedings, confirming three more points for the Cherries. The game had been a much tougher encounter than I had anticipated, with a poor Darlington side defending resolutely and proving to be quite a tough nut to crack. Although it ended in another defeat, caretaker player-manager Paul Ward must have been pleased with his team's performance for his first match in charge. Only a huge slice of luck saved Bournemouth from disappointment.

I stood and applauded my team from the pitch along with the entire Main Stand. The applause quickly shifted to cheers of delight as the public address system announced: 'Middlesbrough 0 Rotherham 0, Notts County 0 Bolton 0, Bury 1 Gillingham 0 and Wigan 3 Swindon 2'.

The Main Stand, notoriously quiet during matches, then instantly burst into life when hearing the other results and began to shout 'The Reds are going up!' – extreme behaviour that I had not witnessed before. Without exception the day's results had gone in Bournemouth's favour. Cherries sat proudly on top of the Third Division table and had opened up a five-point lead over second-placed Middlesbrough.

Port Vale v. Bournemouth – Tuesday 31 March

With ten matches remaining, I realised that Bournemouth were now on the verge of making history and achieving promotion to Division Two for the first time ever. But ten more matches meant 30 points were still at stake and Cherries were far from assured of achieving that coveted promotion place. Looking at the League table I took a deep breath to calm my excitement and mentally acknowledged the fact that Bournemouth were now mathematically safe from relegation this season! Eric Idle taught me to 'always look on the bright side of life' and his advice has often been one of my sources of optimism.

Having played 36 matches already and with only ten remaining, it was slightly odd that Bournemouth were only now about to meet Port Vale for the first time during the season. This situation was due to the original fixture in November being postponed because of a flu virus in the Vale camp. The Valiants were managed by ex-Cherries star John Rudge who stated he 'still had great feelings for his old club and his old team-mate Harry Redknapp'. Vale had experienced a mediocre season with the highlight being a money-spinning two-leg tie with Manchester United in the Littlewoods Cup. They sat comfortably in mid table thanks mainly to their athletic goalkeeper Alex Williams and goal-machine Andy Jones, who had notched 27 League and cup goals already, including a hat-trick in the recent 6-0 drubbing of Fulham at Craven Cottage. Jones' success had resulted in him being selected for the Welsh International squad who were due to play Finland the following evening after the visit of Cherries to Vale Park. His inclusion in the international arena meant that he was unable to play for Port Vale against Bournemouth. How unlucky for Cherries not to be able to have their defence tested by the unstoppable Jones!

Midweek travel to the potteries was not feasible due to work demands and so once again I tuned into BBC Radio Solent for a sports special programme, my umbilical cord to the Cherries match. There was an unusual difference to this broadcast because Cherries were the only side in action that evening and so Bournemouth fans had the luxury of Solent's sole attention. The broadcast followed a familiar format, music based, with coverage from Vale Park limited to a series of bulletins at twenty-minute intervals. A goal by either side would be heralded with a crowd-cheering jingle disrespectfully interrupting the singer, albeit a recording, performing at that precise moment. I sat in the kitchen and cradled a mug of tea. With terrible echo and crackling static on the broadcast, the team line-up was announced. The impartial BBC Stoke reporter battled to be heard above the Vale Park public address announcer. Shouting, he confirmed that Redknapp had persevered with a winning formula, naming the identical starting eleven that had narrowly overcome Darlington three days earlier. For the record he also confirmed Andy Jones' place had been taken by Darren Beckford, who would be making his first start of the season for the Valiants, on loan from Manchester City.

Another mug of tea and fourteen minutes later 'Rockin' all over the world' was halted by the crowd cheer. After weathering an early Vale storm, Bournemouth had taken the lead courtesy of a Newson header. Report over, it was back to the Quo again. The clock ticked on and I nervously made another full mug of tea. On the half hour Newson struck again and thankfully saved south coast listeners from the horror of the full version of the Bay City Rollers' 'Bye bye baby'. In a carbon copy of the first goal the BBC match reporter described how Newson had risen majestically above the Vale defence to connect with a Richard Cooke centre – Port Vale 0 Bournemouth 2. In my excitement I

141

thumped the kitchen table so hard that the wooden surface flexed, sending a mug of hot scalding tea skywards. Tea dribbled down the kitchen walls as I hastily mopped up the flood. Normality had returned by the half-time report when it was confirmed that Cherries had a commanding lead, but only because of some fine goalkeeping by Bournemouth's Gerry Peyton.

After the interval the music continued with contributions from the Beach Boys, Alison Moyet, Mental As Anything and Sheena Easton. As I began to relax Easton's '9 to 5' was interrupted with the crowd-cheering jingle. Vale midfielder Ray Walker had pulled a goal back with twenty minutes remaining.

I stared at my mug of tea and, not wishing to repeat the previous cleaning operation, just silently muttered 'Shit' to myself. The remaining twenty minutes seemed to last a lifetime and the closing stages were unbearable. I ripped through my fingernails, chewing aggressively at each one in turn. My father joined me to listen to the final stages of the broadcast. The Solent presenter confirmed that Vale and Cherries were playing stoppage time before exclaiming, 'It's all over at Vale Park and Bournemouth go eight points clear at the top of Division Three.' My father headed straight for the kettle, singing out loudly 'Boscombe, Boscombe'.

The three points had been a close call, but were earned thanks to a series of heroic saves by Peyton, including a last-minute wonder save from Walker. Redknapp was ecstatic: 'This was a great result and a tremendous performance.' He praised captain Newson for the superb execution of two set pieces and added that keeper Peyton was magnificent, stating 'It was his best game for the club' and describing his performance as 'International Class'.

The following evening in the European Championship qualifying matches Andy Jones scored on his Welsh debut during the 4-0 thrashing of Finland at Wrexham. Selected for international duty and so unable to play for Port Vale, Bournemouth had once again been on the receiving end of another huge stroke of luck, the second time in just three days! Someone somewhere was finally smiling on Bournemouth.

Elsewhere Peterborough's 1-0 defeat at Torquay assured Northampton of promotion to the Third Division. Such was their dominance of Division Four that they had secured a promotion place with still ten matches to play – a quite remarkable feat. I scrutinised the Cobblers' position and achievement with envious eyes, dreaming of what it would be like for Bournemouth to emulate their runaway success.

142

With just nine matches remaining, the prospect of Bournemouth playing in Division Two was now so close it was within touching distance. I could even smell it! High on a wave of enthusiasm my promotion thoughts and mood turned a little sombre as I recalled the 1971/72 Bournemouth team who, under John Bond, managed to let promotion slip from their grasp towards the end of the season. Even today the thought of that disappointment and failure still hurts. Now eight points clear and nine games remaining, I shivered at the terrible thought that Bournemouth could still falter and miss out on their promotion chance.

APRIL

Carlisle v. Bournemouth – Saturday 4 April

Middlesbrough had decided to appeal to the Football League over being ordered to play a postponed home match with Wigan on Wednesday 6 May. Manager Bruce Rioch felt strongly that it would be tough on his side to play four games in eight days at the end of the season and argued that it could influence the outcome of the Third Division promotion race. His appeal was unsuccessful and subsequently turned down by the Football League.

For the first three days during the week I desperately tried to swap my scheduled overtime rota with a colleague so that I could travel to Brunton Park. Each time I approached a potential candidate I was turned down. Frustrated, I accepted the commitment with the one consolation that I would not have to experience the 340 miles, six and a half hours journey from Dorset to Cumbria, and then the reverse journey of the same length and duration.

Up the creek and without a proverbial paddle is a polite way to describe that Carlisle were in a spot of bother. To articulate the situation accurately, they had been relegated the previous season and now sat third from bottom with 31 points, firmly entrenched in the relegation zone again. Operating without a reserve side meant that talent had to be bought or brought in and even free transfers were creating financial difficulties. Scott McGarvey and Mick Halsall were two players who had lined up for the Cumbrians in the Dean Court encounter back in November, but both had recently been sold to alleviate the financial problems. To add to Carlisle's problems Ian Bishop, who had impressed at Dean Court, was also missing due to injury.

143

While I sat in the air-conditioned office processing more insurance paperwork Bournemouth and Carlisle battled out a goalless draw witnessed by a poor attendance of 2,005 spectators. Matches that record a 0-0 score line usually indicate a drab affair and it was an accurate assumption in this case. Listening avidly to the post-match report courtesy of Radio Solent, the full extent of the challenge unfolded in a three-minute summary.

Determined Cumbrian hosts, a Brunton Park gale and a pitch with no grass, all contributed to the stalemate. Both sides could have nicked a goal, but it was on-loan Tony Sealy who was guilty of wasting the best opportunity for Bournemouth. Sealy in space beat the offside trap, rounded home keeper Eric Nixon, but then failed to execute the move as his weak shot stalled in the goalmouth mud only to be hacked away by the panicking Carlisle defence. In his post-match interview Redknapp gave his view highlighting that, 'The conditions destroyed the game,' adding that Carlisle were a physical side, impossible to play football against in the strong wind.

A point, however, was a good outcome especially as Notts County had been held to a 1-1 draw at Walsall. Swindon had won 3-0 at home to Mansfield the previous evening and Middlesbrough were scheduled to play their local derby on Sunday. Bournemouth sat top of the Division with an eight-point cushion.

On Sunday Littlewoods sponsored the first £1m League Cup Final, where Arsenal came from behind at Wembley to beat Liverpool 2-1. The defeat ended Liverpool's seven-year record of never losing a match when Ian Rush scored. Of greater consequence and importance to Bournemouth, Middlesbrough could only manage a 1-1 draw at home to bottom side Darlington to give Cherries a seven-point gap at the top. That result made me smile.

Bournemouth v. Walsall – Saturday 11 April

Behind the scenes the AFC Bournemouth management team continued to focus on the future. The decision regarding the club's plans for a new £3m stadium in King's Park was expected to go to a full meeting of the town council. This was because of the size of the proposed improvement, which had been expanded to include further residential development of the five-acre Dean Court site. The application might be considered at the April planning committee meeting and if approved at that level would then go to the full council on 12 May. Cherries Chairman Rodney Barton stressed the importance of this application, adding that if the council approved the new stadium plans the club had 'something definite to build on' and that it would 'help secure the future of the club'. To survive, the club needed better facilities for life in Division Two, which Barton firmly believed would be achieved with promotion. He was confident and firmly believed it, so why didn't I yet share his optimism? The explanation was simple – my scepticism lay in Cherries' unlucky history. Bournemouth had been close before, but somehow had let slip similar opportunities. I would only believe it when it was mathematically confirmed!

Saturday 11 April marked the commencement in the calendar of what was expected to be the sternest test so far in the promotion race. Bournemouth were scheduled to play three crucial games in a week: Walsall at home, Wigan and Swindon away.

It was a beautiful bright and clear south coast afternoon. I pushed my way through the South End turnstile and it gave a tired moan. The turnstile operator handed me a small blue voucher that would be redeemable for entrance to the Easter Monday home fixture with Bristol Rovers. The same voucher system would apply to succeeding matches. Owing to the ever-growing demand for tickets the club had decided to introduce all-ticket matches for the final three home games of the season. Via the public address system club Managing Director Brian Tiler pointed out that the scheme had been introduced at the request of the police to facilitate the safety and comfort of spectators. It also meant that regular supporters who turned up each week would get priority over the floating supporter who only followed a winning side. I nodded my approval.

Looking out across the stadium I felt an air of confidence wafting across Dean Court. Just over 8,600 home fans boisterously boomed, 'We'll be top at five o'clock,' and in his programme notes captain Newson positively stated, 'If we do well against Walsall, Wigan and Swindon we should be almost there.' Ladbrokes had reduced their odds to 5-4 for Cherries winning the Division title and had even trimmed to 250-1 from 500-1 the odds against Bournemouth reaching 103 points. Featured in the player profile of the Cherries match day programme was 18-year-old reserve talent Matthew Holmes. In a series of answers to a set format of questions, Holmes recorded his 'best goal seen scored' as Colin Clarke's goal at Reading the previous year. So I was not the only one impressed by that incredible strike and it transpired that he was one of five players in the squad who came to the same conclusion.

Walsall sat comfortably in mid table with little to play for, but took some pride in the midweek announcement that two of their players, David Kelly and Bobby

Hutchinson, had been selected in the Division Three 'All Star Team' chosen by the Professional Footballers Association during their annual awards ceremony.

Ever-present Cherries keeper Gerry Peyton had surprisingly been the only Bournemouth player to be selected in the team. The top two most coveted awards went to Tottenham's Clive Allen, voted 'Player of the Year' and Tony Adams of Arsenal, voted 'Young Player of the Year'.

Bournemouth started the match at a furious pace. Before Walsall began to find their rhythm Cherries' winger Richard Cooke, inspired by encouragement from the New Stand, accelerated down the right wing with explosive pace and, after some confusion in the visitors' defence, connected at the end of a move by prodding the ball past the stranded £75,000 Fred Barber in the Walsall goal and into the net. Two minutes played, Bournemouth 1 Walsall 0. The South End burst into excitement as the Walsall players pointed accusingly at each other. A voice from behind shouted, 'You'll never catch Cookie, they feed 'im on nitrous oxide!' The goal had arrived very early in the match before either side had really settled down and, despite much creative Bournemouth play that followed, the score remained 1-0 at half-time.

The second period was notable for only one key moment, but it was to be a crucial heart-stopping flash point. The trauma began in the 81st minute when Walsall striker Nicky Cross clearly fouled Cherries' defender Mark Whitlock and then centred for David Kelly to score. The linesman initially raised his flag to indicate an infringement had occurred, but then lowered it. The referee had not seen any of this activity. It was an obvious foul, but referee Darryl Reeves allowed the goal to stand. The Dean Court crowd fell silent in shock and disbelief. Bournemouth players were incensed and, led by midfielder Tony Pulis who had run 25 yards from his own penalty area, began to remonstrate with the official. Pulis, Morrell and Whitlock aggressively demonstrated their outrage as they manhandled and pleaded with the referee to consult his linesman. Like a weak schoolboy bullied into submission, he eventually agreed to do so and was literally marched across the pitch escorted by the furious three. During the seconds that followed a stony silence fell across Dean Court as 8,600 people attempted to eavesdrop on the conversation. You could have heard a pin drop at the ground. A brief consultation took place between the officials before Reeves indicated that the goal had been disallowed, with a free kick to Bournemouth. An emotionally charged Dean Court erupted in delight and I joined in the singing, 'You thought you had scored, you were wrong, you were wrong.' It was now the turn of Walsall players to protest, which they did briefly, but with less venom. Still shaking his head, a middle-aged Cherries fan standing to my right could not believe what we had just witnessed. Clapping at the reversed decision, he said to me, 'It's our year, we're going up! I can't believe our luck. We really are going up this time!'

In today's modern officiated game 'Iron Man' Pulis would have been dismissed for hostile behaviour towards the match official and heavily fined, possibly receiving a ban for several matches. On this occasion, though, he was lucky to walk away with only a caution for his outburst. The game continued and Bournemouth took maximum points with a 1-0 victory.

On Monday at the office I ate lunch with my colleague Roger Parsons, a thoroughly decent guy and a devout Cherries' fan. He and his wife had a male student from Finland staying with them and Roger had taken him to the Walsall match. Stunned by the Cherries' play and the atmosphere at Dean Court, he had decided to extend his stay in the UK so that he could see another match! Watching Bournemouth was contagious and it seemed that the bug had bitten another unsuspecting victim.

In the FA Cup semi-finals Tottenham beat Watford 4-1 and Clive Allen's 45th goal of the season broke Jimmy Greaves's record held since season 1962/63. Watford received some sympathy in the media as Gary Plumley, a 31-year-old wine-bar owner in South Wales and Newport County part-timer, was forced to make a one-off appearance in the Watford goal because Tony Cotton and Steve Sherwood were both injured. Now I could see why Redknapp was so concerned about keeper cover for Gerry Peyton. In the other semi-final Coventry needed extra time to beat Leeds 3-2 and by doing so secured their first Final in their 104-year history – another historical first in this fascinating season.

Wigan Athletic v. Bournemouth – Tuesday 14 April

I decided to take a day's holiday on the 14th. Clutching my complimentary match ticket and my homemade tucker-box full of doorstep sandwiches, I boarded the supporters' coach for the long midweek trip to Wigan. Three months earlier, and I am appalled to admit this, the only useful fact that I could divulge about Wigan was that it had the 'best discotheque in the world', which had been founded by Russ Winstanley, a local man who had been playing Northern Soul music to the locals, and that the club had a membership of 100,000.

I recalled this fact from my Oakmead Youth Club days when, as resident

147

DJ, I had been forced to suffer playing a selection of predictable vinyl singles regarded as Northern Soul. To me, they all sounded the same. Knowing little about the place and having never been close to the town in my life, I now settled in my seat and prepared to visit Wigan for the second time in just over a month. As the vehicle sped along the A338 I flicked through a copy of the Tuesday edition of the 'Bournemouth Evening Echo'. Inside on page 14 I read that Cherries' defender John Williams had been banned from driving for 15 months and fined £250 by the town's magistrates after admitting driving with excess alcohol.

The victory over Walsall had equalled the club record for the most number of wins in a season. Cherries had only ever achieved 24 wins twice before. The first was back in 1947/48 and the second in season 1971/72. On each occasion Bournemouth had missed out on promotion by the narrowest of margins. Victory in the promotion clash with Wigan at Springfield Park would provide Bournemouth with their 25th League victory of the season and therefore pass the existing record.

Travel to Springfield Park followed the same route taken on Saturday 7 March. The one difference this time was the weather: bright sunshine and blue sky for the entire journey. Having arrived in good time at 6.30pm and with it being such a warm pleasant evening, I decided to explore and entered into the Wigan club shop in search of items that might be of interest to a programme collector. The shop was a small wooden hut with one glass window, similar to the type of domestic shed that you can buy and self-erect from B&Q. Space inside was at a premium and I encountered much elbow bashing as I squeezed past the locals to view the merchandise. The air inside was hot and sticky with the wood discharging a mildewed fragrance. The hut was a treasure trove, an Aladdin's cave for old football programmes, badges and memorabilia.

Although I found nothing to add to my personal collection I bought a copy of the Wigan v. Bournemouth match programme and headed towards the visitors 'away' standing enclosure. Five weeks earlier I had sat shivering in the Main Stand in a futile attempt to protect myself from the biting wind. This time I stood behind the goal and leaned on a blue crush barrier and warmed my face on the rays of the setting sun. As both teams conducted their 'warm-up' session I did the same in the fading spring warmth and thought to myself, 'What a contrast!'

The Latics sat in sixth place, just outside the play-off zone for Division Three.

They had experienced a memorable FA Cup run that had taken them to round six, where they were eventually beaten at home by Leeds in front of 12,250 spectators. Looking around Springfield Park it appeared a mystery how they had managed to squeeze that number inside. Since that match and the defeat at Bristol Rovers on 21 March Wigan had entered on a winning run, having secured maximum points from their following five matches, and manager Ray Mathias was confident of reaching the season-end play-off stage and possibly even an automatic promotion spot if Wigan defeated Bournemouth. Call it supporters' intuition if you like, but I knew deep down that this match would be difficult for the Cherries.

Yet the following 90 minutes produced Bournemouth's best and most convincing performance of the season to date. The result was confirmed with a brace of goals from Cherries' industrious midfielder Mark O'Connor. Squinting through the rays of the now rapidly setting sun, I caught the silhouette figure of O'Connor executing superbly ten yards from goal, following a series of one-touch passes between Aylott and Cooke. Eleven minutes of play completed and Bournemouth had taken the lead. Cooke was everywhere sprinting left, right, then left again as he tore the Wigan defence to shreds. Unable to contain him they turned to rough tactics and obliged with a series of vicious stud marks across his body, but still he courageously weaved between them, leaving them for dust. On 40 minutes, with the floodlight bulbs piercing the dusk, O'Connor struck again following a pinpoint O'Driscoll pass. Wigan defenders stood motionless as O'Connor beat the offside trap to round keeper Roy Tunks to score. My travelling companions and I leapt in the air to celebrate. Unfortunately, my celebrations were a little too vigorous and from my pockets spilled car keys, spectacles case and several coins. Minutes later when calm had settled fellow supporters in the close vicinity collected the debris from my celebration and handed the items back. Even the coins were returned. At half-time Cherries were home and dry. Confidence oozing, Wigan had no answer.

The second period was less dramatic as Bournemouth absorbed any Wigan attempt to make a fight of it. Williams and Morrell were booked and keeper Peyton stood firm. Peyton was in a rich vein of form and behind the goal we sang, 'You'll never beat Gerry Peyton'.

As the game faded away in the latter stages we noticed large numbers of home supporters exiting the stadium. As they left we serenaded them with the now customary song, 'We can see you sneaking out!'

To their credit at the final whistle those Wigan supporters who had remained until the end stood and applauded Bournemouth from the pitch. Demonstrating their appreciation, they politely acknowledged defeat by the League leaders – a sincere gesture from one of the most genuine group of football supporters I have ever had the pleasure to share a match with. In a show of mutual appreciation Bournemouth fans expressed their gratitude by returning comparable applause. The 2-0 victory was the 25th win of the season for Bournemouth and had set a new record for a single season. Cherries stood as proud leaders of Division Three – eleven, yes eleven, points ahead of second-placed Swindon Town. Redknapp was ecstatic and full of praise for his players – 'It was a marvellous display by the whole side' – and added that he could not single out any one player as they had all contributed to giving Bournemouth complete control of the game.

I slept throughout most of the journey back to 'Cherry Land', dreaming of that eleven-point gap and the following week's encounter at local rivals and promotion contenders Swindon Town. Bleary eyed, but back at work the next morning after the Wigan trip, I recounted my personal match report many times over to interested colleagues. By 4.00pm I was exhausted and had to go home.

Swindon v. Bournemouth – Saturday 18 April

Easter has always been considered as the critical period when promotion and relegation matters are ultimately settled. This I saw as complete hogwash. Following this match Swindon, with games in hand, still had 24 points to be won or lost, enough to overhaul Cherries if they succumbed to a late capitulation. Anything was possible considering Bournemouth's history and extensive love affair with the Third Division.

This crucial top-of-the-table match was not all-ticket, but advice to travelling fans was quite simply to get to the County Ground early to avoid disappointment. My friend Mark Rawlings from the Lloyd's Bank Sunday football team offered to drive and along with Rich Perry and Chris Pinchbeck I caught a lift with him for the 70-mile journey to Wiltshire. Heeding the travelling advice, we left Bournemouth at 11.15am and arrived on the outskirts of Swindon at 1.15pm.

The journey was unadventurous until we approached the world's ultimate traffic-control system, known as the Magic Roundabout. Until 1972 there was only one Magic Roundabout and it was a children's television programme featuring Dougal the dog, a hippy rabbit called Dylan and the spring-loaded Zebedee. But Swindon's original County Ground roundabout gradually became the motorist's complete nightmare, failing to process the increasing volume of traffic that converged on it from five different directions. The solution, similar to a series of moons revolving around a single planet was to combine two roundabouts in one. The first was a conventional clockwise type and the second revolved inside the first, sending traffic anti-clockwise. The result was a bemusing state of confusion referred to as a multi-mini roundabout that Swindon folk affectionately named the Magic Roundabout. Bizarre, but it worked! Upon arriving at this traffic atrocity Mark et al. had no idea which route to follow and we all scrutinized the options available to traverse and exit the system. As the debate became protracted the answer stood to our left and stared us all in the face. Draped over the colossal twenty-foot-high road sign lay a massive white sheet, an improvised and homemade traffic sign with red arrows pointing in an easterly direction with the following words scribed in thick black ink: 'Harry Redknapp's red and white army this way! → '

After a frightening experience, but successful navigation of the roundabout, we found the approach roads blocked; the congestion was appalling. Most of the cars that queued patiently had red 'AFCB' scarves draped from the windows or tied to radio aerials. I had never seen so many Bournemouth supporters congregate in one space. Harry Redknapp's red and white army was out in force and absurdly I wondered if Bournemouth was now empty.

Inside the ground I stood on the Shrivenham Road visitors' terracing with my friends. Over four thousand Cherries fans had made the trip and were now tightly packed into their allocated section of the stadium. The County Ground was one of the best stadiums I had seen on my travels during the current season; it was mainly constructed of modern concrete sections with the main stand covered with a sweeping projecting roof. Only the terracing behind each goal looked in keeping with the lower division standard. I was a little perturbed by the supporter segregation arrangements. Only two parallel iron railings behind the end section of the Stratton Bank goal provided a channel that divided the two sets of supporters. The magnitude at stake in this match was significant and would be played in a volatile atmosphere. The segregation seemed inadequate, high risk and simply stupid. If there was to be trouble it was obvious where it would flare up. Fortunately I was standing at the furthest end away from the Swindon supporters and tucked in the corner of the terrace.

Swindon had an astounding home record. Since Boxing Day the Robins had played eight League matches at the County Ground, with the following statistics: won eight, goals scored fifteen, goals conceded nil. This incredible run of home supremacy included a 1-0 victory over Middlesbrough on 28 February. In fact the last visiting team to have scored a League goal at the County Ground had been Bristol City on Sunday 14 December.

A crowd of 14,302 – Swindon's biggest of the season and the third highest in the Third Division this season to date – produced an electric atmosphere. Both teams entered the playing area, Swindon in their red shirts and white shorts and Bournemouth in their away strip of all pale blue. It was a magnificent sight, with red and white ticker tape swirling in the breeze and slowly drifting across the pitch. The home crowd cheered their heroes and we matched the hosts and were united in anthem: 'B-O-U-R-N-E-M-O-U-T-H'. After five minutes of anticipation, which included more vocal taunting by each set of supporters, a brisk warm-up period for each team and the coin toss, the game finally got under way, with Bournemouth attacking the County Road end of the ground.

The Cherries looked confident Division Three leaders and passed the ball between one another in neat triangles, maintaining possession as they built their attacks from the back four. 'Boscombe, back of the net' came the cry as Cherries won a second corner kick. From O'Connor's delivery, Bournemouth struck quickly and clinically after only 16 minutes. John Williams headed home from the corner kick, a perfect header that flew into the top corner. As the ball hit the back of the net the terraces containing Bournemouth fans simply erupted and around me young and old celebrated together. The noise was phenomenal and the familiar song commenced, 'The Reds are going up!' Williams' header was the first League goal that Swindon had conceded at the County Ground in the previous 736 minutes of Third Division football.

As Swindon kicked off to restart the game the first stone landed amongst the Bournemouth supporters. A second stone, then a third and fourth projectile flew through the air, having been launched from somewhere deep in the Swindon crowd section. The terrifying missiles came in sporadic waves soaring high into the sky before plummeting like arrows at the battle of Agincourt onto the heads of their unsuspecting victims. Many Bournemouth fans, oblivious to what had started, continued to watch the game, while others like me scoured the horizon for incoming stones. The situation was exacerbated by some now incensed Bournemouth fans who began hurling the stones back from whence they had come, causing mayhem among the Swindon fans. I saw a large stone spin through the air and heading in my direction. It dropped ten feet short of where I stood, but landed on the skull of an unsuspecting Cherries' fan. His legs buckled from the strike and blood poured from a gaping head wound. It was sickening to have observed this behaviour and terrifying for all around. This was supposed to be a football match, not a riot scene from Beirut. The joy and excitement of a top-of-the-table clash between two good football teams had long gone and was now replaced with a terrace battle full of anger and hatred. This is what I had feared at the start of the season. The intermittent volley of stones continued before police officers infiltrated both sets of supporters, dragged out the main culprits and, to everyone's relief, restored order. At this point I heard the shrill sound of a whistle; referee Wiseman had signalled the end of the first half. I had seen only seventeen of the 45 minutes because of the panic and mayhem after Bournemouth had scored. I had no idea of the score, but apparently Bournemouth still held a 1-0 lead.

With calm restored, the carnival atmosphere slowly returned, but I kept a constant watch on the horizon in case of further missiles. At the start of the second half Bournemouth had to withstand tremendous Swindon pressure as the home side fought to get back on level terms. Three corners followed in succession, but the Cherries' defence was resolute. Then, on 53 minutes, Swindon were awarded a free kick following what looked to be an innocuous challenge. From the resulting kick the ball was swung into the penalty area and headed on by Northern Ireland striker Jimmy Quinn, but only partially cleared as far as Dave Hockaday, who swept the ball into the Bournemouth net for his first goal of the season. The roar that followed from three-quarters of spectators in the ground was deafening. The equalising goal forced Cherries on the back foot, so attacks on the Swindon goal became sporadic.

The Bournemouth defence came under increasing pressure, but the back four of Newson, Morrell, Whitlock and Williams defended admirably and, when they were penetrated, keeper Gerry Peyton was in superb form.

Eventually the final whistle sounded and Cherries' supporters close by celebrated what some considered may have been the title clincher. Swindon's awesome home record had been restrained and a point for Cherries was a superb outcome. There had been no further outbreaks of violence and after a ten-minute wait inside the ground to allow the surrounding streets to clear of home supporters we left the County Ground and headed back to Mark's car. We drove back to Bournemouth with four scarves trailing out of the windows, tooting the car horn at every vehicle filled with Cherries fans. The adrenalin was pumping in my veins. It had been a bizarre day, exciting, terrifying and yet fantastic.

Middlesbrough had won 3-1 at York to maintain the pressure in second place, but Gillingham had lost away at Walsall and Notts County had slipped up at home to the draw specialists Chester, the game ending 1-1. The following afternoon, having recovered from a glorious and raucous celebration from the night before, I munched through a delicious Black Magic dark chocolate Easter Egg and scrutinised the Sunday tabloids. Excitedly I read the report in the 'Mail on Sunday' under the heading 'Bournemouth on the brink' and reflected on the fact that Bournemouth were now only five games away from securing a place in Division Two.

Bournemouth v. Bristol Rovers – Monday 20 April

The sun dipped low to the west as I crossed King's Park for the evening Easter fixture against the Pirates. During the day I had eaten enough chocolate to maintain the Cadbury's business for at least a month and, while feeling a little nausea from my over indulgence, it was invigorating to be out in the fresh air. As I crossed the A338 on foot snapshots of the Boxing Day Twerton Park mudfight flashed across my mind and the sickening loss of in-form striker David Puckett.

Playing in the evening gave the small advantage of knowing how Bournemouth's rivals had faired earlier in the afternoon. There was no real benefit, though, as the outcome of these matches only added greater pressure for Bournemouth to secure a victory. Middlesbrough had scraped a 1-0 victory at lowly Carlisle, Swindon had shared the spoils at Brentford drawing 1-1, Wigan had unexpectedly won away at Chester 2-1 and, damn it!, Gillingham had thrashed Fulham 4-1.

With a blue 'Special Voucher' in my left hand and coins to the value of £3.00 in my right, I pushed through the rusting turnstile. In its customary way it groaned when rotating as if to say 'welcome to Court'. The Easter break had been wonderful and I had enjoyed the luxury of two extra days away from work and with the added excitement of the Swindon trip it had been a joyous period. Now it was back to business in the 'Today' League Division Three as Bournemouth went head to head with relegation candidates Bristol Rovers; both sides eager for three points, but for obvious yet different reasons. The atmosphere was electric inside Dean Court with nearly 7,235 more spectators at Dean Court than saw the first match of the season against Newport County. A staggering increase of 360 per cent and proof, if proof were needed, that the town could and would sustain a Division Two team. It was a gorgeous spring evening and the buoyant mood of all Cherries fans, coupled with the volume of bodies inside the stadium, created a Brazilian-style carnival.

'Going up, going up, going up' reverberated all around Dean Court along with 'We love you Bournemouth, we do'. These two vociferous anthems were interjected with short bursts of 'Ooh arr, ooh arr' and 'I'ye can't read, I'ye can't write, but I'ye can drive a tractor!' to work the Rovers fans into a mild frenzy. A quick glance inside the match day magazine paraded skipper Newson as leader in the Player of the Year league table, two points ahead of Peyton, Morrell and Whitlock. Jimmy Gabriel in his column 'From the bench' proudly announced that the Player of the Season trophy would carry the name of Weymouth-born Micky Cave, the popular ex-Cherries' midfield star who had tragically died from carbon monoxide poisoning in November 1985. This was a marvellous gesture from the club in recognition of Cave's dedication to football. In Redknapp's programme notes under 'Harry's Line' the gaffer alluded to the hunger for success at the club – 'the players want the championship badly,' he stated. He emphasised, too, the importance of not placing unnecessary additional pressure on the team, a mistake that manager Alan Ball admitted he had made at Portsmouth during the previous two seasons that had contributed to their consecutive promotion failures.

At the end of the 90 minutes Bournemouth had completed another league double and smashed the statisticians' records again with their 26th League victory of the season.

The excitement began in the second half as Cherries strikers Aylott and Cooke conjured up two separate moments of South American magic. First Aylott struck with his tenth goal of the season as he flicked the ball up with his right foot, then volleyed it into the net with his left – pure Brazilian magic. Seven minutes later Bournemouth's very own 'Little Richard' curled a direct free kick around the Rovers' defensive wall from just outside the penalty box, a strike David Beckham would have been immensely proud of. At 2-0 to Bournemouth the predictable terrace songs exploded into life and as both strikes were executed with flair and precision I imagined that they would have received a virtual polite ripple of applause from Rio de Janeiro. Bournemouth did not have it all their own way though and, like an annoying Jack Russell dog that refuses to let go of your ankles, Rovers continued to gnaw away until they won a penalty in the 78th minute, Williams guilty of fouling Robbie Turner. Phil Purnell stepped up to take the kick, but Peyton blocked it, his third penalty save of the season in League competition. The outcome was twofold: Rovers heads dropped and the air was filled with 'You'll never beat Gerry Peyton'.

Maximum points achieved, Cherries maintained a nine-point lead at the top of the table over second-placed Middlesbrough. With only four games remaining, the door to Division Two was now wide open and at Bournemouth's fingertips. Only a suicidal act or a submission could now stop Cherries achieving what I once believed impossible.

Blackpool v. Bournemouth – Saturday 25 April

'Tangerines versus the Cherries, what a plum tie that was!', 'Cherries pip Tangerines to maximum points!', 'Ref fails to see Mango offside!' and the unthinkable 'Blackpool rock Cherries promotion bid' were just some of the amusing possible post-match newspaper headlines that Roger Parsons and I conjured up and shared to pass the drag of the journey north. From the back seat of the coach an equally appalling rendition of 'Oh I do like to be beside the seaside' occasionally burst into life as we sped along the M6 to Blackpool. At just £11.50 per supporter via the AFC Bournemouth travel club the two coaches had collectively become Cherries on tour! Inside we jeered and cheered as the coach drivers took turns to overtake one another along the motorway. Despite being on the road since 7am that morning we remained in good spirit. Roger was adamant, two more victories and promotion would be secured with just three more for the Championship. I admired his confidence.

Another record could be broken if Bournemouth achieved victory over the Seasiders. Already top of the Division with 87 points, victory at Blackpool would enable the Cherries to pass the current club record of most points in a season (three points for a win) that had been set by David Webb's Division Four promotion squad back in 1981/82.

Blackpool, though, were expected to be tough opposition on their own patch. When the two sides met at Dean Court back in early February Blackpool were pressing for a top six place, but two months on and a minor slump in form had seen the Seasiders drop to ninth place in the Division. Much of the recent decline in form could be attributed to the sale of goal-machine Paul Stewart to Manchester City in March for £200,000. Although I could not describe it, I somehow felt a strange uneasiness about this game, a kind of intuition or sixth sense that was gnawing away at my subconscious, telling me that this game would have a twist. Previous encounters between the two seaside teams had been limited to two Football League Cup ties in seasons 1971/72 and 72/73, Blackpool eventually winning on both occasions despite a marathon series of replays during the latter encounter. Today's game was to be only the sixth Football League meeting. Honours at this point were even: two victories each and a draw. The last and only time Bournemouth had won when visiting Bloomfield Road was on 14 November 1981, back in the Dave Webb inspired promotion season, when Sting and The Police were musically number one with 'Every little thing she does is magic'.

Arriving in Blackpool at 1.30pm gave Roger and I a little free time to explore the local vicinity. Not surprisingly, the respective town councils of Blackpool and Bournemouth had much in common and regularly jockeyed for pole position for the premiere British holiday beach resort. Stringent measures had been attempted to clean the beaches to the European blue flag standards and both towns had hosted conferences for the three main political parties. Like explorers in a foreign yet familiar land, and resorting to what all newly arrived tourists do, we headed straight for the beach. I liked Blackpool, but compared to conservative Bournemouth it was a different world. Blackpool was the Las Vegas of the north with burgers, chips, ice-cream and candy floss in abundance. The brash and bustling Golden Mile was the slot machine capital of Britain and a place where silly hats and tacky T-shirts were the norm. The sea was slate grey and looked uninvitingly cold. It was blustery on the promenade and a young woman walking towards us was quickly parted from her black 'kiss me quick' trilby hat. We laughed aloud as her male companion chased after it; each time he stooped to pick the hat up it blew further along the promenade, a scene reminiscent of a Benny Hill show sketch.

Behind me a bell rang and then rang again, getting louder and ever more urgent. I looked behind and froze as I saw a bloody great tram trundling towards me. I had strayed too close to the tram rail and quickly hopped out of the way of the approaching rumbling iron vehicle. The tram driver said nothing, but his demeanour was obvious from his prolonged intense stare. I translated it to be, 'Bloody tourists!' We strolled a little further, absorbing the diversity of the Victorian façade of the Imperial Hotel, before debating the attraction of the Blackpool Tower and the surrounding roller coaster arena.

157

The powerful aroma then became too tempting and so we stopped at the next fish and chip vendor for a healthy takeaway lunch. It seemed so surreal; our team were about to embark on a tense critical struggle for three more precious points yet we appeared to be without a care in the world and on a jolly boys outing.

I handed over my £2.80 and entered the visitors' Kop of Bloomfield Road. The standing terrace was a massive open sprawl of concrete stepped terracing and faded tangerine crush barriers. The entrance point at the top of the terrace was steep, incredibly steep, but the view from there was excellent. From this elevated perspective the pitch could be seen to be worn and bumpy with blotchy patches of grass, similar to army khaki camouflage colours. My eyes slowly examined the features of the Bloomfield Stadium. I had anticipated and expected my first impression to be one of awe, but instead it proved to be a cold and disbelieving shock.

I studied the view before me in meticulous detail. Faded orange paint peeled from every roof support pillar to reveal ugly rust that lay beneath. Holes were visible in the rusting corrugated roof of the Bloomfield Road home end and advertising boards were dirty and mainly broken. The Henry Street enclosure that ran the length of the pitch to my left was empty, now derelict and unsafe. I felt cheated and disappointed. Was this the arena that Sir Stanley Matthews eloquently graced during the early 1950s when nearly 40,000 spectators regularly witnessed his wizardry? Was it also this bad when Cherries legend Ted McDougall had a spell at Blackpool? It was heartbreaking, the social destruction of football history in front of my very eyes as yet again I witnessed another decaying club that had once seen greater days. With just 2,866 spectators present the stadium was empty.

'Come on you Blues,' we collectively howled as Blackpool kicked off towards the Bournemouth supporters and surprisingly had the lion's share of the first half. On just ten minutes and right in front of the visitors' Kop, Blackpool won a corner and from the corner kick centre half Colin Methven rose above Whitlock to head home. In the visitors' Kop we stood in silence, many with head in hands; it was a demoralising blow. Roger spat his disappointment, 'shit, all this way to let a goal in after only ten minutes'. I tried to reassure him that I had regularly observed this pattern of play on my away travels throughout the season and instructed him to keep the faith, but it made little difference. Cherries' team looked unsettled and, despite brief forays into the Blackpool area, little penetration was evident. The first half ended a depressing

45 minutes, and Roger had remained very quiet throughout. During the break he confessed his concern that the promotion party might be about to go sour. I had my own concerns, too, but kept them to myself.

Sporadically positioned behind the visitors' Kop goal we rallied behind the Cherries, giving generous encouragement but demanding better. Bournemouth kicked off the second period attacking towards us and within twelve seconds had equalised. O'Driscoll's pass set up Carl Richards, who then appeared to stroll through a static Blackpool defence to calmly shoot past keeper Richard Powell. It was just as though Blackpool had decided to give Cherries a free goal; it was unbelievable. As if an electricity switch had been thrown, Harry's red and white army, including Roger and me, burst into life. It was well and truly game on.

Then, on 54 minutes, Cherries received the stroke of luck that I could have only dreamed they might get once a season. Blackpool defender Paul Jones, under pressure from Cherries' Tony Sealy, attempted to lob the ball back to his own keeper. In the blustery conditions the wind took the ball over the keeper's stretching hand and behind the goal; we sucked it into the net. It was a comical event, but a pivotal moment in the game. Roger and I hugged and danced about the open terracing along with fellow Cherries fans. An eerie silence fell upon the home supporters' end and behind our goal we exploited it. 'Sing when you're winning, you only sing when you're winning,' filled Bloomfield Road.

The game continued end to end, with Gerry Peyton making three excellent saves to deny Blackpool an equaliser, while Powell blocked as Richards and Sealy both came close to sealing a Cherries victory. I looked at my watch. The tension was awful; we were now in stoppage time. 'Come on Bournemouth,' I yelled as Sealy again accelerated past the Blackpool defence to find little Richard Cooke on the edge of the penalty area, who blasted a low shot into the bottom corner of the net. As I jumped with delight I turned to celebrate with Roger, but he had vanished, he was nowhere to be seen. In his excitement he had stumbled and taken a tumble down the terrace some 30 steps below and was now dancing about like a kid near the front. No-one cared about kit colours now; the song was unanimous, 'The Reds are going up!, the Reds are going up!'

With the game finally over I stood in wonderment and applauded my team from the pitch. It had been an incredible resurgence of life from a team that looked down and out at half-time. Whatever Redknapp had said at half-time had done the trick, although according to captain Newson it was unrepeatable! Back on the coach the driver had tuned the radio into BBC Sports Report and the coach fell silent as the Division Three results were broadcast with the following reactions from those onboard. 'Blackpool 1 Bournemouth 3' (cheers and applause), 'Bristol Rovers 0 Gillingham 1' (lots of swearing in displeasure), 'Middlesbrough 2 Brentford 0' (sighs of disappointment), 'Swindon 1 Doncaster Rovers 1' (the coach erupted with a roar and rocked violently!). Cherries had now amassed 90 League points, a new club record, and the gap between themselves at the top and Swindon in third place had widened to fifteen points. The experience of this seaside roller-coaster and the excitement on the coach had drained me. Exhausted, I slept the whole journey home, waking at Ringwood.

MAY

Bournemouth v. Port Vale – Saturday 2 May

An air of expectancy and complacency surrounded this match. During the midweek build-up to the game everyone one I had spoken to, especially in the office, seemed to think that promotion was now a formality and would be confirmed after Cherries had beaten Port Vale. It was simply a matter of Bournemouth just turning up to collect the three points and the rewards. I remained unconvinced, especially when I read that four first-team players had been struggling with their fitness as the squad entered the final stages of the season. Giant central defender John Williams had collected an injury at Wigan that had forced him to have his forearm set in plaster. The arm had been fractured in two places, but Redknapp had refused to make the injury public knowledge, preferring to keep it quiet to avoid the alarm of some referees who would have been unhappy with the situation. Winger Richard Cooke had damaged his ankle at Blackpool, midfielder Mark O'Connor continued to be sidelined with a hamstring problem and midfield 'Iron Man' Tony Pulis had his wrist strapped following another fracture. Pulis was constantly being patched up after a variety of war wounds collected during the season and we often joked about him being Bournemouth's bionic man.

Despite the casualty list I felt some confidence in the fact that Williams, Cooke and Pulis would not want to miss the run-in and would hopefully have recuperated in time for the Vale match. In mid week the 'Bournemouth Evening Echo' had printed the player of the season nomination form, promoting the opportunity for all supporters to vote for their star player of the year. I cut out my form, wrote the name Mark Newson in block capital letters and posted it to the Echo Office.

I have little recollection or notes about this game, with the exception of the pre-match mood. The atmosphere before kick-off was electric and the anticipation high. Richards, Morrell and Aylott underwent their respective warm-up routines, breaking off only to sign autographs for a number of young supporters who had gathered at the edge of the pitch by the Main Stand. In amongst the crowd at the South End of the ground, I laughed as a Cherries diehard had obtained a huge roll of red and white striped plastic ribbon tape, similar to the blue and white tape used to mark off the scene of a crime by the police. The end of the red and white tape was passed from supporter to supporter as it wound itself through the occupants of the South End terrace like a massive boa constrictor snake and I, too, was willingly entangled. Progress of the tape was serenaded to the tune of 'Here we go' as everyone sang 'Pass it on, pass it on, pass it on', an instruction that was duly followed by all who came into contact with the tape. It was great fun and there was much amusement at those supporters who attempted in vain to extract themselves from the red and white web. One Cherries fan in a blue denim jacket became a little irritated as he unsuccessfully tried to unwind himself from the confused tangle shouting, 'get me out, I need a pee!'.

I participated along with a whopping 9,559 as we applauded, screamed and willed Bournemouth to victory. It turned out to be an afternoon of sheer frustration as Port Vale denied the Cherries of the victory that would have clinched promotion to Division Two.

Vale, who needed three more points for Third Division survival, had the better of the first half chances but then had to hang on grimly in the second half as Bournemouth pushed everyone forward, with the exception of Sean O'Driscoll. When Cherries did break down the stubborn Vale defence they found England Under-21 keeper Alex Williams in superb form. With time running out, my heart skipped a beat as dangerous Vale striker Andy Jones took a tumble in the penalty area, but the referee ignored any penalty claims. The game ended disappointingly goalless, which meant that Port Vale had become only the second visiting side during the season to shut out Bournemouth in a League game. More importantly the promotion party had been put on hold and the champagne remained on ice.

Hoarse and frustrated, I left Dean Court to learn that Middlesbrough had won 2-1 away at Chester. Infuriatingly, Swindon had hammered Carlisle 3-0 at

161

Brunton Park, but Gillingham had drawn 0-0 at home to Wigan. The outcome of the Third Division results meant that both Middlesbrough and Swindon had closed the gap at the top, while at the bottom Darlington, Newport County and Carlisle had officially been relegated. In the case of Carlisle they had equalled an unenviable record by becoming only the third club to go from the Fourth to the First Division and back. The others had been Northampton and Swansea.

Fulham v. Bournemouth – Monday 4 May

The midday kickoff in south-west London meant an early start from Bournemouth, especially as it was Bank Holiday Monday and we wanted to avoid the expected traffic migration back to the capital. Roger offered to drive and we left Bournemouth at 8.30am sharp, with red scarves flying from the car windows. Nothing would stop us attending the most important game ever in the history of AFC Bournemouth. This truly was history in the making and yet I still felt a little uneasy despite Cherries being on the verge of certain promotion. A win away at Fulham and Bournemouth would be promoted, but defeat meant it would have to be settled on the last day of the season. The thought of a last day cliffhanger was stomach churning. There was also the championship to win and this added pressure lay heavily on my shoulders. An uneasy statistic niggled in the back of my mind. Bournemouth had never won at Craven Cottage. Since 1928 Cherries had been defeated at the Cottage in every League encounter, with the exception of a 3-3 draw in season 1929/30 and a MacDougall-inspired 1-1 draw during season 1969/70.

Even on the day I was born, 26 September 1962, when Cherries visited Craven Cottage for a Football League Cup match as Bournemouth and Boscombe Athletic, it ended in a 0-4 defeat. This was not encouraging.

At 11.05am we queued through the Upper Richmond Road traffic, but after crossing the Thames Roger eventually found side-street parking with no parking meter. Roger refused to have to exit the match at half-time to put another 50p in the meter to avoid a penalty fine and I did not complain. Stevenage Road ran parallel to the ground and was a sea of red and white congestion with the occasional policeman on horseback raised above the walking throng. Twenty-five coaches had travelled from Bournemouth, with thousands more supporters making the journey independently by train or car. I was convinced that Bournemouth had emptied for the day because I had never seen so many Cherries' supporters in one place outside of Dean Court. In good humour shuffling along the street we sang, 'We love you Bournemouth, we do', before Roger and I paid our £2.80 each and filtered through the turnstile onto the densely packed visitors' terrace.

The sun shone between occasional clouds that were rapidly whisked along courtesy of a strong blowing southwesterly wind. Craven Cottage was a picturesque football ground and one of the most neat and tidy in Division Three that I had seen. Looking directly ahead at the pitch I had a perfect view of the surprisingly lush green playing area and to my left, at nine o'clock, behind the stand I glimpsed a four-man rowing team skimming across the tranquil Thames surface. To my right, in the corner of the stadium, stood the original cottage building with its old and rugged timber pillars; it looked quaint, but out of place. Wherever I looked there were Bournemouth supporters and behind the goal there must have been at least 4,000 of us singing our hearts out for the lads. We made a fabulous noise together. I saw the South End inflatable beach ball heading towards me and, demonstrating lightning reactions, I jumped and punched the ball towards the front of our congregation. It sailed over many heads before crashing into the black wire fencing at the front of the terrace surrounding the perimeter of the pitch.

Making a return to familiar territory were Sean O'Driscoll, Gerry Peyton and Tony Sealy. O'Driscoll and Peyton were both influential players during Fulham's 1981/82 promotion season and Sealy had spent a short period on loan at Craven Cottage, scoring 10 goals in 25 appearances.

A huge roar greeted the Bournemouth players as they jogged out of the cottage and onto the pitch. In the centre circle Newson won the toss and chose to defend the goal in front of us, which meant that the team would be attacking the same goal in the second half and be able to extract any advantage from the strong wind. This would provide tired legs with an injection of energy with the wind at their backs as they ran towards the red and white army. Just as Fulham kicked off Roger turned to me, raised his arms to reveal his crossed fingers and said, 'This is it'. I looked towards heaven and quietly whispered 'Please God' and my gaze centred on a British Airways Boeing 747 descending on its path to Heathrow. My focus was regained as a supporter to my left pressed the button on his compressed air klaxon horn and it blasted the air, triggering a ringing in my ears. Although now temporarily deaf I still shouted, 'Come on Bournemouth'.

The first thirty minutes were tense, with Fulham just having the edge with their possession and they chased everything, but neither team had penetrated the other's defence. In the away enclosure we sang our hearts out for the lads, 'We love you Bournemouth we do, we love you Bournemouth we do', followed by 'We're goin' up, we're goin' up, you're not, you're not!' The atmosphere was electric, but the goal I wanted to settle my nerves was not forthcoming. The gusty strong wind was causing the players some problems. My heart was in my mouth on two separate occasions when Fulham keeper Laurence Batty's long wind-assisted kicks bounced directly into the Bournemouth penalty area and were headed out for corner kicks by Williams and Whitlock respectively. Then, on 36 minutes, disaster struck – Whitlock moved to block a shot in the penalty area and the ball struck his hand. It looked completely accidental, but referee Taylor pointed to the spot. This was not in the script. Roger and I looked at each other in despair and he muttered, 'we're gonna blow this'. Behind Peyton's goal we whistled and jeered as Scott stepped back to take the penalty kick. Roger, unable to watch because of the tension, turned his back on the pitch and instead looked straight at me, awaiting my reaction. Scott struck a firm kick towards the centre of the goal, Peyton dived to his right and somehow the ball struck his outstretched left shin, sending the ball spiralling up and over the crossbar. I leapt three feet in the air, grabbed Roger and struck him several times on the head with my rolled match programme repeatedly shouting, 'He saved it, Gerry bloody saved it!' Behind Peyton's goal we were all delirious and loudly sang, 'There's only one Gerry Peyton.'

Roger could not believe our luck; 'We're gonna do it, I know we're gonna do it,' he shouted. More Fulham possession, followed by three poor corners, eventually brought the first half to a close and 4,000 Bournemouth supporters breathed a huge sigh of relief at the 0-0 half-time score.

My nerves had steadied as Cherries jogged out for the second half. This time they would be attacking with the strong wind at their backs. 4,000 voices screamed, 'Come on you reds! Come on you reds!' On 57 minutes O'Driscoll was penalised for a foul. From 35 yards out Peter Scott floated the ball into the penalty area and it bounced awkwardly off Whitlock to Jeff Hopkins, who, from what seemed an impossible angle, managed to slide the ball between Gerry Peyton's legs. John Williams on the goal line was unable to get out of the way of the ball and so helped it over the line. In his frustration he turned and slammed it into the roof of his own net. All around me there were calls of 'oh no!' and 'shit' as the reality of what had just happened began to register. Roger surprisingly was silent, while I sighed, 'Oh shit, here we go again'. Collectively we were distraught, but bravely continued to sing and encourage our team.

The upset was surprisingly short. One minute later Peyton released one of his own long wind-assisted kicks that landed perfectly onto Carl Richards's head. Bruno flicked it goalwards to Aylott, who then nudged it forward to Sealy, who turned the ball back towards the penalty spot to where Richards had continued his run. As he moved to strike the ball, Paul Parker brought him down with a clumsy tackle. Behind the goal our red and white army screamed 'Penalty!' and the referee agreed, pointing immediately to the spot. This time behind the goal we stood silent and motionless as Aylott prepared to take the spot kick. Big Trev coolly sent Batty the wrong way, placing the ball in the bottom corner of the net. The away terrace erupted as 4,000 sang, 'Here we go, here we go, here we go, here we go, here we go, here we go'.

The pressure-cooker tension was released with that goal, allowing both players and spectators to relax. Behind the goal, with every pass I screamed at Bournemouth to push forward and together we shouted 'attack, attack, attack, attack, attack'. The game was finely balanced, although Fulham were having difficulty getting the ball out of their own half, but each time Richards and then Aylott were frustratingly judged offside.

With nine minutes remaining, Richard Cooke was obstructed 30 yards out and close to the touchline. He picked himself up and floated the free kick into the Fulham penalty area. Keeper Batty advanced off his line, but sliced his feeble punch and the ball landed directly in front of the unmarked Aylott, who, with the goal gaping, managed to steer the ball into the back of the net off his shin. The execution was far from meticulous, but it did not matter how the ball ended up in the net; the fact was it was a goal. On the terrace behind the goal a sea of red and white exploded into a frenzy, while on the pitch Aylott was chased, then caught and mobbed by his delighted colleagues. 'Goin' up! Goin' up! Goin' up!' was all I could sing along with everyone else. It looked as though the dream was finally about to come true.

With 86 minutes on the clock, 'Iron Man' Tony Pulis won another midfield duel in the centre circle and steered the ball to Tony Sealy in space. Sealy took two touches, dropped his left shoulder and accelerated past his marker. At 25 yards out he let fly a right-foot wind-assisted rocket that flew into the top corner of the Fulham net. Before he had time to celebrate his stunning strike he was buried under a rugby style scrum by his Bournemouth team-mates.

Behind the goal I experienced a football orgasm as the emotion exploded and I punched the air and shouted 'yes! yes! yes!'. At this historic moment the 4,000 members of the red and white army quite rightly turned their attention to the orchestrator and we sang, 'We've got Harry, Harry, Harry Redknapp on the bench, on the bench'. The game was all but over, yet there was still time for Gordon Davies to send a header against the Bournemouth crossbar, but we didn't care. Bournemouth were up, a fact that was confirmed 30 seconds later when referee Taylor blew the final whistle.

Redknapp sprinted onto the pitch and hugged his players and each one in turn made their way towards us behind the Fulham goal. It was a scene of pure joy with celebrations and back slapping all round. Every Bournemouth supporter wore a grin like a Cheshire cat and I noticed some were hugging each other while others sobbed tears of joy. Roger and I just shook hands, and then I added, 'Mission accomplished'. For the first time since entering the Football League in 1923 Bournemouth had finally exorcised the ghost and won promotion to Division Two.

Our celebrations continued at Craven Cottage for nearly an hour after the match had finished before police and stewards finally encouraged us all to leave the terracing.

Back in the car we tuned into BBC Radio 'Sport on Two' and listened to the post-match interview with a jubilant Harry Redknapp. 'Magic!' he said, praising his players and all associated with the club. The journey home was delightful and relaxing. There was no pressure now, just huge relief and so we paced the journey home with our red scarves flapping from the rear windows. We were constantly overtaken by hundreds of cars whizzing along the M3 sporting red and white scarves waving in the wind. Horns hooted as each one sped by. At Rownhams services on the M27 we pulled into the car park and stopped for refreshments. The services were heaving with Pompey supporters who were travelling back home after their surprise 0-1 defeat at Crystal Palace, a late Ian Wright goal that had put their promotion celebrations on hold. As Roger and I nervously stepped out of the car a group of them came over to us. At first I thought we were in trouble, but each Portsmouth fan approached and shook our hand, offering genuine congratulations on Bournemouth's promotion to Division Two. One Pompey fan with a large beer belly added, 'God knows, you've waited an awful long time for it.'

When I arrived home I recounted the entire match to my father before jumping in the shower and heading into Bournemouth town centre to begin the celebrations. The following day I bought every national newspaper and read the coverage of Bournemouth's success. Wrapped up in my own personal promotion world I had failed to realise that other promotion and relegation issues had also been decided. Everton had become Football League Champions and Middlesbrough had all but booked their promotion place with Bournemouth following a 1-0 victory at home to Mansfield. Brighton had dropped into Division Three and Aston Villa had been relegated to Division Two after losing 1-2 at home to Sheffield Wednesday. I could not believe it; Bournemouth would be playing Aston Villa next season!

Bournemouth v. Rotherham – Saturday 9 May

Surprisingly, I have very few memories of the final game of this memorable season. I do recall that it was now a two-horse race for the championship between Cherries and Middlesbrough. Boro's midweek 0-0 draw against play-off hopefuls Wigan had mathematically confirmed their promotion with us. A Bournemouth victory in the final game of the season would see Cherries crowned as champions. However, a defeat and a Middlesbrough win at home to Doncaster would give the Third Division championship to 'Boro, with Bournemouth runners-up.

In a relaxed mood I entered Dean Court for the final time this season through the South End entrance, having relinquished my ticket to the turnstile operator. It was a beautiful sun-drenched end-of-season afternoon and many supporters had removed their shirts in a vain attempt to tan their bodies. All sides of the stadium were packed, with 11,310 supporters in total, who had come to watch the final piece of history being written during this season to remember. Looking up to my right, I saw a Cherries supporter sitting high in the South End roof structure, presumably having shinned up the vertical iron roof support to get a bird's-eye view of proceedings. His red and white scarf hung down from his right ankle fifteen feet above the heads of his colleagues in the South End enclosure. As I turned back to look at the pitch I felt a soft impact on the crown of my head. The South End beach ball had fallen directly onto the top of my head. Before I could react, the young lad next to me with lightning reflexes sent the ball skywards to my right and we all had a good chuckle at my expense.

Visitors Rotherham had already achieved a safe position just below mid

167

table with little to play for. It seemed as though they had not been invited, but somehow had unwillingly and embarrassingly gate-crashed a family party. Ken Bailey in all his coloured splendour greeted Mark Newson as he led Bournemouth onto the pitch to a standing ovation from both sets of supporters, which was a nice touch. As the carnival and celebrations continued, no-one, except their own travelling fans, noticed Rotherham run out onto the pitch towards the Brighton Beach End.

Two goals in six minutes from Trevor Aylott and Carl Richards gave Bournemouth the Third Division title as they finished the season in party mood. Aylott struck on 28 minutes, rounding off a superb series of passes to score his fourth goal in the last five games, a vital contribution during a crucial period. This time there was no mass hysteria or excitement, just a vigorous round of applause following a good build-up and execution. Five minutes later Carl Richards powered down the centre of the pitch towards the Brighton Beach goal in pursuit of a great ball from Richard Cooke. Skilfully he flicked the ball over Kelham O'Hanlon and finished it off with a neat header: 2-0 Bournemouth. This time the celebrations were a little more animated and cries of 'Bruno, Bruno' rang out.

The second half brought uneventful, but further, near misses at either end, along with a late mini pitch invasion as some Bournemouth supporters at the Brighton Beach End of the ground spilled onto the pitch to celebrate what I believe they thought to be the final whistle. Bournemouth goalkeeper Gerry Peyton was surrounded and mobbed before stewards and police ushered the high-spirited supporters back over the perimeter fence. As they dispersed it became apparent that one over-zealous fan had removed the green jersey from Peyton's back and kept it as a souvenir. Peyton played the final minutes of the match topless, but still wearing sun visor and gloves. Finally referee March blew his whistle to bring the long hard season to a close and signal the party to begin. Players from both sides sprinted to the dressing rooms as Bournemouth supporters from all corners of the ground swarmed onto the pitch.

It was a good-natured celebration and I, too, stepped over the perimeter fence and walked across the hallowed turf towards the celebrating masses who congregated on the halfway line in front of the Main Stand. The players had climbed the steps to the directors' box, where bottles of champagne were opened and excitedly sprayed over everyone in a scene reminiscent of a Formula One grand prix winner's podium. John Williams led the celebrations as players and supporters shook hands and embraced one another singing, 'Champions! Champions!' It was real 'Roy of the Rovers' stuff and I mingled amongst the crowd, taking pictures and joining in with the fun.

The championship was the icing on the cake and slowly I began to absorb this incredible feat of achievement. After 88 years AFC Bournemouth had won the Third Division title under the leadership of Harry Redknapp, who had assembled a side that had become record-breakers and capped it all by reaching 97 points, beating the previous Third Division best set by Oxford United in 1983/84. The team had cost Bournemouth less than a £100,000 and included a series of bargain buys and free transfers.

Elsewhere the end of season climax had produced the usual surprise, joy and heartache. Manchester City and Leicester City followed Aston Villa in exiting the First Division and would all be playing AFC Bournemouth next season. Derby and Portsmouth had won promotion to Division One. Middlesbrough had beaten Doncaster Rovers 2-0 to end the season as runners-up, having pushed Bournemouth all the way during the Third Division title race.

Swindon, Wigan and Gillingham each secured a play-off place and Swindon would eventually go on to secure promotion to Division Two at Gillingham's expense, via the play-offs. Automatic relegation from the Fourth Division made for a nail-biting finish and, in a bizarre twist of the tale, Torquay escaped the drop thanks to one of their players being bitten by Ginger, an over-excited police dog. In the stoppage time added on to deal with the injury Torquay scored a last-gasp equaliser in their match with Crewe to condemn Lincoln to the Vauxhall Conference. Neil Warnock's Scarborough won automatic promotion to the Football League from the GM Vauxhall Conference.

As Harry Redknapp celebrated Bournemouth's championship success with his players he commented, 'You've got to enjoy the good times in football, because you get some bad ones as well.' It was ironic that Redknapp's first match in charge of the Cherries was that 9-0 reverse at Lincoln City in 1982. Now Bournemouth had just won promotion to Division Two for the first time in their history and Lincoln had just dropped out of the Football League. Football, it's a funny old game!

World headlines went unnoticed in Bournemouth, but for the record the news in May focused around West German teenager Mathias Rust, who flew through heavily defended Soviet airspace and swooped over the Kremlin before landing his light aircraft in Moscow's Red Square. He then got out and

169

signed autographs before being arrested. British Telecom upset traditionalists by starting to replace classic red phone boxes with plastic booths in a bid to beat conservation laws due out the following year. Closer to home, much of Bournemouth and the surrounding area was blacked out by lightning, which included a direct strike on a house in Bransgore.

9.
Division Two, here we come!

As the champagne began to flow the club were deluged with letters, telegrams and messages congratulating all at Dean Court on their historic success. Included in those messages were a number of congratulatory messages from ex-players and exiled supporters around the globe. For once it was marvellous just to enjoy the moment and bask in the glory. The Mayor of Bournemouth, councillor Dan Crone, had been a Cherries supporter since moving to the town in 1966. He described the team's success as 'The best thing since sliced bread. It is tremendous news for the town.' A House of Commons motion congratulating the team on reaching the Second Division was tabled by Bournemouth East MP, David Atkinson, and seconded by Bournemouth West MP, John Butterfill.

Bournemouth fans who had backed their faith with hard cash were able to recoup their rewards. Ladbrokes confirmed that one lucky punter had £75 on AFC Bournemouth to win the championship at 25-1 and was due to pick up almost £2,000.

At a special lunch at the Savoy Hotel in London Harry Redknapp was crowned Third Division Manager of the Season, winning £1,000 and an inscribed silver salver for leading the Cherries to the championship and into the Second Division for the first time. At the same Football Association lunch AFC Bournemouth were presented with a cheque for £12,000 for winning the Third Division championship.

A celebration disco at the Academy nightclub saw goalkeeper Gerry Peyton complete a hat-trick of trophy triumphs. The Player of the Year award was decided on a popular vote of Cherries fans and so Peyton won the Micky Cave Memorial Cup and collected similar awards from the AFC Exiles and AFC Travellers.

On Monday 18 May Ken Brown returned to Dean Court with his First Division Norwich City side to play a friendly celebratory promotion match at which the League Division Three trophy was presented by Ken Bates to captain

Mark Newson. I remember proudly clapping the team as they received a standing ovation and undertook a lap of honour around the perimeter of the pitch. The match, refereed by local official John Carter, ended in a stunning 4-2 victory for the Cherries, thanks to goals from Sealy, Aylott (2) and Tony Pulis at last!

On Thursday 21 May at 7.00pm AFC Bournemouth players boarded an open-top Yellow Bus en route to a civic reception at the Town Hall. The bus travelled from Dean Court along Holdenhurst Road, Bath Road and Exeter Road, through to the Square to the reception. It was a colourful procession and the streets were lined with applauding fans wearing red and white. I wore my red and white scarf with pride and as the team entered the Square their arrival was heralded by a troupe of dazzling majorettes, and I captured the moment on film.

* * *

The odds on Bournemouth winning Division Two the following season were given as 16-1, while odds of 10-1 were quoted on Bournemouth, Portsmouth and Southampton all being in the First Division for season 1988/89.

On 17 June it was announced that AFC Bournemouth would fence in supporters at the Brighton Beach and South End at Dean Court. Dorset Police instructed the club to erect fences and introduce closed-circuit television cameras, following a meeting of all police forces set to cover Division Two matches. This effort was supposed to beat soccer hooligans and would cost the club more than £100,000. A further increased expense would be the rise in police charges for covering matches at Dean Court. It would cost AFC Bournemouth nearly £3,000 per match, an increase of £2,000 per game. Promotion had come at a high cost to the club.

Pre-season friendly matches were quickly lined up against First Division Tottenham Hotspurs and Watford, with away matches at Brighton and Oxford United. Colin Clarke would also make a brief return to Dean Court in a Southampton side for the testimonial match for long-serving Cherries physiotherapist John Kirk.

The new season League fixtures were published on 21 June. Cherries would start their Division Two campaign at one of the best grounds in the Football League with an away trip to Sheffield United. I made a careful entry of each match in my diary and vowed not to miss the season opener at Brammall Lane. Later Bournemouth would be hosting Aston Villa, Leeds United and Manchester City. At a cost of £60.00, a season ticket would guarantee my entrance to all League home games during the new season on the South End terrace. As I scrutinised the fixture list I pinched myself just in case it was a dream!

172

Appendices

Season statistics:

1986/87 'Today' Football League Division Three Final League Table

	P	W	D	L	F	A	Pts
AFC Bournemouth	46	29	10	7	76	40	97
Middlesbrough	46	28	10	8	67	30	94
Swindon	46	25	12	9	77	47	87
Wigan Athletic	46	25	10	11	83	60	85
Gillingham	46	23	9	14	65	48	78
Bristol City	46	21	14	11	63	36	77
Notts County	46	21	13	12	77	56	76
Walsall	46	22	9	15	80	67	75
Blackpool	46	16	16	14	74	59	64
Mansfield Town	46	15	16	15	52	55	61
Brentford	46	15	15	16	64	66	60
Port Vale	46	15	12	19	76	70	57
Doncaster Rovers	46	14	15	17	56	62	57
Rotherham	46	15	12	19	48	57	57
Chester City	46	13	17	16	61	59	56
Bury	46	14	13	19	54	60	55
Chesterfield	46	13	15	18	56	69	54
Fulham	46	12	17	17	59	77	53
Bristol Rovers	46	13	12	21	49	75	51
York City	46	12	13	21	55	79	49
Bolton Wanderers	46	10	15	21	46	58	45
Carlisle	46	10	8	28	39	78	38
Darlington	46	7	16	23	45	77	37
Newport County	46	8	13	25	49	86	37

1986/87 AFC Bournemouth goalscorers

League (76): Richards 12, Aylott 10 (2 pens), Puckett 10, Cooke 7, Newson 7, O'Connor 7, O'Driscoll 5, Savage 4 (4 pens), J. Williams 3, Howlett 3, Morrell 2, Sealy 2, Heffernan 1, Whitlock 1, own goals 2.

Milk Cup (1): Aylott. FA Cup (7): Puckett 3, Richards 2, Aylott 1, own goal 1.

1986/87 AFC Bournemouth match statistics

Date	Opponents	Score	Attendance	Peyton	Newson	Morrell	Coleman	Pulis
23/08/86	Brentford	1-1	3856	1	5	3		2
26/08/86	Bristol City (LC 1)	0-1	2631	1		3		2
30/08/86	Newport County	2-1	2799	1	5	3		2
02/09/86	Bristol City (LC 1)	1-1	4776	1		3		2
06/09/86	Notts County	1-1	3610	1	5	3		2
13/09/86	Bolton Wanderers	2-1	3031	1	5	3		2
16/09/86	Chester City	2-0	3027	1	5	3		
20/09/86	Mansfield Town	1-1	2841	1	5	3		
27/09/86	Bristol City	2-0	5975	1	5	3		12
30/09/86	York City	0-2	3769	1	5	3		12
04/10/86	Darlington	3-0	2006	1	5	3		2
18/10/86	Bury	1-0	2453	1	5	3		12
21/10/86	Doncaster Rovers	3-2	4195	1	5	3		12
25/10/86	Wigan Athletic	3-1	4911	1	5	3		12
01/11/86	Middlesbrough	0-4	10710	1	5	3		12
04/11/86	Walsall	0-2	5056	1	5	3		
08/11/86	Carlisle United	2-1	4284	1	5			3
15/11/86	Fareham Town (FAC1)	7-2	4759	1	5	3		14
22/11/86	Chesterfield	2-0	4312	1	5	3		
02/12/86	Gillingham	0-2	7756	1	5	3		
06/12/86	Orient (FAC2)	0-1	4353	1	5	3		
13/12/86	Rotherham	2-4	2092	1	5	3		
16/12/86	Wolves (FRTP)	3-4	1923	1	5	3	12	
26/12/86	Bristol Rovers	3-0	3573	1	2	3		9
27/12/86	Fulham	3-2	6670	1	10	3		9
01/01/87	Swindon	1-0	10537	1	11	3		9
03/01/87	Chesterfield	1-1	3029	1	11	3		9
06/01/87	Cardiff City (FRTP)	1-0	1482	1		3	11	9
10/01/87	Brentford	1-1	4682	1	11	3		9
24/01/87	Notts County	3-0	6022	1	2	3		8
28/01/87	Swindon (FRT 1)	2-2*	4524	1	6	3		8
31/01/87	Bolton Wanderers	1-0	4219	1	2	3		8
03/02/87	Blackpool	1-1	6242	1	2	3		8
07/02/87	Chester City	2-2	2838	1	2	3		8
14/02/87	Mansfield Town	4-1	5261	1	2	3		8
21/02/87	Bristol City	0-2	14539	1	2	3		8
24/02/87	Newport County	1-0	2143	1	2	3		8
28/02/87	York City	3-0	5804	1	2	3		8
03/03/87	Middlesbrough	3-1	13835	1	2	3		8
14/03/87	Bury	1-0	6806	1	2	3		8
17/03/87	Doncaster Rovers	3-0	1777	1	2	3		8
21/03/87	Gillingham	1-2	7304	1	2	3		8
28/03/87	Darlington	1-0	6370	1	2	3		8
31/03/87	Port Vale	2-1	3228	1	2	3		8
04/04/87	Carlisle United	0-0	2005	1	2	3		8
11/04/87	Walsall	1-0	8626	1	2	3		8
14/04/86	Wigan Athletic	2-0	4391	1	2	3		8
18/04/87	Swindon	1-1	14302	1	2	3		8
20/04/87	Bristol Rovers	2-0	10034	1	2	3		8
25/04/87	Blackpool	1-3	2866	1	2	3		8
02/05/87	Port Vale	0-0	9559	1	2	3		8
04/05/87	Fulham	3-1	9234	1	2	3		8
09/05/87	Rotherham	2-0	11310	1	2	3		8
18/05/87	Norwich City (F)	4-2	6113					

* Lost 2-4 on penalties

Heffernan	Savage	Whitlock	O'Driscoll	Aylott	Cooke	Puckett	Howlett	Richards	Williams J	O'Connor	Lewis	Williams K	Sealy
	4	6	7	9		11	8	10		12			
5	4	6	7	9		11	8	10		12			
	4	6	7	9		11	8	10		12			
5	4	6	7	9		11	8	10		12	14		
	4	6	7	9		11	8	10		12			
	4	6	7	9		11	8	10		12		2	
	4	6	7	9		11	8	12		10		2	
	4	6	7	9		11	8	12		10		2	
	4	6	7			11	8	9		10		2	
	4	6	7			11	8	9		10		2	
12	4	6	7			11	8	9		10			
	4	6	7	9		11	8	10		2			
	4	6	7	9		11	8	10		2			
	4	6	7	9		11	8	10		2			
	4	6	7	9		11	8	10		2			
2	4	6	7	9		11	8	10		12			
2	4	6	7	9		11	8	12		10			
2	12	6	7	9		11	8	10		4			
2	12		7	9		11	8	10		4			
2	12	6	7	9		11	8	10		4			
2	9	6	7			11	8	10		4	12		
2		6	7			11	8	10		4		9	
2		6	7			11		10		4			
12		6	7			11	8	10	5	4			
2		6	7				8		5	4			
2		6	7				8	10	5	4	12		
2			7				8	10	5	4	6		
2			7					10	5	4	6		
2		6	7				8	10	5	4			
12		6	7	9	11			10	5	4			
2		6	7	9	11		14	10	5	4	12		
12		6	7	9	11			10	5	4			
		6	7	9	11		12	10	5	4			
12		6	7	9	11			10	5	4			
		6	7	9	11		12	10	5	4			
12		6	7	9	11			10	5	4			
		6	7	9	11		12	10	5	4			
		6	7	9	11		12	10	5	4			
		6	7	9	11		12	10	5	4			
		6	7	9	11			10	5	4			
5		6	7	9	11			12		4			10
5		6	7	9	11			12		4			10
		6	7	9	11			12	5	4			10
		6	7	9	11			12	5	4			10
		6	7	9	11			12	5	4			10
		6	7	9	11			10	5	4			
		6	7	9	11			10	5	4			
		6	7	9	11			10	5	4			
		6	7	9	11			10	5	4			
12		6	7	9	11			10	5				4
		6	7	9	11			10	5	4			
		6	7	9	11			10	5	12			4
		6	7	9	11			10	5	12			4

THE BEST TEAM EVER?

Was the team of 1986/87 the perfect Cherries dream team? To even attempt to answer that question my personal judgement can only be based on the teams I have observed since following AFC Bournemouth in 1970. That alone immediately limits the breadth of my choice to make any accurate comparisons, so my analysis is flawed. Despite this limited window of observation I will make a feeble attempt at the impossible.

Although before my time, the team of 1947/48 that finished as runners-up in the Division Three race in the days when only the champions were promoted must be strong contenders as the Cherries best ever team. The team of 1961/62 must also be considered as they just missed out on a promotion spot by finishing the season in third place. Then, of course, there was the 1971/72 team under the leadership of John Bond which also missed out despite amassing the highest ever number of points for a team not promoted from Division Three. It may be cruel, but they all have one thing in common and that is failure. Despite much expectation they all failed to deliver and it is often remarked that no-one ever remembers who comes second or third in a race.

When reviewing and comparing the exploits of these good, but unsuccessful, teams it is clear they also have a number of positive qualities in common. These included strong management, individual players of quality and bags of commitment, but this was still not enough to achieve the ultimate goal of delivering Division Two promotion to the success-starved football fans of Bournemouth. Despite their respective potential capabilities, these strong sides who valiantly strived to achieve the dream all seemed to be missing a vital ingredient.

I remain convinced that Redknapp was the prime locator of the missing ingredient and the key to unlocking and releasing the collective power of teamwork and team spirit throughout his successful team. I believe that it was simply a matter of the team performance consistently exceeding that of the total sum of the individual parts. The championship squad of 1986/87 were undeniably a group of very skilful and talented individuals, a mix of youth, raw talent and experience, but there were no obvious recognised star performers.

The weight of expectation on young shoulders may have been slightly less of a burden than for those who had gone before them. For example, unlike the high cost of Bond's squad, nine of Redknapp's players were signed on free transfers, with the remainder all low-cost acquisitions. Yet it was Harry Redknapp's handpicked selection of this talented group of individuals and his ability as a manager to combine their creative resources together that somehow made the difference. Even viewing from the terraces it was obvious from the outset of the season that there was a sense of something different, a new team spirit in the camp, with everyone pulling together.

A successful promotion campaign demands consistency over a prolonged period and is based on courage and stamina throughout. Combining their resources together as a cohesive unit, the 1986/87 AFC Bournemouth team achieved more than any other Cherries side before them and the statistics prove the point. The team won a club record 29 of its 46 matches, drawing 10 and losing only 7. Dean Court was a fortress as they won all but four of their home games, losing only one and achieving this with only sixteen regular first-team players. Unlike McDonald and Milligan from 47/48, Dowsett from 61/62 and MacDougall from 71/72 there were no single goal-scoring heroes. Six of the 86/87 team took responsibility for scoring seven or more goals each during the season with three of those players reaching double figures, including David Puckett who missed half of the season due to injury. Others contributed valuable goals, too, and only one regular outfield player, Tony Pulis, failed to get on the score sheet. Three players – Newson, Peyton and O'Driscoll – were ever present throughout the League campaign, while Whitlock and Morrell missed only one game each.

Did manager Redknapp ever doubt his side's promotion capabilities? He had admitted that he once had doubts that his team could win promotion from Division Three. But those doubts disappeared with the signing of centre half John Williams: 'Until John came, I didn't think we were good enough to get promotion. He suddenly made such a difference. From the first game he played, you could see the improvement.'

Surprisingly, none of the championship-winning squad went on to achieve greater playing success with other clubs, but I have always believed that the character and leadership throughout the team was the solid backbone behind the success. Sean O'Driscoll and Tony Pulis progressed to football management and Newson, Peyton, Williams and Morrell all went on to apply their specialist knowledge in a coaching role.

So were they the best team ever? Well, I personally believe they were and still remain so. They get my vote because of their consistency, teamwork, performance and results. Of course, I admit that over the years there have been many exciting and attractive Bournemouth football teams. These teams have included individual lethal goal scorers like Ron Eyre, Stan Newsham, Ted MacDougall and Colin Clarke. They sometimes also contained the skilful wizardry contribution of individual players such as Tony Scott, Harry Redknapp, Ian Bishop and Wade Elliott. Some teams even had the added experienced dimension that included individuals with international pedigrees such as Tommy Godwin and Luther Blissett. But, at the time of writing, these shining individuals playing in their respective teams have over the years disappointed in one way or another and failed to collectively deliver the goods when it really mattered. The exception to the rule is the team of 1986/87 who remain the only team in AFC Bournemouth's long history to deliver the holy grail of promotion to Division Two and exceed expectation by delivering it as undisputed champions.

I must add that it is not just the playing squad that deserved my recognition. It truly was a team effort and credit must also be given to those behind the scenes at Dean Court who worked tirelessly throughout a long season, yet contributed significantly throughout. Chairman Rodney Barton, Managing Director Brian Tiler, club groundsman John Harriss and trainer/physiotherapist John 'Captain' Kirk all equally deserve my gratitude.

Off the pitch I saw two clear winners during the season. The first was the supporters. At Dean Court we enjoyed some scintillating football that culminated in an incredible home record where 44 goals were scored and only 14 conceded. I was fortunate to see that statistic extended when travelling away from home. The second winner was the balance sheet as attendances at Dean Court home matches went up and up. The average rose in every week but two and increased by 37 per cent compared with the previous season. It was a boom time at Dean Court.

I made another profound diary entry on 26 May 1987. It had taken Bournemouth 87 years to achieve promotion. By my reckoning the next significant promotion season would be in another 87 years, due in the year 2074. Thank God I was lucky to have witnessed the first miracle.

WHERE ARE THEY NOW?

So whatever happened to the record-breaking Cherries team of 1986/87? The following pages provide a brief profile of each player in the AFC Bournemouth championship team of 1986/87 and their career to date.

Harry Redknapp

Managed AFC Bournemouth to the Third Division title in 1986/87. An England Youth international winger, he signed professional for West Ham in March 1964 and played alongside World Cup trio Bobby Moore, Geoff Hurst and Martin Peters. He reunited with John Bond at Dean Court for £31,000 in August 1972 and scored five goals in 101 League games for Cherries prior to joining Brentford in September 1976. He later played for Seattle Sounders and then assisted Bobby Moore at Oxford City before returning to AFC Bournemouth as player-coach. After a brief spell as caretaker boss, he became Manager in November 1983 and plotted that season's FA Cup third-round defeat of holders Manchester United and Associate Members Cup final success. He remained in charge at Dean Court until resigning in June 1992, then assisted Billy Bonds before succeeding him as West Ham manager, for seven years, in August 1994. After a spell as Portsmouth's Director of Football, he became manager in March 2002 and plotted Pompey's 2002/03 First Division title triumph. In 2005 he became manager of Southampton FC.

Jimmy Gabriel

Supported Harry Redknapp as Assistant Manager and helped guide AFC Bournemouth to the Third Division title in 1986/87. Former Scottish international wing-half, he was a key figure in AFC Bournemouth's 1972/73 promotion challenge. He impressed as a teenager with hometown Dundee prior to joining Everton for £30,000 in March 1960. He featured prominently as they won the League Championship in 1962/63 and FA Cup in 1965/66, moving to Southampton for £45,000 in July 1967. Capped twice by his country, he helped Saints to qualify for Europe before John Bond paid £20,000 for him in July 1972. He scored four goals in 53 Third Division games for Cherries and was loaned to Swindon Town prior to joining Brentford in March 1974.

Moving to Seattle Sounders two months later, he coached their side, which included several ex-Cherries, to the NASL Soccer Bowl in 1977. He subsequently coached San Jose Earthquakes before returning to Dean Court as Assistant Manager to Harry Redknapp in March 1987. Rejoining Everton in a similar capacity in June 1990, he has been coaching back in the United States since February 1997.

Roger Brown

Tall, experienced central defender, who spent most of the 1986/87 Third Division title triumph on the coaching staff, but was called upon as substitute in the December game at Rotherham because of Bournemouth's injury crisis. Left the club in March 1987 following the appointment of Jimmy Gabriel as Assistant Manager. Originally signed in February 1978 from AP Leamington for £10,000 by Cherries' boss John Benson, he became a big favourite at Dean Court with a series of dominant displays at the heart of AFC Bournemouth's defence. Sold to First Division Norwich in 1979 for £85,000, then moved to Fulham for £100,000 in March 1980, being ever present in their 1981/82 promotion success. Rejoined Bournemouth in December 1983 and scored eight goals in 147 League games before briefly joining Weymouth in March 1987. Subsequently manager of Poole Town, Colchester United and Bolehall Swifts while working in the family building business in Tamworth. He is now a probation officer in Norwich.

Gerry Peyton

Republic of Ireland international goalkeeper. Won 'Player of the Season' in Cherries 1986/87 title triumph, remained ever present, saving four crucial penalty kicks and kept twenty clean sheets. Initially with Atherstone Town, he moved to Burnley in May 1975 and gained top-flight experience prior to joining Fulham for £35,000 in December 1976. He was a key figure as they won promotion in 1981/82 and so nearly reached the First Division in 1982/83, then was loaned to Southend United before Harry Redknapp snapped him up on a free transfer in July 1986. Also starred as AFC Bournemouth took Manchester United to an FA Cup fifth-round replay in 1988/89. He made 202 League appearances and gained a club-record seven caps while a Dean Court player before following Jimmy Gabriel to Everton in July 1991. He had loan spells at Bolton Wanderers, Brentford and Chelsea prior to briefly rejoining Brentford in March 1993, then reunited with Harry Redknapp at West Ham. Subsequently coaching in Japan and Sweden, he has since been a goalkeeping coach at Southampton, West Bromwich, Fulham and now Arsenal.

John Smeldeurs
Nickname 'The Bear'. Former England Youth goalkeeper who had three spells at Dean Court. Signing professional for Orient in July 1974, he failed to secure a Second Division slot behind John Jackson and joined AFC Bournemouth in July 1979. He made his League debut at Newport County six months later and contested the goalkeeper slot with Kenny Allen before moving to Trowbridge Town in January 1981. Rejoining Cherries from Weymouth for £4,000 in January 1984, he displaced Ian Leigh and set a club-record seven consecutive clean sheets during the 1984/85 campaign. He followed ex-Cherry Stuart Morgan to Torquay in July 1986, then had spells with Peterborough United and Poole Town before returning to Dean Court as non-contract cover for Gerry Peyton in August 1987. Making 98 League appearances overall for AFC Bournemouth, he also played for Brentford, Weymouth and Farnborough Town until a knee injury ended his career in May 1989. He now lives in Corfe Mullen, Poole, and is a driver for Allied Bakeries.

Mark Newson
Nickname 'Captain Marvel' and 'Noose'. Influential right back who skippered AFC Bournemouth's 1986/87 Third Division title triumph, playing in a variety of positions and scoring seven League goals. A former Charlton Athletic apprentice, he signed professional in December 1978, but failed to make an impact at The Valley and moved to Maidstone United in February 1980. He gained England Semi-Pro honours and starred in their 1980/81 FA Cup run, 1983/84 Alliance Premier League title triumph and 1985 Bob Lord Trophy final success. Harry Redknapp signed him in May 1985 and he was ever present in his first two seasons at Dean Court. He scored 23 goals in 177 League games before being sold to Fulham for £125,000 in February 1990. Then played for Barnet, Aylesbury United, Gravesend & Northfleet, Fisher Athletic and Romford. Captain Marvel is now Project Manager of West Ham's football in the community scheme and a part-time analyst for the Press Association.

Tom Heffernan
Featured sporadically throughout the 1986/87 Third Division title triumph, playing fifteen League games and scoring one goal. Popular Irish right back who was an influential figure in AFC Bournemouth's 1981/82 promotion success from Division Four. He initially impressed as a midfielder with Dunleary

Celtic and joined Tottenham Hotspur in October 1977, but failed to secure a first-team slot at White Hart Lane. Alec Stock snapped him up on a free transfer in 1979 and he made his League debut in Cherries' 2-0 win at Rochdale three months later. He was ever present in 1980/81 and became captain before being sold to Sheffield United for £20,000 in August 1983. He then starred in their 1983/84 promotion campaign and returned to Dean Court in June 1985. Scoring 27 goals in 217 League games overall for Cherries, he reunited with ex-Cherry Ian Cunningham at Swanage T&H in July 1988 and then played for Bournemouth 'Poppies', Downton, Sturminster Marshall, Hamworthy Engineering and Parley Sports while employed as a driver for Allied Bakeries in Bournemouth. He is now a painter and decorator in Ireland.

Paul Morrell

Nickname 'Mossie'. Long-serving left back, who was a key figure and the only local lad in AFC Bournemouth's 1986/87 Third Division title triumph. Played in all but one of the 46 League matches and scored two critical goals. Initially with Poole Town, he joined Bath City for £3,000 in February 1980 and moved to Weymouth for £5,000 in July 1981. Then moved to Dean Court in June 1983, scoring in Cherries' 1984 Associate Members Cup final triumph. He netted eight goals in 343 League games until released shortly after his testimonial against Southampton in May 1993. Following spells with Leyton Orient, Bashley and Hong Kong side Sing Tao, he joined ex-Cherry Geoff Butler at Salisbury City in December 1994 and featured in that season's promotion success. He then played for Bournemouth 'Poppies', Sturminster Marshall, Poole Borough and was the boss at Poole Town. Is now currently working in Dorset as a probation service officer.

Mark Whitlock

Central defender who featured prominently in AFC Bournemouth's 1986/87 Third Division title triumph. Played in all but one of the 46 League matches and scored one crucial goal. A former Southampton apprentice, he signed professional in March 1979 and made his First Division debut in September 1981. He was loaned to Grimsby Town and Aldershot before helping Saints to finish League Championship runners-up in 1983/84 and moved to Bournemouth as part of the Colin Clarke deal in July 1986. Scored once in 99 League games while at Dean Court before moving to Reading in December

1988, then Aldershot in 1990 before that club's demise. He has since worked as a security officer, notably at Ocean Village in Southampton.

John Williams
Nickname 'Willo'. Tall central defender who was an influential figure in Cherries' 1986/87 Third Division title triumph, playing 26 League games and scoring three goals. A former Tranmere Rovers junior, the popular Scouser made his League debut at Swindon Town seven months before signing professional in October 1979 and featured in their 1981/82 League Cup run. Joined Port Vale for £12,000 in July 1985 and starred in their 1985/86 promotion success under ex-Cherry John Rudge, moving to Dean Court for £30,000 in December 1986. Scored nine goals in 117 League games until sold to Cardiff City for £15,000 in December 1991. Returning to AFC Bournemouth in July 1993, he was youth team boss prior to assisting Manager Mel Machin and had a testimonial against Southampton in July 1998. He was dismissed in February 2000 and subsequently worked in the licensed trade. He is a match summariser for BBC Radio Solent.

Bobby Savage
Nickname 'Savo'. Featured between August and November in the 1986/87 Third Division title triumph playing fifteen League games and scoring four goals, all from the penalty spot, before being sold to Bradford City for £35,000 in December 1986. Popular midfielder who starred in AFC Bournemouth's 1984 Associate Members Cup final success. Signing professional for Liverpool in January 1978, he was unable to gain a place in Bob Paisley's all-conquering side and joined Wrexham on an extended loan in October 1982, winning 'Player of the Season'. Sold to Stoke City for £10,000 in July 1983, he sampled top-flight football before Harry Redknapp paid £15,000 for him five months later, but a broken leg sidelined him for the 1985/86 season. He scored 18 times in 82 League games. After Bradford City he joined Bolton Wanderers in September 1987 and helped to win promotion in 1987/88 as well as the Sherpa Van Trophy final in 1989. Another broken leg ended his career soon after and he has since coached Knowsley United, Liverpool Schools U-15 side and at Tranmere Rovers School of Excellence.

Keith Williams

A versatile midfielder who featured for a very brief spell in the 1986/87 Third Division title triumph and played six times during Cherries injury crisis in September 1986. Signing professional for Aston Villa in April 1975, he then moved to Northampton in February 1977 and was 'Player of the Season' in 1980/81. Joined Bournemouth on a free transfer in August 1981 and starred in AFC Bournemouth's 1981/82 Fourth Division promotion success under David Webb and became Cherries' player-coach after recurring injury problems restricted his appearances. He scored once in 102 League games while at Dean Court and briefly played for Bath City prior to joining ex-Cherry Roger Brown at Colchester in December 1987. He then played for Swanage T&H before spells with Salisbury, Poole Town and Bournemouth 'Poppies'. Is now managing Bournemouth 'Poppies' with ex-Cherry Shaun Brooks and works as a despatch manager for Bezier Corporate Print in Poole.

Sean O'Driscoll

Nickname 'Noisy'. Influential midfielder who was ever present throughout during AFC Bournemouth's 1986/87 Third Division title triumph, scoring five League goals. He impressed at Alvechurch prior to joining Fulham for £12,000 in 1979. An influential figure as Fulham won promotion in 1981/82. Joined Bournemouth initially on loan in 1984 before a £6,000 transfer that summer, starring in Cherries' 1984 Associate Members Cup final success. Voted AFC Bournemouth's 'Player of the Season' during 1985/86. A former Republic of Ireland International, he scored 19 goals in 423 League games for Bournemouth before a spell as club player-physio, then youth team manager in December 1994. Became first team coach in January 1999 and has been AFC Bournemouth Manager since August 2000, plotting the 2002/03 Third Division play-off promotion success.

Tony Pulis

Nickname 'Iron Man'. Hard-tackling midfielder who was influential during AFC Bournemouth's 1986/87 Third Division title triumph. Played in 35 games, but was the only regular outfield player not to score during the season. A former Bristol Rovers apprentice, he spent a year with Hong Kong side Happy Valley prior to rejoining Bristol Rovers as player-coach in June 1982. He then moved to hometown Newport County for £8,000 in July 1984. Harry Redknapp signed him in August 1986 and he impressed with his tough tackling and versatility before being sold to Gillingham for £10,000 in July 1989. He returned to AFC Bournemouth as player-coach in August 1990 and scored four goals in 90 League games overall prior to succeeding Harry Redknapp as Manager from June 1992 until dismissed in August 1994. Rejoining Gillingham as manager in June 1995, he guided them to promotion in 1995/96 and the Second Division play-off final in 1998/99. He has since managed Bristol City, Portsmouth and Stoke City.

Mark O'Connor

Nickname 'Des'. Hard-working midfielder who played in 43 League games and scored seven goals during AFC Bournemouth's 1986/87 Third Division title triumph. A former QPR apprentice, he signed professional in June 1980. The Eire U-21 international was a member of Terry Venables' 1982/83 Second Division title squad. Reunited with Gerry Francis on loan to Exeter City in October 1983, then joined Bristol Rovers for £20,000 in August 1984. Harry Redknapp paid £25,000 for him in March 1986. He then followed Tony Pulis to Gillingham for £70,000 in December 1989, then reunited with him at Bournemouth in July 1993 and scored 15 goals in 186 League games before following Pulis back to Gillingham in August 1995. Featuring in the 'Gills' 1995/96 promotion campaign, he ran their School of Excellence and also worked under Pulis at Bristol City and Portsmouth, where he is currently youth team manager.

Gary Howlett

Former Republic of Ireland midfield international who featured in 23 League games and scored three goals during AFC Bournemouth's 1986/87 Third Division title triumph before injury limited his selection. Initially with Home Farm in his native Dublin, he joined Coventry in November 1980 and then moved to Brighton in August 1982 and played in the 1983 FA Cup final at Wembley. Joined Bournemouth for £15,000 in December 1984, netting seven goals in 60 League outings. He was loaned to Aldershot and Chester before being sold to York City for £8,000 in January 1988. He joined Shelbourne in February 1991 and starred in their 1991/92 FAI League championship success, also representing the League of Ireland. After a loan spell to Crusaders he moved to Malahide United as player-coach and has since coached at Shelbourne and Monaghan United while working for Aer Lingus at Dublin Airport.

Tony Sealy

Much travelled midfielder who played 13 League games on loan between March and May 1987 during AFC Bournemouth's Third Division title triumph, scoring 2 goals. Began his career with Southampton in 1977 and was then signed by Crystal Palace for £50,000, helping them to win the Second Division championship in 1979 under Terry Venables and then followed his manager to QPR in a £75,000 deal. He then joined Fulham and Leicester City before joining Bournemouth on loan in March 1987, but was not retained at the end of the season. He then played for Sporting Lisbon and Sporting Braga in Portugal, Bristol Rovers, Brentford and Hong Kong side Eastern Athletic. Now coaching Hong Kong Sports Club.

Trevor Aylott

Experienced striker who was an influential figure in the 1986/87 Third Division title triumph, playing in 37 League games and scoring ten League goals. Signing professional for Chelsea in July 1976, he moved to Barnsley for £50,000 in November 1979/80 and starred in their 1980/81 promotion campaign. He was sold to Millwall for a record £150,000 in August 1983 and Crystal Palace in exchange for Vince Hilaire in July 1984. Leading marksman in 1984/85, he was loaned back to Barnsley before Harry Redknapp paid £15,000 for him in August 1986. An excellent target man, 'Big Trev' scored 27 goals in 147 League games for Bournemouth before being sold to Birmingham City for £40,000 in October 1990. Subsequently with Oxford United, Gillingham, Wycombe Wanderers (on loan) and Bromley, he is now a London black-cab driver.

David Puckett

Made a significant contribution to the 1986/87 Third Division title triumph playing in 19 League games, scoring ten goals and two cup hat-tricks before suffering a serious knee injury at Bristol Rovers that curtailed his season. A former Southampton apprentice, he signed professional in November 1978 and made his First Division debut in March 1981 and helped Saints to finish as League championship runners-up in 1983/84. Moved to Bournemouth along with colleague Mark Whitlock in July 1986 as part of the Colin Clarke transfer deal. His Boxing Day injury sidelined him for almost a year and he was loaned to Stoke City and Swansea City before joining Aldershot in January 1989. He was top scorer in four consecutive seasons and rejoined AFC Bournemouth when

Aldershot folded in March 1992. Netting 14 goals in 39 League games overall for Cherries, he moved to Woking in August 1992 and featured in their 1994 FA Trophy final triumph. He has since played for Weymouth, Newport (IOW), Salisbury City, Havant Town, Wokingham, Bashley, Eastleigh and BAT.

Carl Richards

Nickname 'Bruno'. Big Jamaican striker who was leading marksman in the 1986/87 Third Division title triumph playing in 43 League games, scoring twelve League goals and two FA Cup goals. Initially with Dulwich Hamlet, he topped their goalscoring charts in 1983/84 and moved to Enfield in July 1984. He was leading scorer in the 1985/86 Gola League title triumph and gained England Semi-Pro recognition shortly before Harry Redknapp paid £10,000 for him in July 1986. He netted 16 goals in 71 League games prior to joining Birmingham City for £70,000 in October 1988. He was sold to Peterborough United for £37,000 in July 1989, then joined Blackpool for £60,000 in January 1990 and helped them qualify for the Fourth Division play-offs in 1990/91. Following a loan spell at Maidstone United, he rejoined Enfield in December 1991 and featured in two consecutive Diadora League Cup finals. He then played for Bromley and Tooting and Mitcham until injury ended his career. He is now a house husband with two children in Brockley, SE London.

Richard Cooke

Nickname 'Cookie' and 'Charlie'. England U-21 winger who featured prominently in the 1986/87 Third Division title triumph playing in 23 League games, scoring seven goals. Signing professional for Tottenham Hotspur in May 1983, he was loaned to Birmingham City before Harry Redknapp paid £27,500 for him in January 1987. Sold to Luton Town in March 1989, he featured regularly as substitute in the top-flight prior to rejoining AFC Bournemouth in March 1991. He netted 17 times in 125 League games overall for Cherries until a knee injury ended his League career in March 1993. Still lives in the Bournemouth area and is currently working as a London black-cab taxi driver.

David Coleman

Young left back who provided defensive cover during the 1986/87 Third Division title triumph, but played in only one League game as substitute and one cup match. Signed professional for Bournemouth in September 1984 and was then loaned to Poole Town, being briefly recalled during Cherries injury crisis in January 1987. Deputised for Paul Morrell during Cherries' 1989/90 campaign, scoring twice in 50 League outings for Cherries before a knee injury forced him into non-League football. Managed the sports shop at Southampton University until his tragic death from meningitis in May 1997 at the age of 30 years. A team named in his memory competes in the Salisbury and District League.

Morgan Lewis
Young midfielder who provided cover during the 1986/87 Third Division title triumph, but played in only three League games. Former Bournemouth School for Boys pupil who made 12 League appearances for Cherries. Moved to Weymouth in July 1987 where an ankle injury ended his playing career. Settling in Brighton, he taught English as a foreign language and is now a production editor in medical marketing.

Below: The author in 1986, awaiting
Harry's call!

THE END